SERIOUSLY FUNNY

From the Ridiculous to the Sublime

Howard Jacobson

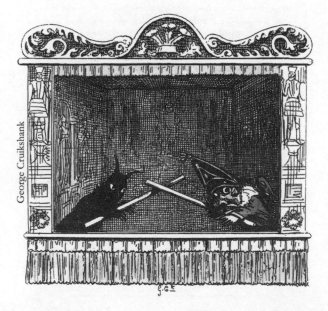

George Cruikshank

VIKING

VIKING

Published by the Penguin Group
Penguin Books Ltd, 27 Wrights Lane, London w8 5tz, England
Penguin Books USA Inc., 375 Hudson Street, New York, New York 10014, USA
Penguin Books Australia Ltd, Ringwood, Victoria, Australia
Penguin Books Canada Ltd, 10 Alcorn Avenue, Toronto, Ontario, Canada m4v 3b2
Penguin Books (NZ) Ltd, 182–190 Wairau Road, Auckland 10, New Zealand

Penguin Books Ltd, Registered Offices: Harmondsworth, Middlesex, England

First published 1997
1 3 5 7 9 10 8 6 4 2

Copyright © Howard Jacobson, 1997

The moral right of the author has been asserted

The permissions acknowledgements on pp. xii–xiv constitute an extension of this copyright page

Some of this material has appeared in a slightly different form in
the *Sunday Times* and *Esquire* magazine.

Set in 11/13.5 pt Monotype Garamond
Typeset by Datix International Limited, Bungay, Suffolk
Printed in Great Britain by Clays Ltd, St Ives plc

A CIP catalogue record for this book is available from the British Library

ISBN 0–670–85546–4

For Conrad Jacobson

Objection, evasion, cheerful mistrust, delight in mockery are signs of health; everything unconditional belongs to pathology.

Nietzsche

Contents

Acknowledgements xi

1 Apes and Angels 1
2 Where There's a Fool There's a Phallus 39
3 The Sibyl's Cavern Or Bum Bum Bum 68
4 Diary of a Visit to a Clown 85
5 The Priceless Gift 103
6 A Brief Digression into Sado-masochism 139
7 How the Devil Became a Holy Fool 149
8 Everyman in His Humour 186
9 The Revenge of the Spider 210
10 Now Get You to My Lady's Chamber . . . 222

Bibliography 243
Index 250

Acknowledgements

The only way to keep this page manageable is to make it niggardly. To have included everyone who has ever made me laugh and therefore made me think about laughter, everyone who has laughed or failed to laugh at me – caused me to reflect on the whole business, either way – the impossibility speaks for itself. Recollections of high-toned conversations at knock-about parties in the company of Terry Collits and Peter Shrubb, Dick Nichols and Joe Hall, back in the Sydney University English department of the sixties, cheer (and of course sadden) my mind still. Similarly, later classes co-taught with Wilbur Sanders at Selwyn College, Cambridge, on the comedy of George Eliot, Joseph Conrad, D. H. Lawrence – we were no conventional grubbers after mirth.

But as far as matters related to this book specifically go, my thanks to Vladimir Alexa, David Drummond, Bruce Kapferer, Brian Kaplan, Matt Leone, Carol Ann Lorenz and Christopher Vecsey.

I have spoken to no one about comedy as much as I have spoken to Rosalin Sadler, and if there is any intellectual daring in this book, she is the person who got it there. The physical daring, too – you try the front row of a circus when the sloshing begins, or a conspicuous table at a comedy club when the comedian turns nasty – was all hers. Not once did she allow me to follow the instinct that had kept me safe and ignorant until then, and run.

My other unpayable debt is to Meredith Levy, who hunted down every idea like a tiger, reorganized my thoughts, and presented her own with such persuasiveness that it cannot be but that many a page of this book is as much hers as it is mine.

PERMISSIONS

Text illustrations and sources

All chapter headings engraved by Jacques Callot (photos: Roger-Viollet).

All remaining Callot engravings from *Jacques Callot Maître Graveur (1593– 1635)* by Pierre-Paul Plan, Brussels-Paris, 1911.

pp. iii, 242: illustration by George Cruikshank from *The Tragical Comedy of Punch and Judy*, London, 1870.

pp. 6, 7: *Distribution of Fool's Caps* by Erhard Schön © British Museum, London.

p. 41: *Able* by Félicien Rops (photo: Mary Evans Picture Library).

pp. 43, 76: from *Lysistrata of Aristophanes*, translated and illustrated by Aubrey Beardsley, London, 1896.

p. 45: Red-figure vase by the Hasselmann Painter showing a woman sprinkling phalluses, *c.* 430–420 BC © British Museum.

p. 54: *The Devil of Pope-Fig Island* by Charles Eisen from *Tales and Novels in Verse* by La Fontaine, London, 1896.

pp. 78, 197: Woodcut illustrations attributed to Albrecht Dürer from *Das Narrenschiff* by Sebastian Brand, Berlin, 1872.

p. 81: Woodcut by Hans Weiditz © British Museum, London.

pp. 104, 124, 161: classical comedian, 'Bucco', Harlequin, illustrations from *La Comédie Italienne* by Pierre Louis Duchartre, Paris, 1924.

p. 150: 'His Wife lies in agony but ... the show must go on!' Anon. (photo: Mary Evans Picture Library).

pp. 154, 155: *Picture Book of Devils, Demons and Witchcraft* by Ernst and Johanna Lehner, Dover Publications, 1971.

p. 157: *The Fool-Eater* by Erhard Schön © British Museum, London.

p. 159: *The Fool-Eater* by Barthel Beham from *Die Holzschnitte Barthel Behams* by Heinrich Rottinger, Strasburg, 1921.

p. 165: 'He Plays with the Worlds' by J. J. Grandville from *The Mysteries of the Infinite*, 1845 (photo: Roger-Viollet).

p. 168: 'The Benefits of Being Small' by George Cruikshank, published in the *Comic Almanack*, 1847 (photo: Mary Evans Picture Library).

p. 179: *Satyr's Family*, by Albrecht Dürer, Rosenwald Collection, © 1996 Board of Trustees, National Gallery of Art, Washington.

p. 202: *Skimmington for Nagging Wives* by William Hogarth (photo: Mary Evans Picture Library).

p. 206: *Devil Playing the Bagpipes* by Erhard Schön © British Museum, London.

p. 213: 'St Vitus' Dance, Pilgrimage to St Willibrod Church in Luxemburg' after Breughel (photo: Mary Evans Picture Library).

Inset photograph credits

1, 2, 5, 26: British Museum, London.

3, 6, 27: Bildarchiv Preussischer Kulturbesitz, Berlin.

4: Metropolitan museum of Art, New York.

7: RCHME © Crown Copyright.

9: Museum of New Mexico, New Mexico/T. Harmon Parkhurst.

10: Hulton, London.

11: Ronald Grant Archive, London.

12: Réunion des Musées Nationaux, Paris.

13: Lebrecht Collection, London.

17: Kobal Collection, London.

18: Camera Press, London/Peter Francis.

19: Kevin Nuble.

20, 21, 24: Scala, Florence.

22: Sotheby's, New York.

23: Camera Press/John Drysdale.

25, 28, 29, 30: AKG London.

31: Tate Gallery, London.

32: Nick 'Spike' Liseiko.

34: Sygma, London/Jillian Edelstein.

QUOTED WORKS

Grateful acknowledgement is made to the following authors, publishers and literary representatives who have given permission to reprint copyright material in this collection:

Extract from *My Gorgeous Life* by Dame Edna Everage, reprinted by kind permission of the author. © Oceania Investments BV, 1995.

Material from *Cracking Up* by Christopher Bollas, by permission of Routledge.

Extract from *Derek and Clive* record © Peter Cook and Dudley Moore.

Material from *The Golden Bough* by J. G. Frazer, by permission of

A. P. Watt Ltd on behalf of the Council of Trinity College, Cambridge.

Material from *Comedians* by Trevor Griffiths, by permission of Faber and Faber Ltd.

Material from *A Trip to Light Fantastic* by Katie Hickman, by permission of HarperCollins Publishers Ltd.

Material from 'A Man and His Dog' and *Felix Krull* by Thomas Mann, by permission of Martin Secker and Warburg Ltd.

Material from *Death in Banaras* (1994) by Jonathan Parry, by permission of Cambridge University Press.

Extracts from *Hopi Journal* by Alexander Stephens. Copyright © 1936 by Columbia University Press. Reprinted with permission of the publisher.

Material from *Show People* by Kenneth Tynan, by permission of Weidenfeld and Nicolson.

Every effort has been made to contact or trace all copyright holders. The publishers will be glad to make good any errors or omissions brought to our attention in future editions.

CHAPTER ONE

Apes and Angels

I

Researching what turned out to be his last book, on show people, the critic Kenneth Tynan went along to Brookside Park, Pasadena, to watch the final day's shooting of the Mel Brooks psycho-spoof, *High Anxiety*.

'Sequence in rehearsal,' Tynan noted in his journal, dated 14 July 1977, is parody of *The Birds*, stressing aspect of avian behaviour primly ignored by Hitchcock: Pigeons pursue fleeing Brooks across park, subjecting him to bombardment of bird droppings. Spattered star seeks refuge in gardener's hut, slams door, sinks exhausted on to upturned garbage can. After momentary respite, lone white plop hits lapel, harbinger of redoubled aerial assault through hole in roof. Brooks's hundred-yard dash is covered by tracking camera, while grey-haired technicians atop motorized crane mounted on truck squirt bird excreta (simulated by mayonnaise and chopped spinach) from height of thirty feet. Barry Levinson, one of four collaborators on screenplay, observes to me, 'We have enough equipment here to put a man on the moon, and it's all being used to put bird droppings on Brooks.'

Nothing in that account suggests that anyone, least of all Kenneth Tynan, thought the technology might have been better employed, after all, sending a man into space. On the scale of human necessity, having a bird dump on Mel Brooks rates higher than a moon landing. The waste justifies the waste. Few things matter more than comedy, and few things are more irreducibly comic than faeces coming out of the sky.

It goes without saying, too, that such conscientious technical absorption in the ingenuities of simulating and squirting faeces only deepens the primary comic disparity between what we would like to be and what we are, between what we aspire to make and what we are made of. A capacity to manufacture the droppings of animals, at great expense, will not liberate us, in the end, from the chore of going on manufacturing our own. Put another way: we can run all we like from the flying excrement of a bird, but we can never escape the excremental animality we share with it.

That's a fate we are pleasurably reminded of – unless we are puritans or coprophobes – when we see Mel Brooks making his shit-scared hundred-yard dash under a hail of mayonnaise and chopped spinach. And it's the reason we laugh at the old joke about the aged cleaning lady who, having spent every day of her working life scrubbing down a pigeon-spattered statue of the Belvedere Apollo, is suddenly offered three wishes; the first of which she uses to become young and beautiful, the second to have the statue come alive, and the third . . . the third she offers, with a deal of exaggerated suggestiveness, to the statue – 'Now your wish, Apollo. What is *your* desire?' – only to hear the god say that for his wish he would like to shit on a pigeon. An ambition, an acknowledgement of membership in the great chain of animality, he enjoys in common with every circus clown and harlequin.

If comedy, in all its changing shapes, has one overriding preoccupation, it is this: that we resemble beasts more closely than we resemble gods, and that we make great fools of ourselves the moment we forget it.

So is it not wonderful how many studies of comedy feel it necessary to begin with an assertion of the very opposite, insisting that comedy is nothing less than the proof of our evolutionary superiority, 'our departure', in Arthur Koestler's words, 'from the rails of instinct' – the whistle signalling that departure (the 12.15 to Refined Disillusion) being laughter itself.

'The first point to which attention should be called,' declares Henri Bergson in *Laughter*, immediately putting distance between himself and the discursive tone of the ass and the rooster, 'is that the comic does not exist outside the pale of what is strictly *human*.'

'Man,' proclaims Hazlitt, opening his *Lectures on the English Comic Writers* with a sonority equally remote from the barnyard, 'is the only animal that laughs and weeps; for he is the only animal that is struck with the difference between what things are, and what they ought to be.'

Try telling that to a dog who has been expecting a walk that doesn't materialize. Try telling it to Alex, the experimental parrot at the University of Arizona, who, when he was about to be left at the veterinarian's for lung surgery – a perfect example, from a parrot's point of view, of things not working out the way they ought to – wailed to his keeper, 'Come here. I love you. I'm sorry. I want to go back.'

In 'A Man and his Dog', a story he wrote in 1918, Thomas Mann dissolves the differences between himself and his short-haired German pointer in exquisite observation of dog mirth.

When I sit reading in a corner of the garden wall, or on the lawn with my back to a favourite tree, I enjoy interrupting my intellectual preoccupations to talk and play with Bashan . . . I rouse and stimulate his sense of his own ego by impressing upon him – varying my tone and emphasis – that he *is* Bashan and that Bashan is his name. By continuing this for a while I can actually produce in him a state of ecstasy, a sort of intoxication with his own identity, so that he begins to whirl around on himself and send up loud exultant barks to heaven out of the weight of dignity that lies on his chest. Or we amuse ourselves. I by tapping him on the nose, he by snapping at my hand as though it were a fly. It makes us both laugh,

(observe the democracy)

yes, Bashan has to laugh too; and as I laugh I marvel at the sight, to me the oddest and most touching thing in the world. It is moving to see how under my teasing his thin animal cheeks and the corners of his mouth will twitch, and over his dark animal mask will pass an expression like a human smile, or at least some ungainly, pathetic semblance of one.

Koestler's conciliatory footnote to his laughter as departure-bell-from-the-rails-of-instinct observation, in *The Act of Creation* –

Some domesticated animals – dogs, chimpanzees – seem to be capable of a humorous expression and to engage in teasing activities. These may be regarded as forerunners of laughter

– hardly measures up to the complexities of self-awareness and mutuality, love and desolation, that find expression in Bashan's laughter. Nor does that slight implied by the idea of domestication – animals learning from us how to blow the whistle on their own instinctivity – meet the satiric contempt of which animals are capable. The parrot we teach to be a miniature airborne copy of ourselves is derisive not in our image, but derisive *of* it. The devilish eye, the rolling gait, the parodies of our voices, down to every wheedling nuance of our accent and pronunciation – what are these but satires on domestication itself?

Masters of derision, tireless mimic clowns and acrobats, the parrots D. H. Lawrence observes in *Mornings in Mexico* cannot leave alone the tame doings of the humans who think they have tamed *them*. With their 'sad old long-jowled faces and their flat disillusioned eyes', they torment Rosalino, sweeping the patio with his twig broom, pretending to be oblivious to their mockery of his own whistling, got off to a T, 'only a little more-so', that *little more-so* containing all there is to know about the sardonical. When they have finished cackling over Rosalino they turn their demonish attentions to the dog, or at least to whoever it is that is calling the dog. 'Perro! Oh, Perro! Perr-rro! Oh, Perr-rro! Perro!' Such 'suave, prussic-acid sarcasm' poured over nothing more contemptible than a human being calling a dog – are we so ludicrous to them? 'Perro! Oh, Perr-rro! Perr-rro! Perr-rr-rro!!' they go on shrieking, their 'strange penetrating, antediluvian malevolence' seeming to make 'even the trees prick their ears'.

Anthropomorphism, this used to be called. Attributing human emotions to the non-human. And much frowned upon by animal behaviourists, butchers, livestock-exporters and fox-hunters, it was. Today, at least as far as the behaviourists are concerned, a little seasoning of anthropomorphism is allowable. Else, it is conceded, we consign animals to the hell of never feeling anything as we do, and therefore never feeling anything at all. But the concession still favours us; the measure of all things is still consciousness as we understand it. Whereas, as far as the comic is concerned, the balance of borrowing and imitation falls quite differently; it is not the animals who must check their satiric *bona fides* out with us, but we who continuously put ourselves to school with them. Off to stag and hen nights we go, when we mean to give rein to the last of what is 'animal' in our natures. There we roar or howl, or even hoot with that laughter which the original jungle roarers and howlers are said to lack the necessary cognitive wherewithal to reproduce. The fool torments us into mirth with a pig's bladder or tickles us with his coxcomb – the feathered crest wherewith a cock struts his arrogance. On his head he wears a pair of ass's ears. Spider-gods play the fool in West African mythology, and a coyote trickster does the same for the North American Indian. Before we concentrated all our beliefs in a single unsmiling deity, from whom every vestige of the animal had been painstakingly removed, we attended religiously (and comically) to the goings-on of goat-men. Thereafter, those same goat-men gave us the tails and horns and cloven feet (to say nothing of the gross sexual appetites and appurtenances) with which to furnish forth our devil. The characters of the Italian comedy, the originators of the English pantomime, took their names and natures from the bestiaries of the medieval imagination: Pulcinella was a day-old chicken, Harlequin might wear a fox's tail, Pedrolino and Pierrot (whom our age has reduced to a figure of sentimentality and kitsch) were little parrots. Derisive birds.

Parrots again. Birds, as the zoologist Alfred Newton described them, highly prized from the first, celebrated by more than one classical poet, and 'reprobated by the moralist'. The admiring classical poets I can find, but the reprobating moralist eludes me. Think of it, though – a philosopher disagreeing with the existence of a bird, on *moral* grounds. For being impolite, presumably. For dropping faeces out of the sky and laughing. For pouring prussic-acid sarcasm over our humanity. For demonstrating our ridiculousness. For being a comedian, in other words.

Way beyond the reach of any moralist or philosopher, high up in the rainforests of New Guinea and North East Australia, the palm cockatoo fashions himself a drum-stick from a paper-bark and beats out his demands for territory and sex. He is the blackest of all parrots. He has a huge Jimmy Durante bill. His crest is high and wild, uncontrollably erectile, a parody of all haircuts, a gross joke on the whole phenomenon of hair – like Ken Dodd's. When he is excited, his face turns scarlet. The gap between his bill and his jaw looks too big. His tongue too loose. Too garrulous. As a consequence, there is something demoniacally half-witted about his mouth. A living creature should be able to close its mouth. For all our sakes. His eye seems to boil in his head. He is utterly ridiculous and utterly fearsome. And he goes on drum-beating his tree. Calling us to the circus, the ludicrous unending spectacle of territorial greed, sexual desire, wants, needs, noises . . . When he opens his wings against the sky he looks like the devil. Not the zoological furry-chinned, wet-mouthed devil whose origins are in the goat-men. *That* devil is still at the mercy of all his bodily wants. Living in hope. A believer. A sentimentalist. No, the devil the palm cockatoo resembles is the real anti-being, the black fiend, the negation of life, the Prince of Darkness, scorning everything . . .

·As a member of human society I am naturally sympathetic to the argument that confines appreciation of the comic to our club alone. The anthropologist Mary Douglas convincingly refuses to let a joke escape the total social situation which alone explains its utterance. In a characteristically teasing article entitled 'Do Dogs Laugh?' she demurs from any

Erhard Schön

scientific isolating of the phenomenon of laughter as a discrete facial signal. 'Laughter is a unique bodily eruption,' she writes, 'which is always taken to be a communication. I suggest that this is because a laugh is a culmination of a series of bodily communications which have had to be interpreted in the usual way as part of the discourse. The finally erupting laugh cannot be screened off because all the changes in bodily posture preceding it have been taken as part of the dialogue.'

Which does not preclude, and is not meant to preclude, the possibility that every dog too has his discourse. But Bergson and Hazlitt both start from the premise that a dog's discourse cannot be ours. The idea that we are the only animal that is struck with the difference between what things are and what they ought to be can be easily refuted at the level of ordinary daily dog expectation and disappointment; but that doesn't address the more philosophical, if you like the more metaphysical, discourse which both Bergson and Hazlitt take for granted. And that is the discourse which assumes the Judaeo-Christian myth of the Fall.

In *The Essence of Laughter*, Baudelaire spells out with satanic glee the cultural consequences of our having invented a garden and then locked ourselves out of it:

It seems certain, if we adopt the orthodox view, that human laughter is intimately connected with the accident of an original fall, of a degradation both of the body and the mind . . . In the Earthly Paradise, that is to say in a setting where it seems to man that all created things are good, there can be no joy in laughter. Man being there afflicted with no pain, the expression of his face remains uniform and unchanged, and the laughter which now agitates the nations, brings no deformation to his features. Neither laughter nor tears are to be seen in the paradise of all delights. They are both of them the children of suffering . . .

6

By this token, it is not only the animals who are excluded from laughter, but whoever is not by culture a Judaeo-Christian monotheist believing in mankind's original wickedness. No paradise lost, no diabolic mirth. If you wonder where that leaves the pagan comedy of Greece and Rome, to say nothing of the causes of laughter in Bali or Tibet, well Baudelaire wonders too.

As to the grotesque figures that have come down to us from antiquity,

he is reduced to arguing at last,

the masques, the bronze statuettes, the figures of Hercules, all muscle, and those of Priapus, with tongues stuck out and pointed ears, all head and phalluses – I am convinced that these things once had a high seriousness . . . My own view is that the ancient world was full of respect for drum-majors and strong men of every kind, and that the extravagant fetishes to which I have drawn attention, were no more than symbolic objects of adoration, or, at most, of strength, and by no means the products of an intentionally comic imagination.

Which makes the Greeks a pretty uncomplicated lot, unable to be simultaneously amused and awed, capable only of childlike reverence, lacking the capacity to distinguish the grand from the preposterous and therefore precluded from paying their dues to both. No alien culture is safe from such imputations of naïvety, and no species, once you assume that the only cultural discourse capable of complexity is your own. And since nothing is more complex than comedy, nothing is more frequently denied the foreigner than a capacity to understand or make it.

I am not, of course, suggesting that we can ever ignore the specific contributions monotheistic blight, the apple and the Fall, make to our sense of the ridiculous. In an extraordinary scene in his 1928 silent film *The Circus*, Chaplin finds himself on a high-wire with three escaped monkeys. What ensues is as much horror as it is farce. The monkeys swarm about him, climb him, undress him, bite his nose, and – horror to end horrors – cram their tails into his mouth. It is lunatic of Chaplin to be up there in the first place, but the monkeys' incalculability and ferociousness put his lunacy to shame. Compared to monkeys a man can only be middlingly mad. But to be so closely compared to monkeys at all, to be at moments indistinguishable from them, up there in the ether, in a medium which is more theirs than yours, where they have being and you don't, high above a hysterically laughing crowd, is a grotesquerie whose degree of fearful-funniness is bound to be determined by whether you are a Hindu or a Christian, whether you consider monkeys to participate in the divine, or whether you believe you were created to enjoy proud dominion over them but have subsequently let your creator down. How and where we laugh at Chaplin monkeyed on the high-wire is all a question of the cultural baggage we are carrying. Yet some of the comic effect must still be attributed to the doings of the monkeys themselves. The 'penetrating, antediluvian malevolence' of the New Mexican parrots seems to Lawrence to belong 'to the ages before brains were invented'. So does the malevolence of the monkeys.

'If you come to think of it,' Lawrence goes on, 'when you look at the monkey, you are looking straight into the other dimension ... There's no rope of evolution linking him to you, like a navel string. No! Between you and him there's a cataclysm and another dimension ... He mocks at you and gibes at you and imitates you. Sometimes he is even more *like* you than you are yourself. It's funny, and you laugh just a bit on the wrong side of your face. It's the other dimension.'

Hence the persistence of what is animal in what is comic. It is not simply that comedy reconciles us to the animal in ourselves. That bit's easy to see, and easy to say. Reconciliation trips off the tongue. And evolution is an acceptable concept so long as you're the ones who have evolved. Harder for us to take, so in love with our own cultural determinants are we, is the idea that comedy scratches and jeers at us from quite some other place and from quite some other time.

'Are they really human at all?' (*they* being circus clowns) speculates Thomas Mann's confidence trickster, Felix Krull, those basically alien beings, fun-makers with little red hands, little thin-shod feet, red wigs under conical felt hats, their impossible lingo, their hand-stands, their stumbling and falling over everything, their mindless running to and fro . . . which bring the crowd to a pitch of mad merriment. Are these ageless, half-grown sons of absurdity . . . human at all? With their chalk-white faces and utterly preposterous painted expressions – triangular eyebrows and deep perpendicular grooves in their cheeks under the reddened eyes, impossible noses, mouths twisted up at the corners into insane smiles – masks, that is, which stand in inconceivable contrast to the splendour of their costumes – black satin, for example, embroidered with silver butterflies, a child's dream – are they, I repeat, human beings, men that could conceivably find a place in everyday life? In my opinion it is pure sentimentality to say that they are 'human too', with the sensibilities of human beings and perhaps even with wives and children. I honour them and defend them against ordinary bad taste when I say no, they are not, they are exceptions, sidesplitting monsters of preposterousness, glittering, world-renouncing monks of unreason, cavorting hybrids, part human and part insane art.

Here may be the reason why, with one or two very rare exceptions, biographies of clowns and comedians tell you so little of what you want to know – by what means and to what end they are so funny. The answer does not lie in any narrative of their daily lives. You may as well, with the same expectation of success, write the biography of a palm cockatoo.

Hard, when it comes to comedy – where we believe we have garnered up our humanity – hard to accept the persistence of the non-human and the pre-human. But necessary. And as thrilling in the end as Marlow's acceptance, in Conrad's *Heart of Darkness*, of his 'remote kinship' with the 'wild and passionate uproar' of the jungle. 'Ugly. Yes, it was ugly enough; but if you were man enough you would admit to yourself that there was in you just the faintest trace of a response to the terrible frankness of that noise, a dim suspicion of there being meaning in it which you – you so remote from the night of first ages – could comprehend. And why not? The mind of man is capable of anything – because everything is in it, all the past as well as all the future. What was there after all? Joy, fear, sorrow, devotion, valour, rage – who can tell? – but truth – truth stripped of its cloak of time.'

Some men have to journey to the Congo to find truth stripped of its cloak of time. I'm more of a stay-at-home myself. I propose we find it in the comic. Always remembering how much of the Congo comedy comprehends.

II

And then there are the angels . . .

The little angels. Piping down the valleys wild, Piping songs of pleasant glee, laughing on a cloud. The holy innocents of laughter, trailing clouds of glory, the infant equivalent to the hare running races in its mirth.

What are we looking for when we scan a baby's face for any semblance of a smile, hoping against hope that this time it isn't wind? Are we searching for some intimation of immortality, some happy baby recollection of the heaven he has just vacated? Do we want a sign that he is ready now to take pleasure in *this* life, that he has successfully negotiated the distance between there and here? Or is it simply love we want to see, a smile of love for us?

When a Navajo baby laughs aloud for the first time he gets a party. All the family is invited. Food is provided and paid for by whoever was the cause of the baby's amusement or was with him when he gave vent to it. A prayer of thanks for the laughter is given by a grandparent. And the baby hands out salt and sweets to all the guests, a promise of continuing good humour and generosity.

Very different, as a way of expressing appreciation for what is free and joyous in childhood, from such Judaeo-Christian traditions as swaddling and circumcision. But then the Navajo do not understand the story of their creation as a process of falling off. They progress, they do not retard. They make a little too free, ancestrally, with other people's wives and husbands, and this keeps them moving from world to world, but they are always ascending, are born out of corn at last as First Man and First Woman and suffer no fundamental rupture with the creative powers. They do not, therefore, as a matter of cultural obligation, habitually measure the difference between what things are and what they might have been. So they might fairly be said – speaking metaphysically, not socially or politically – to have more to be pleased about. (Whether they have more to *laugh* about depends on whether we believe laughter proceeds from an apprehension of pleasure or a recollection of pain, and we have yet to resolve that one.)

In July 1995, I went to Window Rock, the Navajo capital, just on the Arizona side of the New Mexico/Arizona border, to film a first-laugh rite. Baby Calvin had been born on the very morning we first rang the Navajo from London. No other baby was in the offing. Aristotle reckons you can start expecting a baby to laugh from about its fortieth day, and the Navajo agree with Aristotle. Yes, we could come and film the party, but there are no guarantees with laughter. You can say when you should start expecting it but you can't say for certain when it's going to happen. Some babies take longer to find the world laughable than others. They were prepared to delay the party for a day or two if they knew we were on our way, but they wouldn't fake it if Calvin hadn't laughed before we got there. You don't play fast and loose with first-laugh rites. You don't tell lies around laughter. We, however, had to plan the trip weeks in advance. A crew has to be booked. Dates have to be fixed. And we had other appointments to keep in the vicinity. We couldn't hold everything for Calvin. So we had no choice but to risk it.

When we left London, forty-two days later, Calvin still hadn't laughed. The Navajo had our itinerary. Every hotel we were staying in. Every airport we were passing through. Calvin's laugh was a matter of great urgency to us. If there was news we wanted to hear it right away, even if we were 30,000 feet above sea-level and it meant the Navajo ringing the pilot.

But no news came. Each morning over breakfast the first question the cameraman asked was, 'Well, has Calvin laughed?'

We were four days in New York, two days in West Virginia, a day in Albuquerque, four in Santa Fe. We were getting closer. Now the cameraman *and* the camera assistant *and* the soundman were asking before *every* meal, 'Well, has he laughed yet?' And finally, just 'Well?' We went to bed with no other worry on our minds; we rose with no other question on our lips. We were even beginning to get angry with him. Laugh, you little bastard! Laugh!!

Then, two nights before we were due to drive to Window Rock, laden with woolly toys and funny masks to *make* Calvin laugh if we had to, word arrived. He'd done it. Sat up suddenly in his crib, or whatever the Navajo use to rock their babies into contentment, and chortled. No mistake about it. Really thrown back his head and laughed.

The Navajo had their own joke going about Calvin's timing. They'd known he was ready. They'd felt the imminence of the laugh. Heard it brewing in his belly for days. But given that the person in whose company or on whose lap he laughed would have to cough up for the party, and given how tight money was right now, they'd been passing him furiously from one to the other. As in pass the parcel.

Poor little Calvin. He had an unconscionable number of people, friends and foreigners, and a fair bit of equipment, waiting on that first laugh. But then who knows? – maybe that was what finally tickled him into delivering.

The party itself was a muted affair. How could it be otherwise with cameras and microphones poking into every conversation? And there'd been too much expectation; only a Saturnalia could have adequately recompensed all that uncertain waiting. Or at least something in feathers and fancy-dress. It's a shaming fault to confess to, but I confess to it anyway: I am no better than any other white European when it comes to meeting an Indian – I am disappointed by the lack of war-paint. I want to see him in buffalo skins, not jeans. I want to see him smoking a peace pipe outside his hogan, not playing basketball in a trailer park.

In fact, I'd had my share of the ethnic-picturesque on the morning of the party. I'd been standing in the forecourt of the Navajo Nation Inn, looking around, enjoying the dry desert heat, holding my hat in my hands so that a little sun could get to my forehead, watching a couple of local youths come rolling out of the scrub, kicking stones, falling into each other, the taller of the two in a wide stetson, playing blues on a harmonica. I suspect I was smiling. Enjoying the *experience*. Not quite war-paint, but close. In truth, closer than I'd realized. The harmonica player approached me. 'Why are you holding your hat out, man?' he asked me. 'You begging?' I laughed. A good joke. That was exactly how I was holding my hat. He put his hands in his pockets and brought out a bunch of keys and a coin, a small coin, probably a dime. 'You want me to make a contribution?' I laughed again. Even better joke. 'Go on,' he said, 'choose.' What did I say in return? Something like, 'I couldn't possibly.' Something stiff. But still smiling. 'Go on,' he said, 'take one.' I looked at him hard. He was about nineteen. Small eyes. Pigtails so black they appeared to be shot with grey. A narrower face than most of the Navajo I'd seen. In the main they are handsome people, high-shouldered, with broad Alaskan features. They still look what they once were: fierce nomadic raiders from the north. Quite distinct from the smaller, more secretive Mexican Indian with whom they now peaceably, give or take the odd territorial squabble, share these parts. But my friend's features were more pinched, and not at all peaceable. 'OK,' I said. 'I'll take this.' And I made as if to take the dime. The trap closed on me immediately. 'Typical white man,' he said. 'All you see are dollar signs.' I laughed again. A different laugh, this time. Same sound, different motive. Or maybe not even the same sound. Maybe you could hear the fear. *White man?* We all knew what the white man had done. Was I going to have to take the blame? 'Hang on,' I said, 'you've set this up entirely. I wasn't thinking dollars. I was just standing here, minding my own business . . .' He moved closer to me. I thought I saw his hand about to come up. 'I'm a Navajo, man . . .' Yes, I was going to have to take the blame. But when a hand did come up it belonged to neither of us. It belonged to a Navajo policeman, who just happened to be Calvin's father.

Calvin handed out the salt and sweets at a festive table set up in a space shared by a number of mobile homes and curious goats a dozen miles or so from Window Rock. Fort Defiance, the military-minded white men called this spot. Tsehotsoi, the Navajo knew it as – Meadow Between Rocks. A marvellous vermilion canyon, fed by permanent springs and with air as dry as a whip. Of course Calvin wasn't able truly to hand out salt and sweets himself. He was still too young for that. And spent most of his party asleep. But a pretend dispensation worked just as well. Perhaps better. A first-laugh rite, after all, is a form of drama, and drama requires the structure of pretence.

It was a quiet affair. Only by straining my ears and trying to blot out all other sounds was I able to hear Calvin's grandmother give thanks for his 'first laugh'. She kept her eyes lowered throughout the prayer. As much in shyness as devotion. Everyone was shy. The way people should be. The way people were, I like to think, before the tyranny of the idea of social ease and familiarity. Now we have to tolerate the linguistic junk associated with 'space' and 'personal time', as people endeavour to restore the old distances. It's impossible to imagine such a thing as a first-laugh rite in a society that has trouble recognizing reserve. You have to be diffident to appreciate the naked intimacy of laughter. You have to be apart before you can be brought together. Laughter has to come hard to you if you are to acknowledge its shocking force.

You laugh some time after your fortieth day, Aristotle says, and then you become a human being. That was what we were doing in the Meadow Between Rocks – celebrating the fact of Calvin having laughed himself into humanity. Which is a tougher proposition than piping songs of pleasant glee, When the green woods laugh with the voice of joy/ And the dimpling stream runs laughing by/ When the air does laugh with our merry wit/ And the green hill laughs with the noise of it; but not so tough

as Blake's alternative version of infancy, wherein the struggling and swad-
dled babe makes a political decision in favour of simulated mirth:

> When I saw that rage was vain,
> And to sulk would nothing gain,
> Turning many a trick & wile,
> I began to soothe and smile.

The trouble with the innocence/experience dichotomy is that it makes
us too unforgiving of calculation. If Blake's wily infant's smile informs
the parents that their child has mastered the politics of the emotions,
shouldn't that in itself be a reason for them to celebrate? Isn't that
soothing smile the proof that his chances of social survival are good?
Among the many things it signifies and promises, isn't laughter also a sign
of worldliness, a sort of pledge of at-homeness in the world?

Perhaps that too was what we were honouring at Calvin's place. A
covenant between Calvin and the laughter-gods, guaranteeing him owner-
ship of the earth. Sealed with salt, as was the covenant between King
David and the God of Israel. According to the Jicarilla Apaches of northern New Mexico, the earth and the underworld and the sky were created
by the Black Hastshin, who, when he made man, ordered him first to
speak, then to laugh, then to shout. '*Now* you are ready to live around
here,' he said.

On the face of it, this would seem to be altogether too positive an interpretation of infant laughter for the psychoanalyst Christopher Bollas. In
the final chapter of *Cracking Up*, extracts of which I heard him read in
1994 at a conference on humour organized by the Freud Society and held
at the Comedy Store – a conference which the comedian Arnold Brown
took by storm with hostile wit, and the once-genius-comedian John
Cleese depressed with conciliatory melancholy – Bollas offers small comfort to those who would read a baby's smile as a token of either a paradise
remembered or a paradise to come. Wherever there's a scientifically
minded optimistic psychoanalyst there's a baby wired up to a computer;
but, says Bollas,

however clever infant researchers are in finding an infant's skills, the euphoria
surrounding this research is reminiscent of the dolphin hysteria of the 1960s. An
entire generation thought that it was merely a matter of a decade at most before

dolphins would speak, write autobiographies about life at sea, move from Sea World to Parliament. Baby worshipping – a kind of mangerophilia – would have us believe that infants are on the verge of a similar breakthrough, but in fact baby *is* rather stupid. He smiles because he does not *know* what a miserable situation he is in. And the Great Clown in the sky

(that's mother he's talking about)

knows this; when she puts on 'showtime', she is luring him away from his true predicament into the world of make-believe. She believes she's with a sucker who will laugh because he doesn't know better. He is the first true ingenue: too ignorant to know that he is being taken in.

In fact – and Bollas is wise to this – the saving of baby from his own stupidity, that's to say from the *charge* of stupidity, is already implicit in this account of it. If he's so stupid, how come he knows so well where his own best interests lie? Smart of him – isn't it? – to grasp that make-believe, the dramatic structure of comedy, enables him to escape the actual miseries of his situation. 'In its origins,' Bollas goes on, 'a sense of humour takes pleasure in inadequacy. A mother who is amused by baby and who can get baby to laugh at himself before he consciously knows what the joke is all about helps to develop a sense of amusement in the human predicament well before the self comprehends his condition.' That stupid laughter, in other words, is nicely on the way to becoming a vital piece of psychological equipment. Without thinking about it much, we take the absence of a sense of humour in someone else to be a serious impoverishment for them and an almost unpardonable affront to us. Let RADAR – The Royal Association for Disability and Rehabilitation – do all it likes to get us to refer to the handicapped as people with 'sensory impairments', or a dwarf as a 'person with restricted growth'; a humourless little shit will always be a humourless little shit.

Bollas is chillingly good – apocalyptic enough to frighten off any conscientious parenter – about what a mother whose pitch and timing are not right, who is not the clown she should be, may do for baby's sense of the ridiculous for ever. And the implication of that is that she performs an inestimable psychic service for the baby when she gets it right. Taking 'into herself . . . that internal madness which shakes up baby – as it were, absorbing and transforming the element of shock and disturbance'; deflating 'the baby's grandiosity . . . building into the infant's psychic structure that pleasure which is intrinsic to the self's follies, that relief we all need from the tedious demands of a grandiose state of mind'; bringing 'under temporary human control something that is in fact beyond human influence'; reconciling what is him, no less, to everything that is not. A tall order. And all this, in his apparent stupidity, in his blank unknowing misery, the infant greedily accedes to, laughs like a drain and cannot wait to laugh again.

Given what is at stake, given that it is emotional survival we are talking about, his greediness for laughter should be no more surprising to us than his greediness for milk.

III

A word more about humourless little shits. Who, curiously, in the infinite number of myths and fairy stories in which they figure, are almost always female.

Though then again perhaps it is not at all curious. For those stories about unsmiling princesses, of which every culture throws up examples, from riddling sphinxes to moon-mad Turandots, are in fact stories about frigidity, and whoever heard of a frigid man? What then becomes curious is the identification of the laughing organs with the sexual ones. Why wrap up a moral about a woman who will not yield to anyone sexually in the narrative of a woman – usually royal, invariably rich – who cannot crack a smile? Somewhere in all this, I suspect, Christopher Bollas still lurks:

A sense of humour – which takes pleasure in the contradictory movements of two objects (two people, or a person and the environment, or a word and its other meanings) – incorporates the plastic and the wooden, the fluid and the fixed.

Ditto whatever is the opposite of a sense of frigidity. The woman who refuses to yield sexually – or to initiate sexually, if the idea of yielding is now absolutely *hors du jeu* – manifestly takes no pleasure in the contradict-ory movements of two objects. She is wooden, not plastic; fixed, not fluid. Only grant the premise of the fairy story – to wit, the unsmiling princess has a problem in the area of relating self to not-self – and you can start looking around for blame. Was it mother's fault? Did mother get the comic timing wrong? Was the baby princess never eased into that dramatic structure of mutual make-believe which is the secret both of good comedy and good sex? Most times there isn't a mother around at all; the one doing the worrying, the one who issues all the edicts offering the princess's hand in marriage to whoever can coax laughter out of her is the father, the rich man, the king. Too busy ruling, or making money, ever to have put in time cracking baby up. Too dignified ever to have played the Great Clown in the sky.

But first let's consider some of these folk or fairy stories, or jocular tales as they are sometimes designated.

A Norwegian version – *Taper-Tom Who Made the Princess Laugh* – lays out the social and psychological conditions of the inaugural frigidity without any ado:

There was once a king who had a daughter, and she was so beautiful that she was known both far and wide; but she took herself so seriously that she could never laugh, and then she was so haughty that she said 'No' to everyone who came and courted her. She would not have anyone, no matter how fine, whether he was prince or gentleman. The king had long since tired of this, and felt that she could get married like the others; she had nothing to wait for, she was old enough; nor would she be any richer, either, for she was to have half the kingdom which she had inherited from her mother.

So there it is. The princess is motherless, grandiose, humourless and loverless; a chain of interlocking deprivations that can be broken only by the intervention of a third party, of necessity a stranger, usually a bit of an ass, without money or breeding or dignity or even competence, in this case Taper-Tom 'who knew nothing and did nothing, but only sat by the hearth like a cat and poked in the ashes and whittled pine torches'. Not to put too fine a point on it, stared into the fire and pulled his pud.

Meaning that there are now *two* lots of perfectly good genitalia going to waste.

To bring the one to the other, and cut a long story short, Taper-Tom procures a golden goose whose splendid feathers shine so powerfully that they remove all necessity for pine torches and the obsessive whittling thereat. What is more, whoever so much as touches the bird becomes glued to it, provided Tom remembers to say, 'Hang on, if you want to come along!' Just in case we have still not cottoned on to what the golden goose portends, the cook of the royal household into which Taper-Tom has succeeded in gaining access, reaches out a hot and greedy hand, pleading, 'May I stroke that lovely bird you have?' She is not the only one who would like to grab a feel or steal a feather. And pretty soon Tom has a whole procession of the avid and the concupiscent, the irascible and the boorish, including the king's blacksmith with his tongs, and the lickerish cook with her pot and ladle, stuck fast to his incandescent goose. Seeing this 'gang of scarecrows', the princess laughs so long and hard that the king has to hold her up . . .

'So Taper-Tom gets the princess and half the kingdom.'

Addressing another version of this story – *The Golden Goose*, as related by the Brothers Grimm – Bruno Bettelheim ascribes the princess's laughter to the hero's 'making people who normally command respect look ridiculous'. This is a sort of carnival reading of the tale. And certainly Taper-Tom effects a carnival-like procession. But clerical personages are among those held fast to the goose in the Grimm version, sextons and parsons, people who patently do command a degree of local veneration; whereas Taper-Tom's haul includes no one more worthy than a cook or a blacksmith. So the mirth he generates cannot really be explained away communistically. Nor is it quite clear, on this reading, why the princess must yield up her body to the hero, just because he is a good organizer of street festivals. For there to be a marriage, the hero must be simultaneously funny and erotic in his own person. This is where the democracy comes in: the laughter he occasions must be as brutish as his origins, the very antithesis to those *beau monde* refinements which are keeping the princess stoppered. Call him a dope, call him a ne'er-do-well, the boy who makes the princess laugh is always a bit of rough.

Jack and His Bargains, an English variant, and one of the *Jack and the Beanstalk* cluster of stories, makes no bones about the best way for a northern lad to melt th'ice in an uppish posh girl's 'eart. This hero doesn't come a-courtin' with a golden goose; in order that there should be no mistake at all, Jack is armed with a singing bee and a magic fiddle and a stick which belabours people of its own accord, provided Jack remembers to say, 'Up, Stick an' at It.'

Now the King's daughter in them parts, 'ad never bin known to smile, an' the King said as anyone as could make 'is gal laugh three times should marry 'er. There was Lords an' Squires, an' Kings an' Princes an' wealthy men cum from all parts of the globe, but nary a one of 'em could make 'er smile. So up goes Jack in 'is ragged clothes, an' with 'Up, Stick an' at It', an' the Bee, an' the Fiddle. An' the Bee sings 'is dear beautiful songs, an' she smiles. An' then the Fiddle plays the 'lightfullest music as you ever 'eard, an' she smiles again; an' then the stick up's amongst 'em all, an' knocks 'em about all ways, an' she laughs outright. It would 'ave made the Devil laugh . . .

That's to say the stick would. The bee is worth a smile. So is the fiddle. But it's the anarchic stick that draws the laughter. Not even Sergeant Troy, flourishing his blade in the hollow amid the fens, achieved so killing a demonstration of phallic indiscriminateness and aplomb. Though as Bettelheim is quick to observe, the story isn't over yet. Jack has still to spend three nights in the princess's bed, as unresponsive as a stone, before the marriage is agreed. 'By such behaviour,' Bettelheim moralizes, 'he demonstrates his self-control; with it he no longer rests his case on the display of phallic masculinity . . . Jack at first has made her only laugh, but at the end he has demonstrated not only (sexual) power but also (sexual) self-control, he is recognized by her as a proper man with whom she can be happy and have many children.'

At first he made her *only* laugh! A laugh, to a princess who has never laughed before, to be passed off as an *only*! You can see why so many comedies call it a day at the point of betrothal. Get into responsible parenting and sexual maturity and it's all up with mirth.

It is laughter that opens the gates of the princess's icy prison. She laughs, she is sexually aroused, and she is free. The process is indivisible. The laughter is the arousal is the freedom.

Let whoever doubts the sexual potency of laughter remember what it is like to have a woman he loves laugh at another man's jokes. Let him only recall the fuel which a misplaced smile or, worse, an overheard laugh, can pour on jealousy. Sexologists tell us that men relish making a woman blush because in the act of blushing her face and neck become gorged with blood, her temperature rises, her skin itches and prickles, exactly as in the act of sex. How much more so, then, is laughter a foretaste and a re-enactment of sexual abandon. Now, not only do the face and neck compete to see which can fill with the more blood, not only does the temperature soar, and the skin itch and prickle, but the lips part, the teeth are bared, the cheeks are drawn upwards, the naso-labial furrows curve, the head falls back, the throat arches, the chest heaves, breath comes quickly, catches and then comes again, queer spasmodic sounds over which the utterer has no control pour from the mouth, the eyes roll, water and, ultimately – if the joke is truly one to remember – they close. Embarrassment and shame then follow: the body's confession of exposure, conscious that it has momentarily yielded all authority over itself.

We give a lot away when we laugh.

This self-surrender to laughter must be what Marceau, the poacher in Renoir's splenetic (and once banned) 1939 movie, *La Règle du Jeu*, has in mind when he divulges the secret of his success with women. 'Well, sir, whether I want to love them or leave them . . . I always try to make them laugh. A laughing woman is disarmed, you can do what you like. Why don't you try the same, sir?'

'Marceau,' replies the count, 'one needs the gift.'

The gift. Not the knack, as Ann Jellicoe understood it in her famous play of that name. Not a technique for subduing the other sex; not the Don Juan undertaking, to whose success laughter is, if anything, injurious. More a genius for prosperity. The sexual equivalent to green fingers. A fertility gift.

For my part, I remember young manhood as a perpetual frenzy to make a woman laugh. My own late teenage years were nothing short of that, an unrelenting demon-driven green-woods maypole-dancing monomaniacal frenzy, which no amount of success could ever assuage, and no amount of cold weather could ever temper, to get women to throw back their heads and show me their throats. That's all. Just show me their throats. But show *me* their throats. Should they show them to someone else, my frenzy turned into a universal violence; I grew fevered, raving, delirious, distracted enough to kill.

All comedians must be familiar with this condition.

Given the comedic enterprise as I've adumbrated it (and leaving until a later chapter the question of where exactly this leaves the female co-median) we are now in a position to understand the immemorial ambition of the funny-man – from the first clown to the latest stand-up – quite literally to make a prick of himself. Up, Stick an' at It! When Loki, the evil spirit of Norse mythology, is presented with the challenge of yet another congenital unsmiler in the shape of the giant's daughter, Skathi, he pulls off an act of the most pure and quintessential clownishness, incorporating the animal and the divine, the reckless and the calculated, the self-aggrandizing and the self-demeaning, but more to the point enfolding the phallic in the farcical . . .

. . . he ties his genitals to the beard of a goat.

Now, Skathi, see if you can hold your face together when the goat begins to buck.

Risk your manliness to this degree to make a stoneface princess smile and your rage when she laughs at another man's efforts is surely allowable. But then a comedian is *always* risking himself to this degree, whether or not he employs a goat. Because of the sex that there is in laughter, silence inevitably feels like a sexual rebuff. Hence the cruel satisfactions we find, as neutral third-party observers, when comedians compete. The pleasure we derive from a television programme such as 'Have I Got News For You' is in direct relation to the pain and humiliation each of the regular comic personages evidently suffers when the other is funnier than him. One goes into a pet; the other changes colour and averts his eyes – now A, now B, wounded like a discarded suitor by the fickleness of that bitch-princess the audience.

In the heyday of American vaudeville, the entrepreneur Willie Hammerstein, son of Oscar, capitalized brilliantly on the idea of the unsmiling princess *and* the castrated comedian. Hammerstein ran the Victoria, a 'Nut House' or freak show, on the corner of Broadway and 42nd Street. Here he installed the ultimate mirthless woman, Sober Sue – a sort of Madge Allsop of the times – and offered a thousand dollars to anyone who could make her laugh. The best comedians of the day lined up to try. Everybody who was anybody in comedy. All failed. *Ouch!* Rebuffed. Not their fault. Hammerstein knew he couldn't lose. Sober Sue's face was paralysed. But a rebuff is still a rebuff.

The same diabolic principle, somewhat less freakishly applied, was the inspiration for the ABC's 'Make Me Laugh', a TV game show which Bob Monkhouse briefly graced in 1958, and confessed to in his autobiography, *Crying with Laughter*, thirty-five years later.

One of this show's star panellists was the 'King of the One-liners' Henry Youngman, who'd befriended me after I'd introduced him on one of the London Palladium shows as 'a rumour in his own lifetime' and followed his act with 'what a comedian – he has such an original memory'. Henry enjoyed these insults and, as soon as he got back to the States, he recommended me to executive producer Mort Green, who booked me as one of the three guest comedians who took turns at trying to make a blank-faced contestant laugh within one minute. For every second the punter didn't laugh, he or she won a dollar. I took part in three shows in one evening and, during each of my twelve one-minute efforts to crack their resolve, my contestants won their full money. As I was leaving the studios to crawl in shame back to my hotel,

(*shame*, note)

Green stopped me and said, 'I knew you still had shortages in Britain but I never figured you were all out of funny.'

If Monkhouse did as badly as he claims, it was almost certainly because he was not, in the American way, blue enough. In its later 1970s version, anyway, the show teased its viewers with the imminence of male co-medians, acting singly or in packs, talking dirty – cute-dirty; America is always America – to someone's wife or girl-friend. Occasionally, in order to give an impression of balance, men were hauled out of the audience, but immediately all the racy suggestiveness leaked out of the programme. For the show to work contestants had to be female, not to say feminine, young, good-looking, distinctly Catholic or Jewish (discernibly principled, that is), but not prim, not at all blank-faced, just sufficiently strong-minded to be able to cross their legs and set their jaws for a minute at a time, and for us to feel, when they went in the diaphragm, that they had been made to go, against their principles, but not against their natures, by an irresistible comic force.

And what got the one was what got them all. A fine-boned darkly brooding New Yorker, not unlike Susan Sontag around the eyes, not a million miles from the young Anne Bancroft around the mouth, sat stoni-ly through a couple of inept monologues. No sweat. She looked as calmly contemplative as Simone de Beauvoir. What chance did the final duo have with her, a squeaky pair in lemon trousers and funny ties who imitated animals in the ads, beavers, racoons, woody-woodpeckers? I'd have backed them sooner to get a rise out of Hannah Arendt, Simone Weil, Julia Kristeva, the Dworkin woman even. Not this one, though; not Susan Sontag around the eyes, not Sober Sue. But then, forty-five seconds in and getting nowhere, they hit on squirrels, and nuts – NUTS, get it? And she was gone. Head back, throat exposed, naso-labial furrows curved, hot and vaporous gasps escaping from between her moistened lips.

What looks were *then* exchanged between the comedians, the victors and the vanquished, those who'd made a princess laugh, and those who hadn't. The cocks and the gulls.

One of the latter, a crestless sparrow-boned ineffectual quipster, came to grief, if I have my dates right, just one week later, 26 November 1979. The contestant on this occasion was a celebrity, a fruity, all-moving-body-parts night-club singer with a record just released and no powers of resistance whatsoever. The squeaky pair had broken her down in seconds. Ditto a gigolo comedian with an ironic take on self-appreciation. Then it was the crestless sparrow-boned comic's turn. He too, he believed, could have her going in two shakes of a goat's tail. He stood over her. Prodded her. Bullied her. Ha, ha, got you. 'I didn't laugh,' she protested. She appealed to the audience. Did I laugh? Hard to say, bubbles of per-petual laughter being integral to her style of vivacity. But she didn't go for the sparrow-boned guy. A personality clash. Just one of those things. Would not accept that *he* could ever have got a laugh out of *her*. That *she* had ever parted her lips for *him*. 'I didn't laugh!' So now he is hurt. Him alone she doesn't find funny. 'You did. You laughed. Didn't she laugh?' Her face is closed and sullen now. His too. We're into you did, I didn't. These could be divorce proceedings. And in the end the judgement goes against the guy. He didn't, he hadn't, he couldn't have made her laugh. Not man enough. He points a last enfeebled phallic finger at her. And retreats. His mouth disfigured. His self-esteem in tatters. Sexually, utterly destroyed.

Taper-Tom who couldn't make the princess laugh.

IV

Granted the potency of laughter, then, whether we let the laugh out or hold the laugh back, would it not be surprising if there were not a single creation myth which recognized laughter as the First Cause and Primal Agency?

We are familiar with the irresponsible junketings of the gods of the classical and the near-eastern worlds. Zeus in all his pleasures, lending his Latin name to conviviality itself. The Babylonian deities making merry in the broad precincts of their new home, sitting down to festive drink and banquet the moment their houses have been completed. Elsewhere, too, there has never been a shortage of divine high spirits and bawdy. Ganesh, the Hindu elephant-god, trailing his comic trunk; Siva, his benevolent *lingam*. Wakdjunkaga, the quasi-divine Winnebago trickster, detaching his phallus so that it may the more independently enjoy itself. Legba, the trickster god of the Fon, rutting riotously during his time on earth, tricking his mother, the High Goddess Mawu, into returning to the higher place, while he helps himself to whichever woman takes his fancy here below.

But having a good time, in a spirit, so to speak, of *noblesse oblige*, while taking full advantage of all your aristo-divine privileges, is not quite the same as laughing the world into being. For that we have to go to a single papyrus, housed in Paris, which relates how a Godhead of almost certain Hellenized Egyptian extraction (the best of both worlds) laughs aloud seven times – Ha-ha-ha-ha-ha-ha and ha – and thereby sets creation in motion. Out of each laugh wonderfully leaps one of the seven functional gods of the universe. When the Godhead laughs for the first time, light appears, and the god of fire and the cosmos is born. When he laughs for the second, the waters are so amazed they separate, and the god of the abyss makes his appearance. Thereafter, as bitterness and sadness have their way with him – for no one can laugh seven times and not falter in his cheerfulness – more fateful gods are thrown up. Until at last, with the emotions fairly balanced, he whistles mightily to the earth which labours to bring forth a being of its own, a dragon by the name of PHOCHOPHOBOCH, the shining one, the cause, ultimately, of Phobos – terror.

The primal laugh does not make the world an unmitigatedly breezy place. There are tears in laughter. But at least, in this myth, the usual fear and trembling are tempered. Whatever comes later, we get off to a vigorous guilt-free start.

One of the Grimm fairy stories has the created world returning God's favour. Not the same God, of course; though you would expect the thank you to be passed on. According to this fancy, the creator falls ill and comes to convalesce among the people of the earth. While he is down here he encounters a group of jugglers and tumblers. Their antics make him laugh, and his laughter makes him well.

Laughter the best medicine.

Laughter the best . . .

Where our Graeco-Egyptian god was content to laugh seven times and call it a world at that, the modern god of self-help medicine – Man-His-Own-Apothecary – has become so taken with the creative potential of laughter that there is no silencing Him. Wherever there is illness, now, there is a cavorting minor god of mirth. Clowns haunt the wards of

American hospitals, Disneying the young and badgering the old. Some hospitals have humor rooms. Most show the comedy channel. There is a proliferation of books and articles with titles such as *Humor and the Cardio-vascular System*; or, *Alimentary, My Dear Doctor: Medical Anecdotes and Humor*; or, *Epinephrine, Chlorpromazine, and Amusement*; or, *Humor and the Surgeon*; or, *The Use of Humor by Pediatric Dentists*; or, *Mirth and Oxygen Saturation of Peripheral Blood*; or, *Humor and Immune-System Functioning*; or, *Neuroendocrine and Stress Hormone Changes During Mirthful Laughter*; or *Frivolity in Medicine: Is There a Place for It?*

Newsletters carrying the optimistic message of laughter's link-up with long life are sent around the world. You can subscribe to the *Humor Hypnosis and Health Quarterly*, or *Laughter Prescription*, or *Carolina Health and Humor Association Newsletter*; or *Punch: Digest for Canadian Doctors*, or *Achoo!*, the report of the latest doings at the Gesundheit Institute, in West Virginia.

There is a Laughter Therapy organization in Studio City, and another in Santa Barbara. There is a body called Jest for the Health of It in Davis. There is a Health and Humor Association in Norfolk, Virginia, and an-other offering Comedy Improvisation for Healing, Learning, and Com-munication in Denver, Colorado. In New Jersey there's Laughter Remedy; and in Portland, Oregon, Nurses for Laughter.

In 1994, driven by a curiosity that had nothing healthy or remedial about it, I attended the Ninth Annual International Conference on 'The Positive Power of Humor and Creativity', run by the Humor Project Inc. (founder and director, Dr Joel Goodman) in Saratoga Springs, N.Y. Though not specifically a medical conference, the good news *from* medi-cine, trumpeting laughter's prophylactic properties, guggled up into every happy happening and loony lecture. A home health care nurse ran a workshop whose theme was 'Laughter is the Jest Medicine'. An ex-probation officer addressed 'The Connection Between Heart and Hearty Laughter'. Dr Christian Hageseth, who in another age would have been a preacher-man, took us through a double session (with a break for bagels) on 'Healthy Humor: The Art and Psychology of Positive Humor in the Face of Adversity'. And Michael Christensen, founder of the Clown Care Unit and a practising clown himself, comprehensively and unambiguously entitled his lecture, 'Healing Clowns, Clowning Heals: The Red Nose Touches the Heart'.

Many of the delegates were health workers. Those who weren't were counsellors. All were in need of counselling. The only intelligent conversation I recall was with a funeral director. Everyone, of course, was overweight. Few were in possession of anything an Englishman would recognize as a sense of humour. Thousands of homey little sayings, of the *Reader's Digest* sort – laughter *is* the best medicine – found their way on to the walls of the conference centre, into the pages of the conference literature, out of the mouths of the conference lecturers. Dr Goodman himself was a salted mine of used-up puns and burnt-out homilies, a production-line of pithless apophthegms. 'By using humor, you can move from a "grim and bear it" mentality to a "grin and share it" orientation.' 'Love may make the world go round, but laughter keeps us from getting dizzy.' 'Humor can be a wonderful way to add years to your life and life to your years – by preventing a hardening of attitudes.' And countless more. But all, somewhere at their heart, medical. Commonplace beyond the dreams of common men, but still curative.

In the intervals and bagel breaks, delegates heaved their bulks into the book and resource shop where they were able to buy *Epinephrine, Chlorpromazine, and Amusement.* To say nothing of SMILE! badges and red noses and Groucho spectacle-and-moustache sets and, mysteriously, menageries of cling-on, fling-their-paws-around, cuddly toys. What did cuddly toys have to do with humor and creativity? Did these lame and halting delegates think cuddly toys were *funny*, in the way that Rabelais or Aristophanes are funny? Foolish of me even to ask. Of course they didn't. Cuddly toys have to do with making yourself well, finding something to hold, maybe even to love, and making yourself well was what this conference was all about. Humour as I understood it, humour with a u, was of secondary, even minimal importance. Had this been a conference on 'Cuddling and Creativity', or 'Velcro and the Cardiovascular System', the same people would have turned out for it, and the same lectures would have been delivered. Americans aren't looking to laugh, they're just looking to live longer.

What started all this was an article, 'Anatomy of an Illness', which appeared in the December 1976 issue of the *New England Journal of Medicine.* The author was Norman Cousins, a layman, himself editor of the rather more accessible *Saturday Review*, and the illness he was anatomizing was his own. Twelve years before, he had returned from a trip to the Soviet Union 'with a slight fever' which had rapidly deepened into something far more debilitating. The doctors diagnosed ankylosing spondylitis – a collagen disease, a disintegration of the connective tissue in the spine.

'Collagen is the fibrous substance that binds the cells together. In a sense, then, I was coming unstuck.' The chances of his making a full recovery were computed at about five hundred to one. Though his specialist did not in fact personally know of a single patient who had made any kind of recovery from this disease.

Cousins decided to take a hand in his own fate. Looking back over the possible causes of his condition, of which metal-poisoning in the Soviet Union was one, he reasoned that he had been struck down, while others similarly exposed had not, because he alone had been suffering adrenal exhaustion, and that had lowered his resistance. Very well then; if he could see the way down, he could see the way up. Get his adrenal glands to work again. He had read that adrenal exhaustion could have emotional causes, that it could be sheeted back to a massing of negative emotions. 'The inevitable question arose in my mind: what about the positive emotions? If negative emotions produce negative chemical changes in the body, wouldn't the positive emotions produce positive changes? Is it possible that love, hope, faith, laughter, confidence, and the will to live have therapeutic value?'

And that's where we, and all the annual international conferences on the positive power of Humor and Creativity, come in. *Laughter*. Cousins' account of how he effected his momentous cure was interesting to holistic health philosophers in all its details, but it was the laughter part that excited popular curiosity. Not least because it was a popular sort of laughter – a popular sort of laughter inducement, anyway – that did the trick. Watching 'the spoofing television programme "Candid Camera"'. Having the nurse pull down the blinds and play him old Marx Brothers films on a borrowed projector. Being read to out of a *Subtreasury of American Humor*.

'It worked. I made the joyous discovery that ten minutes of genuine belly laughter had an anesthetic effect and would give me at least two hours of pain-free sleep. When the pain-killing effect of the laughter wore off, we would switch on the motion-picture projector again, and, not infrequently, it would lead to another pain-free sleep interval.'

That laughter is good for you, that a party is as necessary as prayer, that 'people must be amuthed, thquire', that a 'merry heart doeth good like a medicine' – all this is the common stock of knowledge. But just *how* a merry heart doeth good like a medicine, just how laughing at 'Candid Camera' could put a disintegrating man back together again, became, after Cousins, a question which scientific research could no longer leave to novelists and theologians.

The findings of that research now trip lightly off the tongue of every humor-nut and stress-manager in America and every NHS funster and clown-carer in Britain. To wit: laughter positively affects the circulatory system, the respiratory system, the cerebral system, the immune system. Just as jogging stimulates the muscles of the abdomen and the chest and the shoulders and the face, so does laughter – hence the coinage 'stationary jogging', for which we have to thank a Dr William Fry of Stanford. ('Funniest novel I've ever read; I jogged till I cried' – Fay Weldon.) Laughter accelerates breathing, raises blood pressure, increases pulse rates, improves ventilation. It can increase adrenalin which in turn may activate the release of endorphins and enkephalins, a pair of narcotic peptides – happy-dust – instrumental to the suppression of pain, the relief of depression, and the writing of lectures for humor conferences. And then there are the catecholamines, which play a part in enhancing blood flow, reducing inflammation, and generally whipping you into a state of cheerfully expectant arousal.

These are powerfully persuasive arguments both for laughter and for comedy. And now that the researchers have done their work there is an even more powerfully persuasive argument for them to leave the laughter-making itself to those whose profession it is. It was the Marx Brothers who put Norman Cousins back together, not an intern in a funny hat. But there seems to be some infection of triviality in the discovery of endorphins and enkephalins which ensures that whoever alludes to them must end up sounding like Joel Goodman. In an inauspiciously titled little self-help chuckle book – yes, I fear so, *Laughter the Best Medicine* – Robert Holden, founder of the first free NHS Laughter Clinic in Great Britain (courtesy of the West Birmingham Health Authority), scuttles through all the familiar physiology, breathing, pulse rates, catecholamines, only to lay out a programme of laughter medicine exercises which makes you despair for the future mental health and overall well-being of humanity.

He proposes, for example, the creation and maintenance of a LAUGHTER LOG of your life,

in which you record 'happy highlights' of each day . . . Jokes, celebrations, witty sayings, humorous anecdotes, joyful events, entertainments, funny moments, slip-ups, successes, thrills, moments of inspiration (also known as *eurekas!*), romantic adventures and silly stories can all make excellent entries. In no time at all your laughter log will become a most precious transcript of your personal history – a true blessing.

And then there is TRANSCENDENTAL CHUCKLING,

the silliest of all the creative growth games that we play at the Laughter Clinic.

To perform transcendental chuckling you should, on waking each morning, sit in a cross-legged, upright position before a mirror and embark upon two minutes of laughing for no reason whatsoever. Life will never be the same. Anyone who sends a tape of his or her two minutes' unconditional laughter to the Laughter Clinic receives a Certificate of Membership to the Happy Human Being Club. Now *there's* an incentive!

For a wild moment or two one toys with the possibility that the italics and the exclamation marks proclaim a man sending himself up. Just to be on the safe side I telephoned him, and listened to his take on silliness. 'I've explored the concept of silliness, the history of silliness. You know it used to mean to be blessed, to be unconditional.' Yes, I knew. *Selig*. German for blessed. Hence Woody Allen's *Zelig*. Selig/silly talk is almost as common among humorologists as endorphins are. Even more common when the humorologist is also a churchman. But *unconditional* as a meaning of selig I was not familiar with. That was a gloss all of Holden's own. So he could do more with words in the flesh, so to speak, than on the page. And he proved that again when he continued, 'Today we have to work off this wanting to be normal. We need frolic. I teach infringement . . .'

I allowed the pleasure I take in the word frolic to hold me back from saying that transcendental chuckling didn't sound to me like an infringement of anything very much. Besides, I wanted to tackle him on another matter. What he called 'superiority humour'. He had quoted Hobbes in his little book. The usual bit of Hobbes, haranguing laughter for being that 'sudden glory arising from a dawning belief in some eminency in ourselves, by comparison with the infirmity of others . . .' An interpretation of the motive force of laughter which has nothing remotely healthful or selig about it. We might differ over the justice of Hobbes's definition of laughter as a joyful self-irradiation of spite and malice, but by no reasoning could his meaning be twisted into what Robert Holden wanted it to mean – 'When we laugh we tend to feel good about ourselves, and when we feel good about ourselves it is much easier to feel good about our experiences, our future and our lives in general.' What had happened to feeling good because someone else was feeling bad? Why all this baby talk? Why the determination never to address the intractable in humour? Why wouldn't he admit that we often laugh out of the worst of motives?

And that we sometimes *need* to do that, as much as we need to do the other thing?

'People with good self-esteem are usually laughing *with* people,' he told me. 'People with low self-esteem are usually divisive.'

Which was more or less where we left it. I admired his logic and persistence. And he might have been right. I might indeed have been drawing my conclusions as to our needs and nature – as Hobbes might have been drawing his – from precisely that pathic model of humanity which the laughing medics mean to fix up with endorphins.

Except that you have only to lightly quizz a laughing medic to discover that he fears (though would rather not say) that a black laugh may release as many healthful endorphins as a white one. Norman Cousins had made himself better watching the Marx Brothers *and* 'Candid Camera'. What's so benign about 'Candid Camera'? Doesn't 'Candid Camera' get its laughs from exposing unknowing people to a host of cruel indignities and spying on their confusion? Doesn't the pleasure of watching 'Candid Camera' – if a pleasure it is – originate in exactly that 'sudden glory' of which Hobbes speaks? Namely, the 'dawning belief in some eminency in ourselves' – *we* have not been made to look foolish this time – 'by comparison with the infirmity of others'.

In the first of their now well-known, even somewhat cultic Health and Comedy Seminars, held in London in 1993, the comedian Arnold Brown and the physician Brian Kaplan – the comedian in his chartered account-ant's suit, the physician with a fish through his ears – discussed the marriage, but as often as not persuaded us of the misalliance, of comedy and medicine. Kaplan has an airy demeanour, a lightness of voice, a sweetness of mien; he gives the impression of having conversed, quite recently, with the angels. You would want him by your bedside were you in pain. Brown looks the way a comedian should look: much like Pulcinella, uncomfortable in his clothes, surprised to be in possession of a body, a fugitive from some colony of hobgoblins and devils. You would want him by your enemy's bedside, were he in pain. He talks about comedy as revenge, comedy as death-centred, comedy as misanthropy. All this by way of illustration of Kaplan's argument that comedy is good for you. He also interrupts Kaplan regularly, on the pretext of a joke having occurred to him, but for no other reason really than that an interruption is a com-edian's stock-in-trade. A second or two that goes to you is a second or two that doesn't go to him. Naturally, Kaplan frequently finds this galling but has to swallow it. After all, comedy is good for you.

As far as mixing acid wit with holistic wisdom goes, as far as a civilized afternoon's entertainment in London's teaching-hospital district goes, the Kaplan–Brown Health and Comedy Hour cannot be faulted. But when I was present, at least, the logic of their conjoined arguments was not pursued. If comedy is indeed, as Arnold Brown would have it, a black spider's web of misanthropy, greed for vengeance, subversion and morbidity, and if it yet contains, as Brian Kaplan would have it, the most marvellous curative properties, then it must follow that there is something our systems positively respond to in the expression of misanthropy, greed for vengeance, subversion and morbidity.

This is not merely a question of balancing the benevolent with the splenetic, of admitting that we all sometimes enjoy a brackish laugh. Far more is at stake. For if we once acknowledge that black and hostile comedy (laughing *at*, not laughing *with*) fulfils an important physiological function, we are well on the way to understanding how it also fulfils an important social one.

Go to Bernard Manning's Embassy Club in Manchester on a Friday or Saturday night – go soon, before the Manchester equivalent of the happy-badge wearers of Saratoga Springs shuts it down – and deny, if you can, that some sort of communal purgation is at work. Manning is not the most charismatic of comedians. Nor is his material always of the freshest. Some nights he is feeling good and he can make it sing, some nights *taedium vitae comicus* seizes him and you feel you are at a wake for a wasted life. 'They say you are what you eat – I'm a cunt,' he avers, one week with the most buoyantly innocent zest, bonding in boyish gluttony with every member of his audience, the next with so little attack he may as well be saying his prayers. Either way, and no matter how many times they've heard it, the busloads of mauve-collared drinking men who are his fans laugh uproariously. It's good to hear someone say cunt in a public place. It's good to be reminded that there's a bit of a gourmand and a bit of a pig in all of us. If the joke comes out ugly, if you can detect the fatigue and the self-hate in it, well that too takes a bit of the strain from off *your* heart. Good to see another man in an emotional fix. Good to share it.

Down, down they go, these fagged-out hunter-gatherers, harried in and out of work and marriage and fatherhood, mostly white, mostly gentile, mostly heterosexual, down, down they go into the basements of their own natures. Like Norman Cousins, laughing for their lives.

The cliché has it that this is comedy operating as a safety-valve. A metaphor taken from pressure-cooking: letting the steam out. Or from

Jacques Callot

the chemical industry: the controlled escape of dangerous gases. Fine, as far as the idea of build-up of pressure goes, but a touch too genteel as regards the build-up of bodily poisons. It's back to the infirmary again. Comedy in a club like Bernard Manning's lances the boil. It enables the pus to run.

Forget transcendental chuckling and laughter logs; if you want to see a laughter clinic in operation visit the Embassy Club on a Friday or a Saturday night. And wonder why *it* isn't on the National Health.

But Manning is in trouble as I write. Not for saying cunt but for saying black. An undercover television programme, working with a hidden microphone and a hidden camera (the latter so hidden it couldn't get any pictures), caught him saying black a few too many times to an audience of almost exclusively white off-duty policemen. The low-quality press, famous for its unvarying humanitarian stand in matters of race relations, took exception to this breach of ethnic manners. Both Manning's and the policemen's. The less low-quality press searched its whited soul and wondered whether there might be a case for censorship after all. The argument that Manning was giving the policemen not just what they wanted but what they needed – lancing the boil, allowing the pus to run – was nowhere advanced.

Jacques Callot

We behave more intelligently than we talk. The wisdom of acquired social knowledge lingers longer in our actions than in our speech. Hence the value of ritual: it represents the victory of our accumulated experience over our aberrant individual stupidity. And an assembly of men, all belonging to the same profession, gathered on a particular night for the purpose of eating and drinking and laughing in unison, is ritual or it's nothing. Over that assembly the comedian presides like a priest. That his jokes should be familiar, or that they should evoke predictable responses – Amen! Hallelujah! – is of the essence. Every member of the congregation understands the formalized nature of the occasion. That it bears upon the everyday but is not itself everyday. That there is artifice at work. Drama. Play. And that the play transfigures actuality. In the event of expression of hostilities, that the play is a substitute for the real thing. Saying the unsayable in place of, and in preference to, doing the undoable.

Alexander M. Stephen's account of the Hopi having ritual fun at the expense of their neighbours the Navajo suggests a more spirited occasion than the coppers' dirty night out, but the mechanics are the same.

While the ninth dance was in progress, entered from Pen'dete two grotesque characters representing a Navajo medicine or song man and his wife. He wore a grotesque whitened false face and dilapidated overalls, and at his back an old pouch, representing the fetich pouch, with a bunch of long eagle wing feathers projecting from it. The man personating the wife had also a grotesque whitened mask and ragged old skirt ... Two of the clowns say that they are ailing, have pains in their belly and their limbs. The song man says he can drive the pains away with his medicine, but first wants his fee ... The chanter ties a bit of string round the head of each patient and in it thrusts several twigs of spruce ... He next takes out a large cloth ball wrapped with string ... he throws it once on each of their backs, knocking the wind out of them, and of course producing a laugh from the spectators ... He then made his patients lie down flat on their bellies and, stripping off their breech cloth ... gets a handful of the grass pulp and slaps it on the anus, and then pretends to insert an eagle feather in the anus, really thrusts the quill between their legs, leaving the feather upright.

The other clowns then ask to be treated, and he causes them all to lie down side by side on their bellies and treats them with the grass pulp and feather, and all the people shout with laughter ...

Racism? Is that racist laughter? Laughter at the speech, appearance, supposed avarice, belief-system, cultural backwardness, of another people?

But hold! It gets worse. Ageist jokes ... handicap humour ... transgression of the rules of hospitality ...

In an interval while the clowns were squatted and eating, a real Navajo family chanced to ride through the court, returning home from Walpi where they had been trading. The old man of the family is partly paralyzed and they invited him to sit down and eat with them, which he did. As he was leaving, the clowns made free to play pranks with the old fellow, putting his crutches away and pretending to throw him down ...

Stephen doesn't leave it there though. 'But in fact,' he goes on, 'they were very careful not to hurt the old man who seemed to enjoy the fun as much as they or the spectators.'

The single black policeman at Manning's function also reported having enjoyed the fun. As a participant in the ritual, he grasped the difference between make-believe rudeness and the real thing. We are still in a theatre of cruelty; but it is cruelty not hate, and it is theatre not actuality.

What enables an Irishman who has been hurt by Paddy jokes at work to successfully prosecute a lawsuit is the persuasion that jokes told by one nation about another invariably intend damage, and invariably cause it. Of all the unquestioned assumptions on the politically correct agenda, this is the most indurated: jokes with an ethnic content promote the rhetoric of racism.

Trevor Griffiths's play, *Comedians*, set (deliberately, one must suppose) no more than a hop, step and a jump from Manning's Embassy Club, bogs down in this very assumption. In a dour, dramatically unlikely riff, Eddie Waters, the determinedly has-been comedian of the principled good old kind, travesties the tumble of racist stereotypes with which the un-principled audience-pleasing comedian of the *bad* old kind seeks to ani-mate his act.

They have this *greasy* quality, do Jews. Stick to their own. Grafters. Fixers. Money. Always money. Say Jew, say money. Moneylenders, pawnbrokers, usurers. They have the nose for it, you might say. Hitler put it more bluntly: 'If we do not take steps to maintain the purity of the blood, the Jew will destroy civilization by poisoning us all.' The effluent of history. Scarcely human. Grubs.

Undoubtedly well-meaning as social criticism, this is inept as a parody of racist comedy, supposing there to be such a thing, for the simple reason that it mimics neither comic content nor comic strategy. 'Say Jew, say money,' is no more like a joke than is 'If we do not take steps to maintain the purity of the blood, the Jew will destroy civilization by poisoning us all.' Or than are Griffiths's own unthinkingly stereotypical stage-directions, come to that:

(SAMUELS, *forty-one, fat, Manchester Jewish, cigar, heavy finely cut black overcoat, homburg, white silk scarf, black attaché case . . .*)

Say Jew, say fat, Trevor. Say Jew, say homburg. Say Jew, say cigar.

(This is not the place to examine why I, a Jew, feel far more threatened by those who would wipe out ethnic jokes than by those who unthinkingly make them. But it may be the place simply to record that I do.)

In fact, the failure of Griffiths's racist-comedian satire points up nicely the difference between the brute simplicities of mere ideologic statement – and Griffiths is himself culpably an ideologue – and the strategic com-plexities of even the most basic joke. When, for example, a comedian says

'Take my wife', we know he does not mean *his* wife. We know when we listen to a joke that we are entering, of our own volition, a world of dramatic make-believe, that we are lending ourselves to a fiction, that the I of the comic narration is not the I of the comedian's actual private life. And, by the same token, that the comedian is not the hero of his own narrative. So, when Bernard Manning invites musical requests but says no to any of that 'fucking nigger music', preferring instead something by 'the great Nat King Cole', we do not suppose for a moment that he doesn't know the joke's on him. That is unless we are the unsmiling princess who interviewed Manning for the *Sunday Times* Magazine at the height of his troubles, heard the word nigger in his club, then heard the name Nat King Cole, and adduced this sophistical boomeranging gag as proof that 'his lack of understanding is almost touching'.

Audiences that do get jokes are well versed in their artifice. They are familiar with the dramatic conventions – including the convention of coming to a profane place where profane time holds sway. They know that jokes don't say what they mean or mean what they say. They know that a joke has a plot, a set of characters, is a complex of warring voices. Else, like the *Sunday Times* journalist, they would never laugh.

This is not to wish away what is gross in the joke's raw materials. There would be no virtue in the transfiguration if there were not first something base to transfigure. Nigger. Yes, we heard that. Lance the boil, lance the boil. But the joke, by virtue of being a joke, turns on the teller and bites its own tail. The man who thinks he hates 'fucking nigger' music is revealed as a lover of it.

'I'm not a racist,' proclaims Roy 'Chubby' Brown three times a week in season, at the end of the South Pier, Blackpool (also a profane place), 'I just hate every cunt.' How can you be more even-handed than that? In comedy the hyperbole of hate makes an instant ass of intolerance, while not denying you the extravagant pleasures of indulging it.

Once accept that a joke is a structured dialogue with itself, that it cannot, by its nature, be an expression of opinion, and you have conceded its unlikeness to racist discourse, which by *its* nature is impermeable and cannot abide a contradiction. Had Hitler come to the microphone in flying goggles, danced a little on his toes, and assured the assembled half-million, 'I'm not a racist – I just hate every cunt,' instead of declaiming, with that terrible univocal monotony, 'If we do not take steps etc. etc.,' his audiences in Nuremberg would have responded differently, and so, probably, would history.

*

As though to make the same point by other means, the northern comedian John Thomson has built a droll and ingenious act out of the wild fantasy of a cleaned-up, ideologically sound Bernard Manning. Calling himself Bernard Righton, and coming out to the microphone in an atrocious frilled dinner-shirt, with a pint of beer in one hand and a lighted cigarette in the other, to say nothing of a flurry of little-finger rings, Thomson wonderfully confirms all our worst expectations –

There's a black feller! . . . . . .

Only to confound them more wonderfully still:

. . . a black feller . . . a Pakistani . . . and a Jew . . . in a nightclub . . . having a drink
. . . . What a fine example of an integrated community!

What's funny is that it's not. Jettison the cargo of offence and you jettison the joke.

V

And this returns me to my disagreement with the healers and the badge wearers. Why must it always be *nice* laughter, silliness, clowning about, goofing, that restores us to ourselves? Why, when it comes to more tendentious comedy, the faintness of heart? Why the fear of the derisive parrot, when it may be precisely derisive parroting that makes our hearts strong?

We each draw our own lines. Even Arnold Brown, bedfellow of all things black and murky, felt that he had to pull back a little, in that first Health and Comedy Seminar, from all the swearing that his contemporaries favoured. 'Einstein,' he protested, 'didn't say "A over C equals 4 B squared – fuck off!"'

No. Einstein didn't. But then Einstein wasn't a comedian.

And you yourself, if I am not mistaken, Arnold, just enjoyed saying, 'Fuck off!'

It will be the argument of this book, even when it is not the natural argument of my own timorous disposition, that there can be no drawing of lines with comedy. We cannot argue for its restorative powers, and then pretend it is milk and water that restores us.

Let the story of Iambe and Demeter be our exemplar.

In some accounts Iambe is the daughter of Echo and Pan – a child born of the union of Chattering and Lustfulness. In others she is simply an old obscure woman from Halimos. Whatever her antecedents, Iambe's achievement remains the same: it is she who makes Demeter, the unsmiling goddess, laugh again.

Demeter, goddess of the sprouting corn, is inconsolable. Hades has carried off her beloved daughter, Persephone. He has entombed her with him in the world below, leaving the earth wintry. Demeter wanders her kingdom, veiled, robed as an old woman, unrecognizable, ungoddesslike, searching in vain for her daughter. At length she arrives in Eleusis, where she accepts neither food nor drink. She sinks upon a rock named 'Unsmiling' and mourns. She does not speak. She does not move.

Until Iambe appears in her presence. And pours from her mouth a stream of obscenities. Jests. Ribaldry. Mockeries. Indecencies. A over C equals B squared – fuck off! You are what you eat: I'm a cunt.

'Iambe's conduct,' in the words of the French scholar Maurice Olender, 'becomes *athyros*' – he is quoting Nikander – 'literally, "doorless", "unrestrained", no longer respecting even for an instant the limits and thresholds that regulate the tensions of sexual life in a society of mortals.'

She becomes, in other words, a comedian.

And in the face of her comedy, Demeter's despair evaporates. She rises from the rock named 'Unsmiling'. She laughs. She eats. She drinks. She comes alive. The recumbent earth stirs again . . .

Just to tweak the story further, iambic poetry was the Greeks' chosen form for the expression of rudeness and abuse, mockery, irony, contempt. To iambize means to satirize or deliver invective. To do as Iambe did.

Those mourning for the dead, like Demeter, require more than pleasantries to pull them through. Transcendental chuckling won't do the trick. Nor will badges and red noses. Innocuous laughter, by its nature, lacks potency. It is through comic obscenity that we triumph over the body's mortality. Where the body dies and its deathfulness is mocked, there it is reborn.

The same process works for all our passions. We gain ascendancy over what is vile in us by relishing it with coarse laughter.

CHAPTER TWO

Where There's a Fool There's a Phallus

I

Strip away all that is fairy in the universal legend of the unsmiling princess, and we are left with the story of an anhedonic aristocrat recovering her joy in life when an oaf shows her his penis. Not through the

sight of the penis alone is her emotional release effected; it also has to amuse her by its antics.

Now remove the anhedonic princess from the picture and what are we left with?

The example of Hippoclides, for one. Hippoclides, who flashed and frolicked away a dynasty, and made the expression 'All one to Hippoclides' a catchphrase for supreme indifference.

The story, for which Herodotus is the source, goes like this:

Wishing to marry his daughter, Agariste, to the best husband that can be found in the whole of greater Greece, Clisthenes, tyrant of Sicyon, puts out a proclamation inviting all those who deem themselves worthy to be his son-in-law to come forward within sixty days and be tested. There is no reference to his daughter having difficulties smiling, and precious little mention of anything else about her hereafter. First and foremost, you may say, this is a story about men.

Suitors arrive plentifully, men of 'exalted position and lineage' from Italy and from Thessaly and from the Ionian Gulf and from Aetolia and from Trapezus and from Paeus and from other places in the Peloponnese. And of course from Athens. The wealthiest and most handsome of the Athenians being Hippoclides, son of Tisander.

In order to make trial of their tempers, their accomplishments, their dispositions, and their skills on the running-track and wrestling-ground, King Clisthenes keeps the suitors with him for one whole year, sometimes drawing them apart to test their conversation, sometimes bringing them all together for sumptuous meals. Bodily skills and strength may be of the first importance in choosing a son-in-law, but so is deportment around the dining table.

Partly because of his 'manly spirit', and partly because he is of good family, Hippoclides pleases the king best of all. Whether or not he pleases the king's daughter we are never told. This, as I have said, is a suitor story without any significant suitee. The final choice, anyway, is to wait upon a wedding-feast, at which the whole population of Sicyon will be present.

The appointed day arrives. A hundred oxen are sacrificed. The suitors are regaled. And after dinner is completed, they vie with one another in music and in public speaking. As the drinking advances, Hippoclides 'comes to dominate the company'. He calls for the flute player and requests a jig. And then he dances to it, taking great delight in his own performance. A judgement which is not shared by Clisthenes, who now begins to look upon his favourite with distaste. After a pause to get his wind back, Hippoclides orders a servant to bring him in a table . . .

and when it was brought, he got on it and did a Laconic clowning dance and then an Attic one, and thirdly he stood on his head on the table and made gestures with his legs . . . [Whereupon] Clisthenes gave up all thought of having him for a son-in-law, because of his dancing and immodesty.

If that seems a trifle humourless and harsh, consider Greek costume and the likely manner of its fall when a man stands upon his head and gestures with his legs. Immodesty not simply in the sense of arrogance. Immodesty in the sense of impropriety. Immodesty in the sense of impudicity.

It's the sight of the upside-down Hippoclides, shamelessly waving his legs in the air, that makes it impossible for the king to countenance him as a husband to his daughter. Whatever *she* might think.

'Son of Tisander,' says he at last, 'you have danced yourself out of a wife.'

Comes back the reply, 'It's all one to Hippoclides.'

In an alternative translation, 'What does Hippoclides care?'

And why would that phrase, translated whichever way you like it, have become, as Herodotus assures us it did, *a byword ever since*? Perhaps because of how much it whistles away. Perhaps because of its upside-down delivery. Perhaps because of its conjunction with Hippoclides's gross exposure. Genuine expressions of the sublimely carefree are hard to come by. Mainly they are idle boasts. But Hippoclides truly reverses his calculating and his pleasure-loving organs, puts his manhood where his mouth is, and fixes inescapably the association of clowning, the nether body, and indifference.

Another of the reasons – perhaps the very first of reasons – why we go on seeking out lewd priapic farce: it connects us to the grand democracy of things, where it's all one, where nothing matters.

Comedy, Aristotle assures us, originated with the phallic songs.

When I was at school I gathered from that that it was the phallus that did the singing. Not so impossible, given the apotropaic phalluses you find in any good museum: phalluses with wings, phalluses with feet, phalluses with eyes and teeth and claws; dog phalluses, goat phalluses, Leviathan phalluses, phalluses that rise up snarling at their owners, phalluses in a basket, phalluses with phalluses of their own. Compared to those, a lyric tenor phallus is not that wild an extravagance.

Félicien Rops

Hardly wilder, anyway, than a phallus that is sung *to*.

Either way, by effectively ascribing a phallic origin to all drama – comedy growing out of the songs, and tragedy out of the hymn to the wine god, Dionysus – Aristotle had sown the dragon's teeth. Up until very recently it has been impossible for classicists to accept bawdy and buffoonery, drunkenness and the genitalia, as the motive forces for the creation of the first western dramatic art. 'It is extraordinarily difficult to suppose,' wrote the near godlike authority, Pickard-Cambridge, in 1962, 'that the noble seriousness of tragedy can have grown so rapidly, or even at all, out of the ribald satiric drama.' To which the quick answer is, drop the word 'noble' if you really wish to gain access to the serious. But it was not just tragedy Pickard-Cambridge found hard to square with ribaldry; he didn't like to think that comedy had begun that way either. Faced with the famously indecent red-figure phylax vases of southern Italy, whose relevance to the Old Comedy he was simply not prepared to countenance, even when they demonstrably depicted familiar comic scenes, Pickard-Cambridge took the 'noble' course and looked the other way.

If the view here taken of the substantial independence of the phylakes from Attic comedy is correct, it is unnecessary to discuss the former more fully here. A large number of the vases are figured in their full hideousness and disgustingness in several easily accessible publications . . .

Meaning, so you look at them *there*, if you must.

And the nature of their hideousness and disgustingness? They showed comic actors complete with padded phalluses.

Altogether, as the Oxford classicist Oliver Taplin argues brilliantly in a recent polemical volume, *Comic Angels* – the only gripping book about vases that has ever come my way – the common understanding of the phylax play as a rough species of knock-about farce, indigenous to southern Italy, and bearing no more than a passing resemblance to the real Greek thing, has been of immense convenience to scholars eager to save Athens from any imputation of indecorousness. A convenience which Taplin means now to deprive them of: 'This fobbing-off of the padding and the phallus on to South Italian phylakes not only fails to appreciate the cultural sophistication of Megale Hellas, it fundamentally misconceives the whole nature of Greek comedy. The grotesqueness is of the essence.'

Not just in the origin, but *of the essence*. Few classical scholars today

AUBREY BEARDSLEY

would deny the Old Comedy its padded and protrusive phalluses. That they were sometimes worn still stiffer than that must also be allowed, if such frequent allusions to engorgement in Aristophanes, as

> A man, a man! I spy a frenzied man!
> He carries Love before him like a staff

or

> COMMISSIONER:
> So what are *you* doing? You men?
> MESSENGER:
> What d'you think? Going round, bent double:
> You'd think we were carrying candles in a gale;

are to make any dramatic sense at all. Bums, too, were padded up and swollen. Bellies were bloated. Costumes representing the naked bodies of women were sported by men and fondled, fingered, exposed to the ridicule and raillery of the audience. Puns on all organs and functions of the body abounded, but the penis, both as a moving spectacle and a verbal paradigm of instability and capriciousness, of diminution and of growth, dominated the proceedings. The entire experience of theatre-going, for the Greeks, was phallus-centred. A statue of Dionysus, or a phallus in his honour, was paraded to the theatre, where it was installed in a position of prominence for the duration of the performance. The comedy you watched was burlesque-priapic. The satyr play which rounded off the day was priapic-tragic. Your only relief from the pendulum oscillations of the phallus came in the tragedies themselves, when you could watch the Bacchae ripping Pentheus to pieces, or King Oedipus putting out his eyes – gestures which, as any psychologist will tell you, symbolize castration.

That fructification was the name of the game originally, when ecstatic revellers danced behind the sacred member, and women worshippers of Dionysus strode out to keep appointments with their cults, phalluses tucked underneath their arms like fresh baguettes, is almost too obvious to state. But for the sacred and obscene rites to have hardened into formal art – on vases or in poetry or on the stage – one must suppose the addition of something in the spirit of 'All one to Hippoclides', the phallus as site of comic forgetfulness, irresponsibility, freedom.

And for the phallus to be really free and forgetful, it needs to be

attached to an animal or a god. Somewhere between both comes the satyr.

A satyr play was the final dramatic offering, the last oblation to Dionysus, on any day at the Greek theatre. 'Noble' in his seriousness though every great Greek tragedian was, his work was not finished until he'd provided a satyr play, as a sort of afterword to his three tragedies. Whatever were the last lines of the satyr play, those were the last lines you heard from an actor that day. In the case of the only surviving satyr play, the *Cyclops* of Euripides, those lines promised an escape from vassalage to the one-eyed Polyphemus, and a return to the freedom of the wine. 'From now our orders come from Bacchus.'

Starting from a Sophoclean fragment, the poet Tony Harrison recently, and to my mind with complete success, essayed a modern version, *The Trackers of Oxyrhynchus*, a satyr play *about* satyr plays, a romping justification, in clogs and Yorkshire accents, of satyr nature and satyr function:

> SILENUS:
> But a satyr, good people, doesn't just exist
> solely for fucking or for getting pissed.
> We're not just the clowns sent in to clear the ring
> we're here to show surprise at everything.
> We satyrs are on hand to reassess
> From basic principles all you possess,
> to show reactions apparently naïve
> to what you take for granted or believe.

That's a tall order, when you come to think of it: submitting *all* we possess to reassessment. If we are to agree to it, if we are to become Hippoclidean and allow that for the duration of the dance at least, everything is up for grabs, we require a little of that persuasion which accompanies the release of phallic inhibition. So the satyrs may not *solely* exist for fucking and for getting pissed, but they can only do that other thing if they fuck and get pissed first.

Liberating as Tony Harrison's Yorkshire goat-men were, treading the antic hay in their mill-town clogs, their huge cloth phalluses flying about, now like tails, now like flails, they never had a hope of matching the indiscriminate abandon of the satyrs who peopled (or do I mean animated) the domestic pottery of ancient Greece. No living creature is safe from them; not women, not men, not deer, donkeys, not one another, not the goblet or the amphora itself. One pokes his phallus into a wine jug ('From now our orders come from Bacchus'); another performs a feat of spectacular phallic juggling, balancing a vessel on the tip of his penis (a penis which was painted out in Victorian reproductions, so that the vessel levitates miraculously above the satyr's empty groin), while less gifted satyrs prepare to fill the vessel in question with wine.* On a highly elaborate red-figure kylix, which you can look at in Berlin, one satyr breaks the perpetual-motion line of fellatio and fucking to come marauding out of his plane in pursuit of an utterly impassive decorative sphinx. They masturbate without shame, defying whoever looks upon them to come up with a better way of whiling away an hour. Their agility, no less than their libidinousness, is of an order not available to mere mortal man. They can bend further over backwards, and then further over forwards, than is necessary for participation in any known sexual practice, not excluding bestiality, group buggery, or daisy-chains. They are tumblers no less than jugglers; acrobats, contortionists, musicians, dancers. But their first object is always the satisfaction of their tireless sexual voracity.

That their ithyphallicism did not represent a Greek ideal – supposing the Greeks to have been so simple minded as to embrace *an* ideal – hardly needs to be stressed, even though, lest we come to false conclusions and think of taking to the woods, classicists go on stressing it. A little phallus, a *phallo piccolino*, was more the ticket. Something which, bearing in mind pugilistic and athletic considerations, could be tied up and tucked out of the way. But then it was the very *exceptional* nature of the satyr, exceptional as to phallus size and appetite, and exceptional in the sense that he was, to employ anthropological language, transitional – always in the process of leaving one bodily form and meaning for another; ambiguous, un-completed, not classically rounded off, still with his protuberances intact – that enabled him to give the Greeks that holiday from themselves which is the only point of worship and the first justification of comedy.

If that makes the satyr the earliest comedian, later comedians have not failed to learn from him. Herakles has his club. Harlequin his *batte*. Grimaldi his stove-poker. Punch his universal cudgel. The jester his *marotte* and bladder. Ken Dodd's tickling stick is clearly in the ithyphallic tradition. Similarly Chaplin's cane, pursuing an independent life of its own, finding

---

* To this day, in the West Country, satyric Cornishmen dance, to the tune of *The Muffin Man*, with a full beer mug on their foreheads, lowering themselves to a sleeping position and then rising again, never spilling a drop. Only the most literal-minded observer would question the allusion to phallic adroitness and sexual control.

its own way up the dress of a passing *ingénue*. Dame Edna, who strictly speaking has no business being phallic, trembles her gladdies – the tremble being a register of the cross-sexual liberty she is taking. Sir Les Patterson carries something monstrously transitional – part human, part mechanical, part Australian – down one leg of his stained cultural attaché's trousers. In *Up Pompeii*, the 1971 film spin-off of the television series, Michael Hordern sports an erection capable of remarkable long-range no-hands harassment; never actually seen, it is frequently remarked upon by an admiring and envious Frankie Howerd: 'How *does* he do that?'

The same way a satyr does.

I I

Of all phallic clowning, that of the North American pueblo Indian, the Zuni and the Hopi, is the most blatant and the most intriguing. It is also the most frustrating, in that it is no longer something the public is encouraged to see, let alone permitted to photograph, let alone permitted to film. Plagued by puritanical criticism, intrusive tourism, insensitive explication, brute ignorance, the inevitable misapprehensions of the secular imagination, and all those other little niggles to which comic performers feel themselves susceptible, in or out of a ritual context, the Zuni and the Hopi have brought a curtain down on performances whose significance anyway, they say, was always religious. Aided by museum curators utterly at home with every kind of cultural pietism, they have succeeded in removing from public circulation almost all photographic trace of this nether bodily aspect of their rituals.* They have attended to their own censorship, in other words; subjected to closure an activity whose primary function must have been, however temporarily, to open.

---

* Every culture, no matter how reclusive, has its breaking-point; that little soft spot for this or that aspect of an inimical society, its pop singers or its film stars or its sporting idols, for whom it is prepared to drop every principle of unapproachability it owns. Recognizing the actor Henry Winkler – otherwise known as 'The Fonz' – in the plaza one afternoon, the Hopi, who happened to be avid Fonz fans, at once modified their rules relating to the video-taping of ritual performance. No filming permitted, unless you are the Fonz.

Hearing about the existence of the Winkler tape from every Hopi expert I quizzed, I decided to write to Mr Winkler, care of Walt Disney Television. A fax came back promptly from his assistant, Marilyn J. Belknap, wishing me the best of luck with my project but refusing to release the tape on the grounds that Mr Winkler 'holds it very sacred'.

Up to them, of course, that's if any deed can ever be said to be the sole property of the doer, but it does mean that Hopi and Zuni clowning goes on being cast in the shocked language of the first she-ethnographers sent by the Bureau of American Ethnology to Arizona and New Mexico a hundred or so years ago. 'While the scenes at the closing of the initiatory ceremonies are disgusting,' wrote Matilda Coxe Stevenson, only doing her job, 'the acme of depravity is reached after the [great-god kachina] takes his final departure from the plaza . . .'

We'll come, eventually, to what that acme of depravity turned out to be.

Other observers managed a cooler appraisal. Though we wouldn't be as interested in the subject as we are if the extremity of what they saw enacted in the plazas didn't make them sweat just a little bit. As in this, from Alexander M. Stephen's *Hopi Journal*, published in 1936:

Coming back among the six guests [one of the 'women'] tears off their ragged mantles, revealing each of them with a large false penis made of gourd neck, and assisted by another 'old woman' . . . she throws the guests down and daubs their penis with the filth.

She pretends to stamp on the penis of one and he weeps and moans and gives up the ghost. The Pai'akyamu then come and examine him and announce that he is dead. They roll and rub him and strive to revive him, but without avail. Finally they turn him over and placing their mouths close to his anus pretend to suck at it, and he gradually revives and they thump him on the back, shouting, and send him away restored. The 'women' bring out two or three sheepskins from the house and spread them in the middle of the court, and then bring out the girl who pretends coyness, but they lay her down on the skins . . . and bring the groom and lay him beside her and cover them both and all the spectators shout. There is a crowd of spectators, all the surrounding house tops are dense with them . . . Fortunately there are no white people present. Men and women seem to enjoy this very broad farce alike, although there are symptoms of modesty among some of the girls who occasionally turn their heads or look down.

The bride and groom pretend dalliance under the mantle and soon he surmounts her, then some of the Chuku run up and snatch away the mantle that had been covering them, shouting to them to go ahead but that everyone wanted to see the act. Then, it is plain to be seen, the bride exhibits a false vulva and the groom a false penis, these secured in place with strings, and they explicitly perform the simulated act of copulation, and the throng of spectators rend the air with their hilarious shouts.

If the weight of so much ritualized performance seems to have nudged us away from the frolicsomeness of the satyrs, Adolf Bandelier, author of *The Delight Makers*, an archaeo-anthropological novel on the subject of pueblo Indian clowning, published in 1890 to considerable acclaim, returns us to something more like the circus sex of the Greek red-figure vase:

They chased after her, carried her back and threw her down in the centre of the plaza, then while one was performing coitus from behind, another was doing it against her head. Of course, all was simulated, and not the real act, as the woman was dressed. The naked fellow performed masturbation in the centre of the plaza or very near it, alternating with a black rug and his hand. Everybody laughed.

But sacred circus sex. *Sacred.* Just as classical scholars are concerned that we should not adduce a general Greek libertinage from Aristophanes and the satyr play, so are anthropologists of the pueblo Indian quick to remind us of the conservatism of Hopi and Zuni society. The clowning referred to above belongs to religious ceremonial. The Hopi and Zuni clowns are revered figures. Every bit as holy as the priests they mock. Though they feign gross misconduct, sparing neither children nor the elderly nor animals, they pursue, as clowns, an austere regimen. Speaking of the Koyemci, the sacred clowns of the Zuni, Ruth Bunzel describes how 'everyone goes in hushed reverence and near to tears to watch them on their last night [of office] when they are under strict taboo. At this time, from sundown until midnight the following day, they touch neither food nor drink. They neither sleep nor speak, and in all that time do not remove their masks.'

Masks, by the way, from which protrude genital-like knobs stuffed with seeds, and raw cotton, and dust from the footprints of inhabitants of the pueblo. A magical preparation.

And the clowns are a sort of magical preparation themselves, the fruit of an incestuous union between a brother and a sister, each of whom suffers a terrible deformation as a consequence of their transgression, each of whom goes mad at the sight of the other, but from whose coupling come gift-bearing offspring, neither one sex nor the other, neither straight nor askew, neither sane nor mad.

At the heart of the phallic clowning, as at the heart of the solemnity, lies our old friend, fructification. Those phallic singers, to whose influence Aristotle wished us to remember we owed comedy, had a boisterous job to

1. Satyr as acrobat. Red-figure wine cooler
by Douris, *c.* 500–470 BC
(*British Museum, London*)

2. Satyr reduced (for decency's sake) to
mere illusionist. Expurgated print of (1)
(*British Museum, London*)

3. Satyr free-for-all. Detail on a cup by the circle of the Nikosthenes Painter,
late sixth century BC (*Antikensammlung, SMPK, Berlin*)

19. Pulcinella rising Christ-like from his tomb, a tumble of odd bones demanding another day, another bite at the senses. *Apparition at the Tomb of Pulcinella* by Giovanni Domenico Tiepolo (*Collection of Mrs Jacob M. Kaplan, New York*)

do, waking up the spring. But it was a momentous one to boot. Much hung on their success. For the pueblo Indian it is the corn that has to grow. When he performs his phallic antics, simulating sex or spilling seed on to the ground, it is the earth he is fucking. That he may be a moralizer as well, disassembling the ethical structure of the tribe only in order that it should snap together the more firmly, once its elements have been shaken out and reaffirmed, is a matter we will return to. The clown as teacher, like the phallus as a rod of social discipline, belongs to later. For the moment I want to stay with fructification and forgetfulness. 'Longing for something to make her laugh,' goes a pueblo legend, '*Iyatiku* (Corn Maiden) rubs her skin and covers the ball of epidermis with a blanket. From underneath comes *Koshare* (the clowns) to make fun and to make people forget their troubles. *Iyatiku* makes an arch for him to climb up and down.'

Arch presumably equals rainbow, but keep it quiet. Else Joel Goodman will produce the badge: THE SHORTEST DISTANCE BETWEEN A CLOWN AND GOD IS A RAINBOW.

So: if the Corn Maiden can be made to forget her troubles . . . But we know all that, from Demeter and Iambe.

Somewhere between a satyr, a pueblo clown, and Dionysus himself, is Kokopelli, a mythic figure of the Indian southwest whose distinctive en-curved silhouette appears, as a pictograph or petroglyph, in thousands of rocky locations, and more latterly as a doorstop or a candle holder in thousands of Indian arts-and-crafts shops, from Albuquerque to Tucson. He is a twisted insect of a figure, humpbacked, crested like a palm cock-atoo, always with a flute to his lips, and – until the missionaries stopped by and insisted on castration – efflorescent with phallus. But then that affects only the craft shops. Climb the rocks and the phalluses are still where they've been for thousands of years. Like all trickster figures, his reputa-tion rests on an unreliable character, a vagabond temperament, and an insatiable sexual appetite. In this regard, and his flute is no more an incidental than are Pan's pipes, he is totemic in the way that a rock singer is totemic. Those girls for whom a touch of Mick Jagger is still worth risking suffocation, are attending to an ancient call. Music is magic, an appearance of licentiousness is sacred, a humpback has the power to avert the evil eye. That Mick Jagger the private man is no hunchback matters not a jot; the moment he moves into performance mode he becomes, to misapply a phrase from Christopher Bollas, a 'densely fraught tangle . . . like the hunched-over Harlequin of the Middle Ages'. He transgresses the limits of the body; he passes from the rigidity of the normal man into the flexibility of the freak; he becomes lucky.

Visiting Pompeii recently, to see for myself the famous paintings and statues of Priapus, phallic fauns, phalluses carved into paving stones, phalluses carved into the walls of corner houses, the murals in the House of the Mysteries showing the worship of the phallus, Herms – those columns which are all head and phallus, and who cares about anything in between – I became conscious that the Italian fixer super-intending my itinerary might think me, if not fixated on phalluses, at least limited in my curiosity as to other things. I brought the matter up with him in his car one morning. As usual he'd been offended when I forgot his earlier injunction and fastened my seat belt. 'We have so many regulations in this country,' he'd told me. 'At least we can be transgressive in our cars. Please unfasten your seat belt.' 'This phallic business ...' I began '... I don't want you to think ... What interests me about them is the power they once exerted over the popular imagin-ation, as good luck charms, as ...' He checked to see that I really had unfastened my seat belt, honked his horn for no reason that an Eng-lishman could be expected to understand, fished inside his glove com-partment, and brought out a brass key-ring for me to look at. It was a figure of a top-hatted alcoholic hunchback, tuxedo'd above the waist, all red-chilli phallus below. In one hand he carried a horseshoe, with the other he was giving the two-fingered horizontal horn-sign. Covering all eventualities.

'Yours?'

'Mine.'

'Still?'

He didn't understand the question. '*Apotropaico*,' he said.

'I know. I'm just surprised you have one. Is it old?'

Stupid question. You can buy them in every gewgaw shop in Naples. And throughout the rest of southern Italy come to that.

For a day or two I went about in mild shock, a touch sniffy like the anti-quarian Richard Payne Knight, who began his *A Discourse on the Worship of Priapus* with a letter from Naples, dated 30 December 1781:

Sir,

Having last year made a curious discovery, that in a Province of this Kingdom, and not fifty miles from the Capital, a sort of devotion is still paid to PRIAPUS, the obscene Divinity of the Ancients (though under another denomination), I thought it a circumstance worth recording; particularly, as it offers a fresh proof of the similitude of the Popish and Pagan Religion . . .

Knight, too, noted the existence, the *persistence*, of ornaments of dress and amulets worn by the 'women and children of the lower class, at Naples' as a 'preservative from the *mal occhi*, evil eyes, or enchantment'. And reported on the discovery of a 'most elegant small idol of bronze' in the ruins of Herculaneum. 'It has an enormous Phallus, and, with an arch look and gesture, stretches out its right hand in the form above mentioned' – that is to say 'clinched, with the point of the thumb thrust betwixt the index and the middle finger'.

Not, notice, the same arrangement of the fingers as on my Italian fixer's amulet. Not the horizontal horn-sign, but the *fico*, the fig.

And where the horizontal horn-sign is blatantly and self-sufficiently masculine in its suggestions, invoking the power of the bull-god, and no doubt the insouciance of the satyr; the fig – the sign of penetration – acknowledges a little more of the mutuality of enchantment, taking the precaution of including the woman's organs of generation in its dumb-show of bravado and magic. For the female genitals too had the power to shoo away malignity.

And to shoo away the devil himself, come to that. As in Rabelais' story of the old woman of Popefigland, whose husband fears his coming scratching-match with the devil, but which the old woman sees a way of circumventing.

Rely on me, she says. Leave him to me.

When the devil comes to keep his appointment, impatient for the clawing-match, he finds the old woman on the floor, howling. Dying, she cries, of the wound her wretched husband gave her.

How so, enquires the devil.

He told me of his appointment to scratch with you, the old woman tells him. And asked if he might first try out his nails on me. Here, look, he scratched me with his little finger, right here, between my legs. Torn me wide open. It will never heal. Look for yourself . . .

With this she lifted her clothes to the chin, as Persian mothers used to of old when they saw their sons fleeing from the battle, and showed him her what's-its-name. When the devil saw this huge and continuous cavity, extending in all directions, he cried out: 'Mahound! Demiurge! Megaera! Alecto! Persephone! He shan't find me here. I'm off like a streak . . .'

Charles Eisen

Those Persian mothers whom Rabelais remembers, whose drastic response to the cowardice of their sons is lauded in the chapter 'Of the Virtues of Women' in Plutarch's *Morals*, were not dealing in quite the same
magic as the old woman of Popefigland. The shock of the exposure, this
time, is aggravated by the shame of it. The mothers show what no mother
should ever allow to be seen, and the sons see what no son should ever
look upon. The unnatural cowardice of the sons is answered by the
unnatural immodesty of the mothers. Terror and shame, as much as
mockery and jeering, are what drive the sons back into battle. If it means
anything at all to say that magic is unloosed here, it is the magic associated
with the revelation of secrets and the crossing of boundaries. Not simply
sexual secrets and boundaries – no line of limber chorus girls lifting their
skirts would have had the same effect on the faint-hearted Persians – but
secrets associated with the terrors of age and boundaries determined by
the mysteries of birth.

Specific to the action of the Persian women is the fact of their being
their sons' mothers, but the fearsomeness of old age is essential to every
story of this sort, and to every expression of it in art. Mikhail Bakhtin, the
great Russian critic of the grotesque, cannot be bettered on the subject.

In the famous Kerch terracotta collection we find figurines of senile pregnant
hags. Moreover, the old hags are laughing. This is a typical and very strongly
expressed grotesque. It is ambivalent. It is pregnant death, a death that gives birth.
There is nothing completed, nothing calm and stable in the bodies of these old
hags. They combine a senile, decaying and deformed flesh with the flesh of new
life, conceived but as yet unformed.

No wonder the devil, who is as much for completion as any One God
or puritan, runs from the sight. And no wonder, when the old hags cackle
in fairy-stories, that the innocent children and the handsome young
princes – incapable of laughter any of them – shudder. Such unseemliness
– giving birth in death, making new flesh out of old – goes to the heart of
comedy. 'Give me life!' demands Falstaff, when calm and stable nature
expects nothing but repose and death from him. The most riotous of the
satyrs is Silenus, old, balding, paunchy, always drunk, forever young after
his time. That something monstrously transitional which disfigures the cut
of Les Patterson's trousers is the more grotesque for being middle-aged,
clamorous not with new life but with old.

Remember old Iambe, cheering up Demeter and recalling the spring with broad jokes and ribaldry? Well, there's another version of that story. This time the cheerer-up is Baubo, and although there are still the usual disagreements as to her lineage and provenance, all variants concur as to the manner of her approach. Not with jests and verbal obscenities does Baubo persuade the goddess to drink and live again, but by raising her skirts and showing Demeter those parts ordinarily 'veiled by shame'. 'Enchanted by the spectacle,' in the words of Clement, Demeter is relieved of her grief, and smiles.

Enchanted by the unwonted sight of an old woman's sexual organs, the devil flees; enchanted by the same spectacle, Demeter, desolated goddess of the sprouting corn, gives way to mirth. Not much question on whose side the aged vulva plays.

As though to confirm Bakhtin's conflation of deformed flesh and new life, Arnobius, departing somewhat from Clement's account, cranks up just how much Baubo shows.

She takes that part of the body by which the female sex gives birth and on account of which woman is called 'the bearer' and, after long neglect makes it as neat and smooth as a little boy whose skin is not yet tough and hairy.

And only then does she raise her skirts to Demeter.

A brief disquisition on depilation may not be out of place here. Clearly, if Aristophanes is to be trusted, the Greeks had a taste for it. One of Lysistrata's suggestions for heightening seductiveness among the conjugality-for-peace conspirators is that

> We pluck and trim our entrances,
> Like good little spiders . . .

Why? Because then the flies will come buzzing, and not find it easy to escape.

What works for a housewife will, of course, work just as well, or better, for a flute-girl or a prostitute. When Praxagora proposes shutting down the brothels in *Ecclesiazusae*, one of the consequences will be that the ex-prostitutes may sleep with men of their own class and 'let their hair grow where it wants to'. Where *it* wants to, but not, obviously, where their clients do.

This predilection for what Aristophanes makes great play of referring to as *piggies* or *piggy-wigs*, 'not ready for sticking' –

MEGARIAN:

Squeal pig. Squeal, piggy-wiggy, squeal.

Do you want to go home again, empty? Squeal!

DAUGHTERS:

Oink oink!

– is not entirely unknown to our own age. Any soft-porn magazine worth the name ensures that there's a piggy-spread or two among its pages. Some make absolutely no concession to any other taste. Whatever the appeal – and it cannot be a perversion, else contemporary beachwear of the Bay Watch sort would not conspire in it to the degree it does – there can be no denying that one of its elements is the grotesque. A transgression, not simply of decency but of form. Even a young woman's body becomes deformed when it apes a child's.

How much more so, then, the aged body of a Baubo.

So while we cannot know exactly what it was that made Demeter laugh when the old woman's *peplos* was raised, we can guess at the components of the gesture. A breach of all conventionally regulating restraints; a divulging of secrets; an intimation of fecundity where fecundity is least to be looked to; a grotesque parody of both youth and age, defying every signal as to the limitations of either; a grotesque parody of nursing, too, making the place through which the child enters the world a sort of child itself; and a promise of forgetfulness – all one to Hippoclides – Baubo having reversed her organs of reasoning and her organs of pleasure, exactly in the manner of the lewd Athenian dancer. As to the latter – Baubo putting her vulva where her mouth is – only look at any of the terracotta figurines known as Baubos for confirmation of its meaning: no distinction is drawn between her bottom half and her top; no intermediary superstructure of bone or flesh is of any consequence; her smile requires only her genitals to support it. The perfect analogue for the intimate, unmediated relations mirth, magic and the organs of generation enjoy with one another.

That we acknowledge this relationship at some deep and unexamined level, even if we would much rather not, is proved, in an inverse sort of way, by the example of a well-meaning Victorian antiquarian who mistook a Baubo for a clown, blundering (wilfully?) as to the sex, blundering (wilfully?) as to the parts, but being broadly right, if we allow for some sentimentality, as to the ambition.

In a volume entitled *Illustrations of Kilpeck Church, Herefordshire: In a Series of Drawings Made on the Spot (With an Essay on Ecclesiastical Design, and a Descriptive Interpretation)*, George R. Lewis set about recording that 'profusion of decorative sculpture and fantasy' (in Pevsner's words) which adorns one of the loveliest Romanesque churches in Britain. When he came to the exterior corbel table running round the whole church, Lewis noted that it was 'designed to shew good and bad works' – a lamb and cross, a pair of wrestlers, various beasts. Of figure 26, Lewis remarks that it 'represents a fool – the cut in his chest, the way to his heart, denotes it is always open to all and sundry'. An innocent fool, then. An indiscriminate fool. A holy fool.

Lewis's drawing, done, if we are to believe the title of his volume, 'on the spot', shows the fool's heart as open as a church door, square in the middle of his body, his hands paddling backwards, as though he means to swim off the wall, his legs . . . but he has no legs. The figure as it actually was, and still remains, not at all so worn away as to create misunderstanding, is of a she not a he, legs (yes, legs) apart, arms slid behind and through them, each hand firmly gripping a labium majorum, in order that the pudendum should be as wide apart as it is possible, in stone, to make it.

We do not need to go beyond prudery to find an explanation for Lewis's reluctance to record what he saw, or for the measures he took to draw something else – the amputation of the legs, the slapping-away of the wrists, the organ transplant. But prudery alone won't explain the extraordinary imaginative leap that transformed an obscenely immodest devil-scarer of a woman – a Sheela-na-gig as she is called in Ireland, where her type once routinely protected churches against enchantment – into a harmless fool with a gaping heart. Only that ancient affinity between the sexual organs and the comedian, dimly recalled, not completely obliterated even from the memory of a modest Victorian enthusiast for churches, can explain such a thing.

Assuming that Thomas Wright, author of *The Worship of the Generative Powers During the Middle Ages of Western Europe*, is a more trustworthy witness than Lewis, then Lewis wasn't the only person not seeing what he saw when he saw a Sheela. Because of the difficulty of delineating the female organ, Wright argued, scarcely more than twenty years after Lewis drew his fool, 'it soon assumed shapes which though intended to represent it, we might rather call symbolical of it, though no symbolism was intended. Thus the figure of the female organ easily assumed the rude form of a horseshoe, and as the original meaning was forgotten, would readily be taken for that object, and a real horseshoe nailed up for the same purpose.'

More to our purpose is the beginning of an argument advanced in an enthusiastic little pamphlet called *The Good Gargoyle Guide – Mediaeval Church Carvings in Leicestershire and Rutland*, published by the Heart of Albion Press in Loughborough by its author, Bob Trubshaw. What if the more conventionally rude gargoyles and grotesques, Trubshaw wonders – the face pullers, the mouth stretchers, the eye gougers, all of whom the churches of Leicestershire and Rutland represent in abundance – are nothing but polite versions of the Sheela-na-gig? They are comparably confrontational. They mingle the comic with the fearful to exactly the same degree. They appear to perform exactly the same functions on the walls and ceilings of churches, now frightening away evil-doers, now questioning the wintry assurances of religious faith. And most important of all, they employ their hands in exactly the same manner to open what should be closed. Never mind the horseshoe; could it be that Baubo's obscene gesturing has been mischievously kept alive in the face, her ribald function returned to her speaking parts, whence it originally derived, but the more ribald now on account of where it's been?

By this token, those other familiar grotesques of Leicestershire and Rutland, the contortionist with his head between his legs, the tongue poker, the nose distender, become comprehensible as more overt male versions of the spring-inducing exhibitionist. The satyr and the Baubo conjoined. Every year, in mid-September, contenders for the World Gurning Championship gather in the Cumberland town of Egremont and pull faces through a horse collar. 'Gurn' is a variant of grin. It means to show the teeth, dog-like, in laughing as well as in snarling. But competitive gurning often benefits from the complete absence of teeth. The less like a face you can make your face, the better you do. And the funnier you become. 'A bum with teeth in it,' is a coarse insult for an ill-favoured countenance. Take the teeth out and what are you left with? When the All Blacks do their Haka before a match, does it not resemble a sort of facial mooning? A review by St John Ervine of Bert Lahr's performance in *Hold Everything*, in 1928, marvelled at Lahr's capacity to raise laughter simply with his face. 'Believe me, or believe me not, Mr Lahr can obtain laughter by merely distorting his features. *Isn't that the oldest kind of clowning?* It is. Yet Mr Lahr, I solemnly assure you, is able to cross his eyes and twist his mouth and *make people laugh.*'

Jacques Callot

The critic seems to be in some irritation with himself, for laughing at what he is not absolutely certain should be laughable. But he answers his own question.

This is, indeed, the oldest kind of clowning. The art to show the body's lewd construction in the face.

III

Visiting the World Gurning Championships in 1995, I was struck by a singular discrepancy in the gurning practices of men and women. Where the men struggled in their horse collars, affecting reluctance, wildness, ferocity, terror even – evoking the baited fool, the freak in the stocks, the object of a primitive community's cruel derision – the women held still, refused all extraneous histrionics, confident that they possessed in their disfigured countenances alone that which could scare the devil. In this they were more shocking than the men, more absolutely and nakedly obscene. They knew they could trust their grimace to disclose, unaided, its own covert meaning. The long lubricious history of its journey up and down the body.

Jacques Callot

When the women's winner was announced, her husband rushed on to the stage to take her in his arms. 'You're married to the ugliest woman in the world,' she said to him, holding out her silver cup. 'I know,' he said, unable to conceal his pride. 'I know.' And smothered her in kisses.

No beauty queen ever excited such a feverish renewal of passion in the man who loved her, and loved to see her admired by others.

It was difficult to know where to look, so intimate was their encounter on the stage, so much dark promise did it contain.

IV

Women's organs more than hold their own, then, when it comes to a ding-dong with the darker agencies, or a transgressive parley with the lighter ones. Where they lose out to the phallus as paradigms of the comic is in the area of visible play. The phallus rises, and the phallus falls, and Diony-sus willing (like Barkis, Dionysus is always willing), the phallus rises again. Some stylization of Baubo may have made it on to amulets or got itself hammered on to the doors of sheds and farmhouses in rough confusion with a horseshoe, but only the phallus could be taken out for walks, as the

Greeks and Romans enjoyed the fancy, fashioning the organ into every imaginable winged or pedestrian creature, giving it a fantastical predatory existence of its own. An indulgence whose potential for ludicrous narrative the Winnebago Indians of Winipig (People near the Dirty Water) understand perfectly. Wakdjunkaga, trickster-hero of the Winnebago, detaches his penis the moment it is a nuisance to him, puts it in a box and carries it on his back. The advantages of this become manifest when, espying a chief's daughter swimming with her friends, he is able to slip it out of the box and send it skimming through the lake like a torpedo, bound for a destination into which, after one or two false starts, it lodges so squarely that not all the strong men of the village are able to pull it out again. If it is hard, by the time we have come so far, to tell the phallus from the clown and the clown from the phallus, that is because the difference is, at best, only marginal.

In its unpredictability, in its capacity for abrupt movement and sudden change, in its miraculous powers of recovery (or not), the phallus gives the comic its dynamic pattern.

Watching the comedian Lee Evans in concert in Manchester in 1994, where many years before I had watched Norman Wisdom in revue, I was intrigued by the ways that they were, and then again weren't, and then again were, alike. Lee Evans is often compared to Norman Wisdom, but where Wisdom had been all softness and pliancy, a thing of limpness in the audience's hands, imploring pity, Evans made sudden rallies, grew irritated with ingratiation, rounded on us, turned implacable and hard. On the face of it, to the degree that the comedian is the phallus and that a phallus is not much use unless it comes back up, Evans was the more successful. But then Norman Wisdom, too, always rose again from where he'd fallen, and if he cranked up the pathos at last, wasn't that only so that he should lodge in our affections the more? When Wakdjunkaga first sends his penis skimming across the lake it makes waves; he has to call it back and weight it down a little with a stone, calm the velocity of the attack. There's more than one way to ensure you lodge squarely within the chief's lovely daughter. A pitiable pliancy might achieve its end no less certainly than adamant. So maybe both comedians were faithful, in their own fashion, to the sacred ideal of phallic revival.

The main thing is to stay capricious. Comedy turns to tragedy when Fellini's Casanova dances, love-sick, with an exquisite wind-up china doll because sex has now parted company from nature. In the final scene of *Carnal Knowledge* Jack Nicholson berates a whore for departing by a hair's breadth from the only script that will give him an erection. It has to be that way, and no other. Both films chart the professional lover's inexorable decline into phallic inflexibility and mechanism.

In his biography of Fellini, Hollis Alpert reports a conversation between Fellini and Gore Vidal on the subject of Casanova's appearance. 'Fellini described how he wanted the character to look – tall, straight, like a walking erection.' As for Donald Sutherland, who played Casanova in the film, Fellini told Gore Vidal that he liked him 'because he has a wonderfully stupid look. He looks unborn. I want a character who is unborn, still in the placenta.'

Never flexible, never alive.

Bergson states it to be a veritable law of the comic that 'the attitudes, gestures and movements of the body are laughable in exact proportion as that body reminds us of a mere machine.' Thus, clowns make us laugh, in Bergson's view, by virtue of their mechanically repetitive actions. But Casanova in the arms of a clock-work doll doesn't make us laugh. And nor does Jack Nicholson in the throes of an erection that has gone wrong because it has gone unscripted. But then Bergson is pursuing laughter as an external corrective force – abstract laughter, as it were; principled laughter, laughter dealt out rather than laughter induced. We laugh, in his account, at any deviance from the normal. This makes laughter at once a severe critic of aberration and a guardian of what is most alive in us, since what we know to be normal, Bergson says, is that 'a really living life should never repeat itself'. So it comes to the same thing in the end: comedy celebrating nature's eternal changeability, forever mimicking and pursuing the ups and downs of its renewals.

Where mechanical repetition becomes tragic at last, forcing the phallus to do what it would rather not, seeking a renewal that has nothing of nature in it, fear of phallic failure, acknowledgement that the phallus will always have the final word on where it wants to be and when, is one of comedy's most enduring preoccupations. The comic alternative to the big surprise satyric man has in store for women – the 'triple-decker hard-on' with which Peisthetaerus threatens Iris in Aristophanes' *The Birds* – is no surprise worth mentioning at all: the 'limp and withered member' the women scorn in Aristophanes' *Thesmophoriazusae*; George Formby's Little Ukulele; Alexander Portnoy's much abused organ, functionless the moment it arrives in the land for which Abraham sacrificed his foreskin.

Whatever their specific roles in a narrative, anticlimax and bathos (the art of sinking or coming down) always carry the memory-trace of the difference between what a man promises and what he delivers. In a battle-field scene early in *The Great Dictator* Chaplin makes great play of loading and firing the hugest of cannons only to see it squirt, once the smoke clears, the limpest of shells. There is no explosion; the shell feebly arcs, plops, and then fizzles. The desperately swaggering Marquis in Goldoni's *Mirandolina* whips out his sword in order to polish off a rival, only to find that his blade has snapped clean away and that he is left with nothing more threatening than the haft and the pommel. The clown Grock used to drag a giant suitcase behind him, keeping the audience in suspense as to its marvellous contents, offering to open it and then remembering other business, encouraging all manner of wonder and speculation, until finally . . . finally . . . drawing from it a tiny violin.

In time of war it gave the British people immense satisfaction to ima-gine that the Great Dictator fulminating across the channel, holding his own nation in thrall and threatening destruction to every other, was short one testicle.

Playing with the idea that 'those things are comic which are not proper for an adult', Freud admitted to some uncertainty as to where, quite, that left us. 'I am unable to decide,' he wrote, 'whether degradation to being a child is only a special case of comic degradation, or whether everything comic is based fundamentally on degradation to being a child.' An indeci-sion which he was prepared to firm up again in a footnote: 'The fact that comic pleasure has its source in the "quantative contrast" of a com-parison between small and large, which after all also expresses the essen-tial relation between a child and an adult – this would certainly be a strange coincidence if the comic had no other connection with the infantile.'

By making Hitler short one testicle we are of course returning him to an infantile condition. Not yet, not fully, a man. That 'limp and withered member' which the women in *Thesmophoriazusae* mock, belongs to a child but reminds them of his father. Unerect, the man is no better than an infant. Comedy degrades him back to infancy.

Visiting Circus Harlequin a year or two ago, intrigued by the fact that it belonged to the novelist Philippa Gregory and her husband – it may be commonplace for novelists to write about circuses but it is rare for any of them to own one – I was beguiled by a routine performed by the Konyot Clown Company (mummy Konyot, daddy Konyot, and baby Konyot), in which a large clown (daddy Konyot) is bundled into an enormous washing-machine, where he is sudded, rinsed, tumble-dried and spun, and finally disgorged one-tenth his original size (baby Konyot). Considering the act was about shrinkage, it was queerly optimistic. On the one hand we had witnessed a diminution, a degradation, on the other we were present at a birth. Big goes in, small comes out.

In his book *Realism of the Renaissance*, the Russian critic L. E. Pinsky pinpoints Rabelais' comic affect to the 'feeling of the general relativity of great and small, exalted and lowly ... the feeling of rising, growing, flowering and fading, of the transformation of nature eternally alive'.

This is the way to understand Freud's 'quantitive contrast', the part relativity of great and small – large cannon, tiny shell; big case, small fiddle; phallus up and phallus down – plays in comedy. It keeps us continually on the move. It releases us from the tyranny of fixity. It promises the ultimate reduction of even the most mechanically dangerous of men to the soft pliancy of childhood.

V

Where then, if clowning is by its nature phallic, if every comedian is a stand-up on pain of becoming a fall-down, does that leave a woman who would be funny?

Until recently the fair answer to that would have been that it doesn't leave her anywhere. Unless the woman was a sort of honorary man like Mae West, or an actual man in skirts – a camp extravagance of some kind, a dame or drag queen, a parody of a woman – her contribution to comedy was confined to that species of innocuous domestic farcicality typified by Lucille Ball. Dizziness. Daffiness. Qualities which of necessity presupposed the existence of a husband, because it was as a husband that you experienced their inconvenience and as a husband that you learned to find them endearing. 'I Love Lucy'. We *all* loved Lucy. We were all married to her.

True enough, she was cutting-edge in her way. Woman at the centre of things, her own chief in her own domain. Her however many millions of husbands simply taken for granted. Assumed, so that she could get on with being herself. But she was not *that* cutting-edge. She was not, for example, husband*less*.

But then Lucy was American and a sit-comedian, and whoever engineers American sit-comedies once wanted to do a version of 'Fawlty Towers' in which Basil and Sybil hit it off. No need to dwell on the folly of that. We all know that happy marriages and comedy don't mix. Satyrs don't make good husbands. And no husband would let his wife do as Baubo does.

And then there is the problem of beauty. Beauty is not funny. Beauty fades; beauty is pain; beauty is passive, self-engrossed and solemn. Comedy is the god of growth, the god of tomorrow, and what promise for tomorrow has beauty ever held? The only change beauty promises is decay and that's tragedy's reserve. Baubo yoked her old age to her grotesquely shaven vulva in order to get a rise out of Demeter, but the beauty she may once have had was not part of the joke. Phyllis Diller understood that extravagant play with ugliness was the only way for a woman comedian to beat the solemn-hush-of-beauty trap. 'I was at the beauty parlour for five hours – and that was just for the estimate.' Similarly Joan Rivers. 'My body is falling so fast, my gynaecologist wears a hard hat.' Not tragic decay. The body (as far as the conceit goes) was never up to much anyway. When she ran naked through the room her husband Edgar asked 'Who shaved the dog?' Pity poor Edgar. Like Phyllis Diller, Joan Rivers liberated us from marital allure. No one wanted to be *their* husbands. Which left us free to laugh.

But no sooner shut the husband up in the man than you encounter the sister in the woman. Laugh at a woman, and some other woman will tell you you're laughing inappropriately. Women are funny, but they're not *funny*. Or they're *funny*, but not funny.

'The new female comics,' writes Nancy Walker in M. Unterbrink's *Funny Women: American Comediennes 1860–1987*, 'refuse to practice the self-deprecatory humor that seemed the only avenue for those in Phyllis Diller's era, when the put-down of women was a staple of male stand-up comedy.' And Linda Pershing, another contributor to the same volume, cites the example of the feminist comedian Kate Clinton, who 'makes a strong effort not to publicly devalue herself for the sake of a laugh'.

Not to publicly devalue herself! What is the matter under discussion here? How to comport oneself as Principal of Girton College, Cambridge? No clown ever eschewed self-deprecation. No phallus was ever dignified, unless it was Casanova's as Fellini imagined it: tall, straight, stupid and unborn. Comic only in the sense that we ridicule it.

However it goes in America, concern for a lady's deportment has not slowed down the progress of women's clowning in this country. Joanna Lumley became a cult comic figure – camp, but not exclusively camp – the moment she turned her own looks and body into a site of self-derision.

By never letting you forget her fatness, Dawn French succeeds in making an ongoing mockery of thinness. It's as phallic as the non-phallic can get. The same teasing us with the imminence of exposure, the same play with the relativity of great and small.

Gross in her sloppy pig-out T-shirt and half-mast desexualized harlequinade trousers, Jo Brand goes all the way back to the more fearful figures of carnival gluttony and sloth – to Hans Wurst and Jack Sausage and Falstaff and even, since she is lazily libidinous as well, the Wife of Bath. The jokes she tells come without any gesticulations or microphone-savvy and are concluded almost before she's begun them. Who's got the energy or the lungs for a long story? In this comic tradition idleness and repletion are on the side of appetite and appetite is on the side of all our freedoms, especially our freedom to die the way we choose. Why worry about cancer from smoking, she asks, when you're going to die of heart disease from being fat.

At a concert in Bradford, where women were gathered as though for a suffragette convention, dressed only to give support to one another, I watched Jo Brand spin wonderful fancies around the horrors of men who were not gross as she was gross. Little men. Thin men. Fleshless men. With high fastidious distaste she plucked at her own person, as though their fine-splintered bones, shards of small thin man, still clung to her clothing. As for their value sexually: 'You might as well shove the whole bloke up.'

The ultimate phallic joke – the man as phallus entire. And the ultimate revenge on the phallus – you need the entire man inside before you notice that he's there.

At last – pudenda *victrix* – the pudenda out in the world again. Not just frightening the devil and inspiriting the spring, but offering to match the phallus for indefatigability, greed, mobility, indifference. Self-deprecating? Self-aggrandizing rather, in the best Hippoclidean comic spirit – setting the rest of the world at naught.

CHAPTER THREE

The Sibyl's Cavern
Or
Bum Bum Bum

'*Bum, bum, bum . . .*' Kenny Everett to camera, on ascertaining that
the 'Russell Harty Show' he is appearing on is going out live.

I

It seems we are not yet through with old women hitching up their skirts
and showing us their parts. Though this time it is the rear-parts rather
than the fore-parts, the site of the body's death rather than of the body's
birth, that we are obliged to confront.

Rabelais again . . .

Encouraged by Pantagruel to consult an
oracle to find out whether or not he is going
to be happy in marriage, Panurge (in company with Epistemon) visits the old prophetess of Panzoust, whose dwelling is a poorly
built, poorly furnished, poorly ventilated
straw-thatched cottage on the brow of a
mountain, under a spreading chestnut tree.
The old woman herself is 'grim to look at, ill-dressed, ill-nourished, toothless, bleary eyed, hunchbacked, snotty and feeble', and is making soup out
of green cabbage, yellow bacon, marrow bone (and no doubt snot), when
Panurge first encounters her. Once in receipt of Panurge's offering, but
only after having spent the necessary period of time sitting deep in thought
and 'grinning like a dog', the hag sets about the business of divination,
turning spindles, covering her head with her apron, sweeping her broom
three times across the hearth, emitting horrible cries, and at last following

68

the terrified Panurge and Epistemon into her backyard, where she shakes eight leaves off a sycamore tree, writing words upon them with her spindle, and then casting them to the wind. Upon those leaves, if you can find them, she tells Panurge, 'the fatal destiny of your marriage is written'.

After saying this, she retired into her den. But on the doorstep she hitched up her gown, petticoat, and smock to her armpits, and showed them her arse. 'Odds tripe and onions,' cried Panurge as he saw it, 'look, there's the Sibyl's cavern.'

Otherwise – *trou de la Sibylle* – the Sibyl's hole. The gateway *of* the Sibyl and the gateway *to* the Sibyl; and since we associate the Sibyl with the under-world, the Cumaean Sibyl having shown Aeneas the way to get there, we may assume that that too – the entrance to hell itself – is what the hag vouchsafes a glimpse of to the appalled Panurge.

Arse = hell – nothing too difficult about that equation. Not yet ready to accept the anticlimax of ordinary daily life after heaving his wife out of her apartment window, the hero of Norman Mailer's *An American Dream* forces a double entry into the German maid, alternating caverns, now dipping into heaven, as he puts it, now dipping into hell. That the arse, poetically speaking, is a suitable place to visit after a murder hardly needs insisting. It is the graveyard of the body, the House of the Dead.

As for the supreme contempt implicit in the gesture of the Sibyl of Panzoust – a gesture not at all to be confused with Baubo's optimistic and invigorating exposure – is it conceivable that there can be a community on earth that does not recognize the signal or employ similar means for its transmission? From the invitation 'See my arse' to the command 'Kiss my arse' is no distance to speak of. Kikuyu women, seeking to punish a wrongdoer, synchronize the lifting of their skirts in a show of communal disdain. Their buttocks are their reprimand. For Peter Pan's chums – Tootles, Slightly and the Twins – in danger of baying wolves, their but-tocks are their protection. What would Peter do in such a situation? 'Peter would look at them through his legs.' And over the boys bend, proffering the spectacle of eyes where eyes are not meant to be, at the terrible sight of which the wolves 'trot away foiled'. In *Notes on a Cowardly Lion*, John Lahr tells of an episode in the deadly war between two impresarios of midgets, Leo Singer (who was considered exploitative of his clientele) and Major Doyle (who was himself a midget monologist), in which three bus-loads of New York midgets, all in the employ of Major Doyle, parked outside Singer's Central Park apartment, had the doorman ring up Singer and tell him to look out of his window, and at the appropriate moment presented their bare behinds to him – one hundred and seventy of them – as a mark of their esteem. This became known as 'Major Doyle's Revenge'. By way of revenge on those who mounted his wife backwards, face to rump upon a mule, while he was out of town, Frederick Barbarossa of Milan was said to have demanded that on pain of death they retrieve a fig wedged deep into that same mule's rear end, and then return it, each time employing only their teeth. More than one of the miscreants preferred death to this indignity. And while we are on the arse as a weapon of censoriousness and revenge, what about the arse of a cancan dancer? What else is that choreographic frolic for which cancan dancers are most renowned – turning their backs on the audience and like Kikuyu women flicking their skirts over their heads in unison, then wiggling their frilled or even naked buttocks – but a chastisement, a tit-for-tat discourtesy, the ultimate scornful riposte to the ignominious sexual curiosity which keeps them in ignominious employ.

That we may, as culpable spectators, enjoy being on the receiving end of such contumely, is a matter for our individual psychologies and takes away nothing from the contemptuous intention of the action. But it is true, none the less, that no sooner is the hole to hell exposed than we are put in the mood, so to speak, to go on pilgrimages and seek strange lands. Even though we were not privy to the spectacle of one hundred and seventy midgets showing their bottoms to a man they despise, and can do no more, alas, than picture it, the picture is outlandishly inspirational. It transcends our usual expectations of the allowable and the doable. Midgets, as I shall argue later, like dwarfs and hunchbacks, like the prodigiously or the parsimoniously endowed, already work some magical transformations and transgressions of their own, proclaim the looseness, latitude and variety of life. But the *arses* of midgets, and of *one hundred and seventy* midgets at that – what possibilities for renewal and unconfinement do they assure!

Arse = hell = House of the Dead, but in order for the body to renew itself it must first have its funerals. 'Celia, Celia, Celia shits!' wailed Swift, inviting D. H. Lawrence to remind him that it would be far worse for Celia if she didn't. While there is discourtesy in the old woman of Panzoust showing Panurge and Epistemon her Sibyl's cavern, there is also auspiciousness: a Sibyl points the way to the underworld but also to the future; her words are on the wind for Panurge and Epistemon to run and gather. It is interesting how often a hole to hell evokes a sort of answering oracular optimism. When the gainsayer Korah is swallowed up in the desert on Moses' say-so – God opening the earth in an act of exceptional topographical violation – three of Korah's sons are spared because of the repentance in their hearts, and are further rewarded with the prophetic gift. The earth opens and the earth yields. Here the pit, there the prognostication. Even while he writhes in hell, Korah is promised a time when he will return upward. 'The Lord bringeth low,' foresees the prophetess Hannah, 'and the Lord lifteth up.' From low to high. Out of the dark of the Sibyl's arse into the light of prediction, the scattered leaves of futurity, great expectations.

(The greatest of all Great Expectations conform to this pattern. Philip Pirrip's expectations of a new life in a new place – a clean break and a spotless eroticism, free of all former 'taints' of indignity and obscurity – have their source, ironically, in exactly those low dank marshes he cannot wait to put behind him. The visitant who rises from those marshes, showing Pip the hole to hell, is also the benefactor who bankrolls his fantasies of escape. Ironical, because Pip would be shitless if he could.)

Preposterous as was the claim of the art critic David Sylvester that something of Rabelais attached to Gilbert and George's 'The Naked Shit Pictures', first shown in England at the South London Gallery in 1995 – preposterous because Gilbert and George eschew all ribaldry, subsume ostensible merriment under the po-face of camp, lack the taste and aptitude for Rabelaisian abundance – one of the pictures in the exhibition, *Bum Holes*, did for all that manage a sort of carnivalesque confutation of form and shape, that's if you can imagine a joyless carnival. *Bum Holes* shows what it sounds as though it shows, and a little more to boot: the clerks Gilbert and George bending over, one on his knees, one not, each wearing nothing but his wrist-watch, each exposing a sad hang of ageing scrotum, a tired perineum, and the said bum hole. Little of aggression or derision attaches to their posture. This is another of the ways in which they are not Rabelaisian: they would not presume to reprimand or show disdain. They do not have the requisite authority in their bums. But by pulling them open as they bend, the way models in the ruder girlie magazines pull open their pudenda, they shock the eye into an alarming and liberating act of transference. For opened like this, their bums resemble, in shape no less than gesture, the very thing they mean to ape – the vagina.

Not only because of their proximity to the organs of generation, then, are the organs of waste paradoxical. To the confusion caused by neighbourliness we must now add the havoc of resemblance. Cross-sex resemblance at that. Disposed so, an arse may be a cunt and a man may be a woman. 'Split-arses' is a term the comedian Roy 'Chubby' Brown favours for distinguishing the female sex from the male. It acknowledges considerable common ground. Mistress of the euphemism which puts to shame the vulgarity it means to hide, Dame Edna Everage is not above referring to a woman's sexual organs as her 'front botty'. Up and down and round and about we go. A democratization of the flesh which takes us closer than we first imagined to the face/cunt merry-go-round of Baubo and the Sheela-na-gig. And in one sense takes us beyond it. For it is a democratization of gender as well. In the organs of waste, where a man may resemble a woman, women also resemble men. In the bum we are equal.

Equally withering.

Equally sanguine.

II

There is a phenomenon, found in communities we like to think of as more primitive than our own, which scientists of community refer to as dirt-affirmation – the occasional, often ritual embracing of the body's corruptions by people who under normal circumstances go to extreme lengths to avoid all dirt. Quite out of character with the community's habitual fastidiousness, filth, faeces, urine will suddenly be welcomed, ritualized, played with, thrown around, even eaten.

We know more about this than we may think we know. Once again, the pueblo Indians of the American southwest clear a path for us through to our own experience. Though once again we have to turn to the shuddering reports of early ethnologists for the evidence. The last time I invoked the name of Matilda Coxe Stevenson it was to promise a fuller revelation of that 'acme of depravation' as she called it, reached once the great-god kachina took his leave from the plaza. Although she was famous for punching her way into Hopi secrets, this is a Zuni ceremony she is describing, and the clowns are the Newekwe, a curing fraternity, not quite the gods the Koyemshi are, but holy all the same.

The performances are now intended solely for amusement . . . A large bowl of urine is handed by a Koyemshi, who receives it from a woman on the housetop, to a man of the fraternity, who, after drinking a portion, pours the remainder over himself by turning the bowl over his head. Women run to the edge of the roof and empty bowls of urine over the Newekwe and Koyemshi. Each man endeavours to excel his fellows in buffoonery and in eating repulsive things, such as bits of old blankets or splinters of wood. They bite off the heads of living mice and chew them, tear dogs limb from limb, eat the intestines and fight over the liver like hungry wolves. It is a pleasure to state that the Newekwe is the only fraternity that indulges in such practices.

You speak as you find. Alexander M. Stephen found comparable practices among the Hopi clowns.

At 3.10, two men made up in dilapidated costumes of old Hopi women, wearing grotesque masks and grey horsehair wigs, came up ... bearing basins of water on [their] shoulders ... About the same time two young men wearing ... scanty dilapidated shreds of costume began running back and forth ... and each time one passed in front of the old women these tilted a little water from the basins on the runners ... [others] joined in this race, all shouting and anxious to be wetted as much as possible.

After the water was exhausted the two personating old women went towards the Chief kiva court and very soon returned with the same basins, but this time full of foul smelling urine. The two 'women' held these basins in front of them ... and eagerly drank of the urine, rubbing their bellies after a draught and shouting *pash kwa'nwa*, very sweet! Some of the Chuku thrust their heads in the basins, sousing their faces in the stinking urine and swallowing it, as I have said, with all apparent eagerness. While the Chuku were drinking, the 'women' ran among the spectators trying to sprinkle them also, but as nearly all the men standing along the cliff edge of the court were in their gala costume, they – or most of them – ran away and avoided the foul aspersing. Most of the Chuku drank more than once, and as each of the basins held about three gallons, although perhaps half or more was spilled on the ground and on the persons of the Chuku, I am of the opinion that between two or three gallons were actually drunk by the seven participators. It is good medicine (*na'hu*) they say, good for all intestinal ailments.

That these Hopi ceremonial clowns no more drank urine for the internal good it did them than the ancient Israelites avoided bat and lapwing on nutritional grounds, does not need arguing, whatever incidental medical benefits may have accrued from the practice or the avoidance. Matters of the culture, not the stomach, are in play.

It has been observed by all students of both the Hopi and the Zuni people that indecorousness has no part in the normal proceedings of their societies. They do not relish the sight of clowns chucking whatever their bodies manufacture at one another and at bystanders because that is how they themselves would entertain at home. Rather, it is precisely because they are particular in matters of bodily hygiene and hospitality that they look to clowns to be otherwise. In so far as those who are not official performers are drawn into the formal scatological antics of the clowns, their contributions are accompanied by a complex of bewildering emotions. The anthropologist Barbara Tedlock, who has lived startled and wonder-struck among the Zuni Indians for more than twenty years, describes the women of Zuni Pueblo climbing the wooden ladders to the roofs of their houses and pouring buckets of icy water and cornmeal over the 'silly-looking, soaking-wet, half-naked' Mudhead clowns trotting by the windows in single file, all the while shedding – the women shedding, that is – inexplicable tears of grief. True, water is not urine and cornmeal is not shit; but that may just be splitting hairs. Dousing is dousing. And maybe crying is laughing. However we are to understand any of the above ceremonies, it is evident that they entail powerful ambiguities of feeling, that horseplay involving actual or symbolic abominations doesn't lie easily on the Indians' consciences. If the Hopi and Zuni are somehow at war with themselves in these clownish acts of dirt-affirmation, then Mary Douglas's formulation – that some religions make anomalies powerful for good, in the same way that gardeners turn weeds into compost – may explain why.

'Whenever a strict pattern of purity is imposed on our lives,' she writes, in *Purity and Danger*, 'it is either highly uncomfortable or it leads into contradiction if closely followed, or it leads to hypocrisy. That which is negated is not therefore removed. The rest of life, which does not tidily fit the accepted categories, is still there and demands attention.' It is the rest of life, which their categories at other times deny, that the pueblo clowns attend to and affirm whenever they swallow urine or fool around with shit. And by so demonstrating the arbitrary nature of the system which would negate that untidy 'rest of life', and by demonstrating it within a highly structured framework of buffoonery, an activity quite outside the usual business of the community, they prove the freedom of choice which the people have exercised in living as they do.

Call that conservatism, if you like. And call the clowns policemen of the very taboos they violate.

In the process, meanwhile, in the course of all this extraneous wild play with waste and refuse – none of which, it must be said, however conservative in essence, resembles a *Spectator* lunch or a *Sunday Telegraph* drinks party – we have the time of our lives. Watch any pantomime or circus audience: it never laughs more unconfinedly than when the shit starts flying. I only just don't mean that literally. With the example of pueblo clowning before us it is difficult to see those buckets of water that conventional circus clowns employ so liberally, their hoses and their water pistols and their pumps, as anything but tame substitutes for the overflowing bowls of urine and the basins of 'foul aspersion' with which the Newekwe and the Chuku enliven the plazas of New Mexico. Here is the explanation not only for the amount of water that gets sloshed about in circuses, not only for the imminent threat of a dousing inherent in the fool's bladder, but also for all the wallpaper and emulsion sketches we have laughed at, the custard pies, the wobbly cakes, the endless confectioners' creams and treacles. At a performance of the pantomime *Babes in the Wood* in Bournemouth, Christmas 1993, I sat among an audience of adults and children and was swallowed up in laughter which knew no bounds, which seemed to come from lower in the human body than any sound I'd ever heard, which threatened never to end, never to subside into something calmer or less painful, never to release the laughers from their torment, and all because Roy Hudd and Geoffrey Hughes (formerly of 'Coronation Street') emptied a gloopy glutinous mixture of brown slime and chocolate junket into each other's trousers, poured it down then jammed it in then squeezed it through until it squelched out at last through the bottoms of their trousers, a shaming slushy sticky custard the colour of shit.

'The biggest single laugh in the history of the American stage,' according to John Lahr – a full sixty-two seconds it lasted – came when his father, Bert Lahr, finding himself in a doctor's surgery and mistaking what he was required to do when handed a glass for a urine sample, took out his hip flask, measured three fingers of whisky in the glass, and handed it over to the doctor, insisting that that was all he had to spare. 'The house roared and screamed,' a reviewer wrote, 'as I have seldom heard them scream and roar.' It takes nothing from Bert Lahr's own tact and timing to say that it was the reference to the act of pissing, anticipation of the difficulty of pissing to order, and then the appearance of a liquid the colour of piss itself, that had the theatre in an uproar.

'Lavatorial', we call comedy of this kind when we choose to feel superior to it. As though we *have* a choice in the matter. Not all comedy finds

AVBREY
BEARDSLEY.

its material in *our* materials, but laughter is never more itself, never more buoyant, never more transcendental, than when it celebrates these carnival comings and goings of the body. In the shit, in the specimen bottle, we are all equal – king and commoner, woman and man. And if that sounds like equality in degradation – well there we have the reason for our merriment. Every time we void – imaginatively; in comedy – it is like a party, a wake for the dead we were all on the same terms with when living.

The Egyptians believed that the sun was rolled across the sky by a dung beetle. Without dung beetles the world would be overrun with dung. Here is a figure for the role of the scatological clown: he aerates matter, he returns waste to usefulness.

In this he is like the goose of countless fables, fairy-tales and moral satires, who shits a stream of golden crowns. 'And the shitting was such,' in Sir Richard Burton's translation of Basile's *The Pentameron*, that the poor sisters who bought her and loved her and let her sleep with them in their bed, 'began to lift their heads, and to look well fed and happy.' Allow greed to replace natural affection for the bird however, put the gold before the shit, and the goose will not perform. So, when the gossip Vasta out of 'surging envy' steals the goose and lays clean sheets on the floor for her, and bids her walk thereon, 'instead of showing a mint and a coining of crowns, out of her fundament there came forth a sewer of dirt, which covered the bed-linen with a dark yellowish matter, the stink of which filled the whole house . . .' Only after Vasta tries again and is rewarded with a 'new dysentery'; and only after she twists the goose's neck and throws her into the sewer 'into which ordure and filth were cast', where happens to be relieving himself a prince; and only after the goose, who is not dead, fastens herself on to the 'fleshly part of the prince' and will not let go, hanging on like a 'hairy hermaphrodite'; and only after the original sisters successfully persuade their goose to relinquish 'the wretched prince's back parts', reminding her that the 'mouth of a country maid' is a far nicer thing to kiss – only then, after this succession of dungy mishaps, is there a happy outcome, and is the goose able to return to what she does best, turning ordure into treasure.

If the clown is more a dung beetle than a goose, it is because, in order to live, he must first *eat* the shit he processes . . .

Dirt-affirmation. The actors of the *commedia dell'arte* flung flour and water no less freely than pueblo Indian clowns fling what flour and water stand

Attributed to Albrecht Dürer

for. They emptied chamberpots over one another's heads, fell into dung heaps, ate too much and farted, subjected their arses to the scrutiny of doctors and mountebanks, allowed huge clyster-pipes to be inserted so that their bowels would be loosened or even, as in the *Marvellous Malady of Harlequin*, so that Harlequin would the more easily be delivered of triplets.

Among Placido Adriani's collection of *lazzi* of the eighteenth century and earlier – a *lazzo* was the settled piece of comic business around which a *commedia* scene was improvised – can be found

The *lazzo* of fresh urine which is when Pulcinella says that all urine is warm. The maidservant quibbles on the word *fresca* [meaning both 'cool' and 'fresh'] and says it is fresh only when it is made there and then, and she shows him.

And

The *lazzo* of the pulse and urine which is when Pulcinella touches the patient's foot and says 'It is a headache!' He then has urine brought to him, drinks it and spits it out. So that he can write out a prescription he makes Coviello go down on all fours with his backside to the audience. He then asks Coviello to stretch his hand back, makes him hold an ink-pot and then, after dipping his nib in the ink, writes on Coviello's backside, 'Galen, I thank you, *ego medicus*.'

Although we have been taught by *Les Enfants du Paradis* to think of the nineteenth-century French pantomime of the Parisian Funambules as *commedia dell'arte* poeticized – in Théophile Gautier's description, 'vague, indefinite, immense, obscure' – much of the original Italian anal, oral and excretory violence remained alive and well in it, both before Deburau and after him. Robert Storey, the conscientious though censorious historian of Pierrot in French pantomime, recounts a Pierrot of the 1820s demanding milk from a chamberpot; and another, who when asked by a blind man for a loan of his oboe, hands over an enema-syringe instead, the taste of which the blind man notices to be . . . well, peculiar. In a sketch still more reminiscent of the Newekwe, a Pierrot of the 1850s happily gobbles up a rat which Arlequin has slid on to his plate. Very good, he observes – 'A very good dish.' If those examples all share some refined culinary *frisson*, horror confined almost entirely to the environs of the mouth, a pantomime entitled *L'Etoile de Pierrot*, staged at the Funambules in 1854, essayed a far more extravagant revulsion. A house becomes a chamberpot, gigantic clyster-pipes serve as a mast, diapers go up as sails, and in this vessel Arlequin and Colombine go to sea – the Yellow Sea, to be precise. A stage awash with piss.

In this hyperbole, the dramaturge Charles Charton may have been remembering the fart Pantagruel blew, causing the earth to tremble for twenty-seven miles around, and engendering from its fetid air 'more than

Cap. Cardoni. *Maramao.*

fifty-three thousand little men, misshapen dwarfs'. But why stop there?

... and with a poop, which he made, he engendered as many little bowed women, such as you see in various places, and who never grow, except downwards like cows' tails, or in circumference, like Limousin turnips.

An example of fruitfulness in farting so prodigious that Panurge is prompted to wonder why then Pantagruel doesn't join these 'fine clump-ish men and fine stinking women' in holy matrimony, so that they may 'breed horse-flies'. Which Pantagruel – for why stop there? –

did, and called them pygmies. He sent them to live on an island close by, where they have multiplied mightily. But the cranes make continual war on them, and they put up a courageous defence. For these little stumps of men (whom in Scotland they call dandiprats) most readily lose their tempers; the physical reason for which is that they keep their bowels close to their hearts.

If you have ever wondered why minimalist and conceptualist art is never funny, however playful it aspires to be, here is the reason: comedy is invariably on the side of plenitude; it is expansionist not reductive; it wants things never to end; it knows that less means less and only more means more. So while Gilbert and George and Rabelais may have a poop or two in common, the resemblance stops at that; the one – taking Gilbert and George to be one – is already finished, while the other is just beginning to blow.

If hyperbole shows the way to optimism – new worlds at the end of every exaggeration – and defecation shows the way to hyperbole – no end to how much we can squeeze out of ourselves – then defecation is the mother of hope. It is change we celebrate every time we throw a custard pie, or water-pistol an audience; change, renewal and disorder. Our freedom. Proof that we can never be obedient to any single idea of our nature, that we will always spill over, move on like running water . . .

And be devil-proof. A secular farce of the fifteenth century, one of the sort that accompanied mystery plays of the times, tells of how the turd of a dying miller – a man much cuckolded in life – is mistaken for his soul and borne off to hell by an apprentice servant-devil. The soul 'goes out by the backside,' Lucifer had warned his apprentice; 'keep on the look-out for it at the arsehole.' Which he conscientiously did. And once having seen it appear, he seized his prize, bagged it, and carried it down to hell with fiendish and triumphant howls. When the bag is opened below, all the devils are appalled by the stench and 'Lucifer ends the play by a solemn exhortation to all devils never to bring a miller's soul to Hell, as it is nothing but dirt and filth.'

Hans Weiditz

Meaning that the future looks bright for all millers. Thanks to a turd.

Another reading of the story might be that you can't expect to do well, even as a devil, if you allow a dainty stomach to rule your intelligence.

You who would see into the future, the Sibyl of Panzoust as good as tells her visitors, hitching her petticoats up to her armpits, you who would *have* a future, look where the dainty won't! You cannot hope to have a share in what's coming if you do not accept your share of what's been.

'We all dream,' writes John Updike in a powerful passage of thought, a meditation on obscenity and shit, late in *The Witches of Eastwick*,

and we all stand aghast at the mouth of the caves of our death

trou de la Sibylle!

and this is our way in. Into the nether world. Before plumbing, in the old out-houses, in winter, the accreted shit of the family would mount up in a spiky frozen stalagmite, and such phenomena help us to believe that there is more to life than the airbrushed ads at the front of magazines, the Platonic forms of perfume bottles and nylon nightgowns and Rolls Royce fenders. Perhaps in the passage-ways of our dreams we meet, more than we know: one white lamplit face astonished by another. Certainly the fact of witchcraft hung in the consciousness of Eastwick; a lump, a cloudy density generated by a thousand translucent over-lays, a sort of heavenly body, it was rarely breathed of and, though dreadful, offered the consolation of completeness, of rounding out the picture . . .

Witches and shit; Sibyl's arses and the mouths of the caves of our death. The nether world. The more to life. The rest of life that will not tidily fit. Clowns' business. And novelists', of course.

How to keep – is there any, is there none such, nowhere known some, bow or brooch or braid or brace, lace, latch or catch or key to keep it – not beauty, but what may look like beauty's opposite (though is not), is there any way to keep *completeness*; keep it back, keep a sense of it, keep faith with it: that obduracy of life and matter sending up its stalagmites of accreted family shit against the airbrush.

In what feels almost like a companion piece to the Updike – Americans having even more to fear from Platonic forms than we do – Philip Roth's Mickey Sabbath, narrator of *Sabbath's Theater*, argues for the pleasure it gives him to hear Gus Kroll, the service-station owner, relay lewd jokes, however tired.

Gus's impassioned commitment to repeating the jokes had long ago led [Sabbath] to understand that they were what gave unity to Gus's vision of life, that they alone answered the need of his spiritual being for a clarifying narrative with which to face day after day at the pump. With every joke that poured forth from Gus's toothless mouth, Sabbath was reassured that not even a simple guy like Gus was free of the human need to find a strand of significance that will hold together everything that isn't on TV.

For TV read airbrush. For strand of significance read shit.

The shit, the witchery, the jokes, the jokes about shit – if, as I've argued so far, they promise nothing so much as our capacity for change and renewal, they are the warrant, too, of that without which change can have no meaning: our persistence. Call it a holding together, call it the consolation of completeness. They come to mean the same thing and teach the same lesson. Mirthless and clean, we vanish as though we had never been.

Jacques Callot

No scene of literary bawdy that I remember pleased us more as school-boys than Chaucer's Alisoun, the carpenter's wyf, putting out atte wyndow sche hir hole, for the lovesick Absolon to kiss – 'ful savorly'. We savoured that. The idea that not only with his mouth, mistaking it for hers, he kiste her naked ers, but relished it. Wiped his own lips dry in readiness for the job and – aaagh! – really got in there. Fully. Ful fully. With all his taste-buds up and twitching. How we ran around, clutching our stomachs, pretending to be more appalled than we were – a beard, a beard! ful wel we wist a womman hath no berd – doing as the clerk did, wiping from our outraged lips (we should have been so lucky) all memory of the shame, now with dust, now with sand, now with straw. The tale could have stopped dead at that point for us, no matter what the narrative exigencies, so happy were we with it, so eager to feign retching over it again. We didn't need that second ers at the window – the carpenter's this time – nor the fart that 'it let flee' (a fart to rhyme with 'wher thou art'), nor the red-hot poker with which Absolon executed his revenge. But since they were there, we accepted them. Who were we to look a gift horse in the mouth? We were twelve years old. We hadn't kissed much yet. We had farted a fair bit, but we weren't sure what role farts were going to play when other skills were expected of our bodies. *The Miller's Tale* inflamed and calmed us at the same time. It threw a bridge between what we knew and what we didn't. It consoled us with the thought that whatever else we were going to have to do with our bodies in the hot years ahead we weren't going to have to stop laughing at them.

CHAPTER FOUR

Diary of a Visit to a Clown

5 Nov 1993

The newly done-up lounge of the Astoria Hotel, St Petersburg. Mafiosi with no necks sit under the *thé dansant* palms, their hands deep inside the

pockets of their black-market leather coats, insinuating a thread of dismal menace into every new convenience and refurbishment, superintending the comings and goings of the whores, the guides, the porters, the taxi drivers, and ultimately even us – the cultural innocents from the West, here because it is the city of Pushkin and Dostoievsky and Slava Polunin.

Teatime, though there is no tea. I have spent most of the day talking through an interpreter to the person I have come to St Petersburg to see. Another way of putting this is that I have spent the day talking to the person my wife, Rosalin Sadler, reckoned I should come to see. Which is why, for pleasure or for penance, to enjoy reward or to suffer vengeance, Ros is with me. The person we have *both* come to see then – to be even-handed about it – is the above-mentioned Slava Polunin. Clown.

I have devoted a not inconsiderable portion of my life to *avoiding* clowns. Fearing them as a child. Hating them as an adult. Not wanting their sweets or their balloons. Not wanting to be singled out by them. Not finding them funny. Forever trying to summon up the courage to resist their blackmail and not smile. Now I am in one of the most humanly horrible cities in the world, risking the malevolence of the mafiosi, spending money, doing without light, doing without tea, in order to *meet* a clown.

Thus does the whirligig of time bring all things round, as some other clown says.

It's going to take some whirligig to keep the story of Slava Polunin, or at least the story of my coming to see Slava Polunin, in decent order. Did I hear about him at this year's Edinburgh Festival? Did I read that he had been booked to appear by someone who books fringe acts and who had then gone bankrupt, leaving innumerable fringe funny-people without a venue? Or have I imagined that and did I in fact know nothing of him until I saw an ad for his ensemble – The Academy of Fools – in Clapham High Street? And wasn't that the day I ran into Barry Fantoni in the Polish cake-shop – a day, therefore, of Italian-Polishry and Jewishry and Russianry and Foolery?

Round and round the whirligig goes. Why am I making such a fuss of this? Every encounter is preceded by a history of ironic circumstance and accidents. I suppose I'm fussing because I cannot get over the lengths I've gone to – the lengths I've been persuaded to go to – to meet a clown. Maybe I haven't yet rendered the degree to which I loathe and fear them.

Anyway, anyway, I saw the ad, liked the name of the group – The Academy of Fools – (probably because academies were where I'd spent most of my life, finding them on the whole safer than circuses), and as a consequence bowled along to see it at the Hackney Empire. Where I was struck . . .

But rather it was Ros who was struck. By Slava's St Sebastian, perforated with arrows, taking an unconscionable time dying to the music of Rodriguez, now falling, now rising, now down, now up again, staggering, collapsing, rallying, teetering between life and death – no, actually dying in the orchestra pit and then resurrecting on the very backs of the audience's seats. By Slava meaning to hang himself in a fit of clown melancholy, pulling at an interminable rope, and finding a second clown meaning to hang himself on the other end of it. By Slava making ambiguously chaste love to himself through the arm of an overcoat hanging on a coat stand, making two people out of one, defying the pathos of singularity with the reproductive greed of the grotesque. By Slava filling the theatre with giant balloons, huge coloured balls as tall as the dress circle, playthings from another planet, whose enormity drew everyone out of their seats in pursuit of the Brobdingnagian childhood they'd never had. By Slava . . .

But that will do. For my taste he was a touch fey. Belonged too much to the French mime tradition. Chased a few too many butterflies. Relied more than I liked a clown to rely on a sort of sentimental eunuchry. Wasn't visceral enough. Though had he been visceral I still would have complained. How many more times? – I just didn't like clowns. Ros did like him, though. Ros thought him a genius, in his way. And it was her own genius for enthusiasm that got him to meet us in the pub next door to the Hackney Empire, and to give us his fax number in St Petersburg, and to agree to be in to talk to us should we ever see our way clear to being in his neck of the woods.

Which seemed to me a safe enough place to leave it. Fat chance we'd ever be in *that* neck of the woods.

We have lined up a translator-cum-fixer – Sergei. He picks us up from the Mafia-controlled lobby of the Astoria, a little late. Protection-money difficulties, we assume. He is dapper, conceited, leather-jacketed of course, with English pronunciation skills most English people would kill or go to Eton for. All wonderfully rounded 'O's. Lips perfectly pursed for 'prunes and prisms'. Last week he was escorting Ted Turner and Jane Fonda around town. They had come to buy St Petersburg. They must have loved his accent.

He drives us out the way we came in the afternoon before, in the direction of the airport. Which he pronounces ohpert. He parks the car, according to instructions he's received from Slava, outside a book and lemonade shop which has an illuminated sign ordering us to SMILE. We smile. That's to say Ros and I do. Sergei doesn't smile if he can help it.

St Petersburg was built to an Italian model on a bog filched from Finland. The idea was to fill the bog in, but it's showing again today in the courtyard of the Stalinesque apartment fortress through which Sergei uncertainly leads us. The numbers over the rotting doorways have all faded. We turn left, then right, then left again. Sergei has Slava's number but no number is visible. Occasionally a door opens, showing us figures huddled below a rotting staircase. Raskolnikovs wiping blood from banisters. Sergei asks for help with the number. No one gives it. No one knows. No one wants to know. They rush past, heads down in their babushka headscarves or rabbit hats, ankle-deep in Finnish peat, refusing the slightest effort at sociability, resenting us for requiring it of them. If someone were dying out here in the mud, in the already dead morning light, would they raise a mitten to help? No.

SMILE says the illuminated sign in the road. Smile? On our walk down Nevsky Prospekt the afternoon before, I had watched three Russians – two men and a woman – posing for a photograph on a bridge over a canal. 'Try saying cheese,' the photographer had suggested. But they couldn't so much as *think* cheese. Perhaps they'd never seen any. Certainly they'd never seen a smile. Blankly they stood, their shoulders not quite touching, as though modelling for their death masks preparatory to execution. Could this be a clue to Slava's long-drawn-out death of the clown St Sebastian, which brought the house down at the Hackney Empire? It wasn't fancy; it was a St Petersburg street scene, the slow slaughter of the spirit on Nevsky Prospekt any afternoon in winter.

Or any morning, come to that. Still no one helps us with the number. Still they hurry past, not alive enough even to look sickly. All this is galling to Sergei. You can tell he is not proud of his city. He is a fixer. It's his business to know everything. These people are anti-fixers. It's their business to know nothing. Eventually Sergei finds it himself. We were wrong to have turned left. We were right when we went right. In a corner of the first-floor landing a pair of down-at-heels in cheap anoraks are rolling cigarettes out of something that doesn't look like tobacco. One of them seems to have had the fingers of one hand amputated at the knuckles. When I look harder I see that it is not fingers but fingernails he is without. Could be, that over time he has rolled them off.

They look up guiltily when they see us, startled in the performance of some feverish but utterly trivial felony. This is how the citizens of St Petersburg dispose themselves in public places. It is impossible for two or more people to relate spatially in this city without appearing to be up to no good. See a man talking to a woman on a street corner and for all the world he is a ponce threatening a prostitute. See two men out walking together and each is picking the pocket of the other. Even family groups invariably look wrong: the children always on the point of finding somewhere inappropriate to pee, the mother always on the point of abandoning them. No one here knows how to stand naturally in juxtaposition with another; every social configuration is a tableau of petty wrongdoing. For the first time I understand what it means to say a place has lost its innocence. It is not corruption I am describing now, not degeneracy, but a forgetting, a misplacement of the simple civic arts of physical ease and guiltlessness.

So coming to such a place to see a clown may turn out to have a very particular meaning. A clown! Aren't clowns there to remind us of our innocence? And isn't that one of the reasons I've always hated them – because I've never believed in innocence, never believed in it in art or performance at least, always thought of it as false, ersatz, a nonce word – *innononce* – invented by those who would make children's stories out of adults' lives. But here, on the stairs of a cruel Russian tenement block I suddenly see that there might be an argument for teaching it, for bringing it back, for showing a demoralized citizenry how to melt the unease in their spines and consciences, how to go rubbery, flop about, how to hold themselves as if they are *not* petty larcenists.

Is this the explanation, then, for Russia's great tradition of clowns and fools and holy innocents and idiots savants? That Russians have been forever losing the trick of naturalness; that they have always been like this, long before Lenin and Stalin, huddling suspiciously in doorways, up to no good in their heads; and only clowns have been able to laugh them back into simplicity?

Slava the clown greets us at his door. Greet may be too warm a word for what he does. He holds out a hand and averts his face. Shy. And more than a little wary. What do we want with him after all? Why have we come this far to find him? If he were really hostile, I decide, he would not be inviting us into his apartment. But the other side of the why have we come this far query is, since we have, what about some heat? But then again, he isn't that sort of a clown. Not an only-connect clown. More a touch-me-not clown.

He is wearing a black T-shirt with some grotesque festival figure scrawled over it. A souvenir of carnival. He is finely built, but muscular, like a dancer or an acrobat. His hair is wild. On stage it stands out aurorally, as though magnetized by irregular interplanetary activity. Today it is less dramatic, but still electrically charged. He has dark gypsy features and a wide sensual mouth. Bohemian rather than designer stubble. And of course, of course of course, his eyes express sadness. What age is he? Forty-five, I guess. A sad age even if you're not living in St Petersburg.

There is a soothing minimalism about his apartment. This is partly the imposed minimalism of Soviet Socialism and its aftermath. But there is also design in it. Just enough. Just enough pots and pans. Just enough places to sit.

A breakfast bar – Manchester, *circa* 1954 – divides the kitchen from the lounge. Here, four people can sit and talk, half in the lounge, half in the kitchen; close to the tea and biscuits. Tea flows, not from a samovar but in a fashion that reminds me of what I have read of samovars; continuous tea, thin, aromatic, always hot. You don't have to ask; you just get it. No fuss. Slava pours and pours without looking to see what's in your cup.

The floorboards are polished. Light and clean. There's a pleasant but not new wallpaper on the walls, a sort of Celtic horse pattern, two different horses endlessly repeating. We sit under a red light. It's spare, pared down like his act, but not cold. Ros is adamant about this. NOT COLD. I have more trouble around deprivation. I need clutter to be convinced of comfort. I need uselessness and garrulousness, gewgaws, junk – that's a home. But here there's just enough, I'm told, to show heart. Just as Slava's stage act has just enough to convey myth. A transparent telephone lights up when it rings. Transparent! Get it? Simple, functional, no fuss – but it shows its heart. Innards of green and orange and yellow and pink. This is what happens to a phone when it rings – its innards pulse. This is the myth behind the appearance. Keep it simple and true.

So there we are. One of us sees a perfectly pared-down adequacy, exactly mirroring his stage act. The other sees an empty flat.

Apparently – according to Ros – there's much red and yellow about. Slava's colours. The colours he dresses in on stage. The colours of danger in nature. The colours of wasps and blood.

He talks to us about Clownade which I at first take to be something like Bandaid – clowns against starvation in the Third World, clowns against war and racism and brutality and the imprisonment of the innocent – all those things that the rest of us are for. But in fact he means something more like Clownage, the whole art and reason and point and purpose of being a clown. Nineteen eighty-two was an important year in the history of his own Clownade. It was in that year that he set up the first Russian Festival of Mime Action. Mass action, he calls it. Every mime in Russia attended. Eight hundred participants. We digress into romantic pantomime, and names crop up which Sergei is unable, or too embarrassed, to spell for us. Tomaszewski is one. Henryk Tomaszewski, the Pole, founder of the Wroclaw Pantomime Theatre. A combiner of mime and dance, sumptuousness and absurdity, eastern theatre and Faust. Does that help us with the concept of romantic pantomime? Jean-Louis Barrault, then. Marcel Marceau. When Marcel Marceau visited Russia for the first time in the sixties Slava volunteered his services in a lowly technical capacity, just so that he could be close to that most wistful and striped of mimes; be close to him and watch him work. Not one show did Slava miss. Marcel Marceau is *it*, for Slava. The real thing. The bee's knees. Marcel Marceau and Lindsay Kemp.

I don't particularly like where this is taking me. Marcel Marceau and Lindsay Kemp? These were the last personages I had in mind, and theirs the last idea of what constituted comedy, when, as a sixth-former, I planned the first of my many planned books on the cheerfulness of great art, specifically literature, specifically English. *The Genial View*, it was going to be called, as an *homage* to Henry James, who wasn't English but who was Englishified, which was even better, since it meant he had choices and rejected them. Many years later I did get round to writing and publishing an essay on the comedy of *Hamlet*, explaining just what sort of mirth it was that Hamlet himself had, he knew not wherefore, mislaid. And whatever sort of mirth that was, it certainly wasn't the mirth of Marcel Marceau or Lindsay Kemp. Behind Marcel Marceau was Deburau, the nineteenth-century French Pierrot, known to English audiences chiefly through Barrault's depiction of him in *Les Enfants du Paradis* – pale, silent, virginal, moonsick, morbid, murderous. Not robust. Not ribald. Not English.

Not French either, you would have thought, bearing in mind Rabelais and Molière. But that too is part of the story. How comedy comes to lose, it knows not wherefore, all its mirth. How its centre of operation moves from the stomach to the heart. How the devil becomes a holy fool.

So which is Slava, I wonder. A demon or a decadent? Despite his unambiguous declaration of loyalties and antecedents, despite his butterfly-chasing on the stage in Hackney, I sense something more diabolic in him. Something not virginal and moonsick.

Anyway, to return to that 1982 festival of mass mime action, it gave a definite boost, Slava tells us, to the development of pantomime – romantic pantomime – in his country. For thirty or so years before, pantomime had languished in Russia. It had grown stale. Whatever had been alive in it, Stalin had killed. 'Under Stalin,' Sergei carefully translates for us, 'everything above the average was extinguished.' It was in need of a kickstart. And Slava had kickstarted it.

He is, of course, a congenital kickstarter. He has that weary look that all kickstarters get in the end. The look that says, I've done it all for them,

Jacques Callot

I've done nothing for myself. The look that acknowledges that time is running out, that an altruistic life is not a happy one, that kickstarting doesn't feed the family.

Hearing mention of Stalin I ask the obvious question: comedy and subversion, blah, blah . . .

Slava comes back firmly. He doesn't look for political protest of any kind in the theatre. Because the theatre expresses the inner world . . . but – and he is distinct and passionate on this matter; even though I speak no Russian I hear that he is distinct and passionate – this comes to the same thing in the end because expressing the inner meaning of things is ultimately, inevitably, subversive. We've never been involved in political activity, he says, but finally it happens so. Whenever we try to make a world that conforms to our inner world, it becomes protest.

I applaud him in my heart. This is true of all art. And it is the reason why overtly political art – activist theatre, socialist fiction and so on – invariably disgusts. It betrays the power of the medium it employs. It fails to understand that a work which expresses the inner meaning of things needs no other superstructure of combative intent to threaten the equanimity of conformists. But then overtly political artists are themselves necessarily conformist.

Jacques Callot

Gian Fritello.   Ciurlo.

Sitting sipping endless thin tea under a bare red light, I enjoy having my business, the business of being a novelist, explained to me by a clown.

As an example of his own methodology, Slava cites an act he devised in the early 1980s, which became famous 'all over Russia'. 'NEL'ZIA' it was called – meaning NOT ALLOWED. In this sketch NEL'ZIA was the only word that was used. NOT ALLOWED. NOT ALLOWED. A clown approaches a ball. Another clown follows. The moment the first clown attempts to touch the ball the second clown shouts NEL'ZIA! The first clown approaches a table. The second clown shouts NEL'ZIA! Then a chair. NEL'ZIA! Then a phone. NEL'ZIA! Eventually, in exasperation, clown one lunges at the ball. L'ZIA! he cries. L'ZIA! L'ZIA!

This is to be understood on several levels, Slava tells us. An inner voice telling a person not to touch. And, of course, the force of bureaucratic injunction. An absurd world, either way. Tragedy and comedy mixed. 'At any time I make a piece I try to make it a metaphor for the time it is created.'

Talk of balls reminds Ros of the finale to Slava's act as we saw it at the Hackney Empire. The release of the balloons. It was her sense that Slava was in a bit of a snit, professionally, by the end of the night. She'd watched him leave the stage while the giant balloons were bouncing around among the audience, watched him talking to friends at the bar at the back of the theatre, and seen distaste take over his features. Her guess was that children were the problem. Too many of them there that night. Too many of them leaping after his balloons. She wonders if children are not his ideal audience . . .

Bingo! Slava doesn't pause, doesn't bother even to pretend to sugar the pill. 'What I do is for grown-ups,' he says. But there is a problem with the genre. Over the last decades it has been kids who go to see clowns. And it is difficult, he says, to change this attitude. In Russia, on the other hand, 'intellectual audiences come to see my show without children. And professors from academies and military officers' – I check that with Sergei; yes, military officers – 'play with the balloons at the end. The idea is to bring adults back into their childhood.' I think of interrupting him and asking why, if he doesn't much care for the child in the child, he should welcome it back in the adult. But I let him finish. 'It always happens that at the end, when the balls are released, the adults stand up and start playing with the balls.'

As indeed they did at the Hackney Empire, even if their number was diluted by real children. They rose and laughed and cheered and squealed and strained to get a touch of the balls. *L'ZIA! L'ZIA!* When I say 'they' I am making a clear contradistinction between them and me. I didn't rise or laugh or cheer or squeal. I, the historian of the comic, the champion of the funny over everything else, backed off. In truth I was already backed off – ready to flee as I always am in the live theatre, half-out of my aisle seat, up on the balls of my feet, my body at a twist, quivering like a compass needle in the direction of the nearest exit, fully packed and on my mark, set to make a run for it just in case, you know, a comedian (or even a tragic actor come to that: Lear, Coriolanus, Timon of Athens) takes it into his head to point or to allude or to force me on to the stage – so what, this time, I mean by saying I backed off is that I quit my seat, pushed my way through the hooting ballooners, and hid at the rear of the theatre where, providentially, there was a bar – the same bar that Slava had retreated to. The difference between us being that he was sulking because children were being children and I was sulking because adults were. I didn't want a balloon to come my way, forcing me into collusion with another person's smiling eye. *NEL'ZIA!* I didn't want to have to go gaga, communally, over a coloured ball. Recapture my childhood? Me? God forbid!

So what was the matter with your childhood, Mr Jacobson?

The same that was the matter with everybody else's. The mystery is not that I have no desire to recapture mine, but that *they*, the officers and professors from academies, are prepared – no, eager – to go bouncing all the way back to *theirs*.

But I lie. There was something the matter with my childhood. Something happened in it, anyway, that prepared me to be afraid of clowns. I was five or six years old. On holiday in the country, somewhere in the southwest, where my father had been billeted in the war. The village had a village idiot. If I tried hard enough I could probably remember his name. In my mind I associate him with milk and milk churns. Perhaps he sat on one. Perhaps he distributed milk. Perhaps he had a real function in the village other than terrifying me. But he terrified me better than he did anything else. I ran whenever I saw him coming. Ran from his bloated head and his squeaky voice and his unpredictability. I could not understand the universe he inhabited and so I felt I could calculate nothing of what he might do next. What my father did next was make me shake his hand. He's nice. Go on. He means no harm. He's friendly. Go on. Shake. By his lights, my father was doing the right thing. He didn't think one should be afraid of anything. *He* wasn't. But that meant he underestimated my dread. He never knew how close I came to having a six-year-old's heart attack that afternoon, feeling the milk-sweet fingers of the village simpleton in mine. Or how much *more* frightened of him I was thereafter.

I don't get into any of this with Slava. Ros, I know, would rather that I didn't. And Slava probably knows what I think without my telling him. Can see it on me. Smell it on me. The enemy-of-clown-and-unpredictable-simple-person odour. And if it came right down to it, would I trust his attitude to his own childhood? What clown has ever convinced you of the soundness of his relations with the infant in himself? So it's best to leave it. This is theory we're discussing, after all. And in theory it's OK to regress. Everything about the comic is OK in theory. It's practice that gets you into hot water every time. As, for example, while we're on the subject of water, Slava's ensemble spraying water at the Hackney Empire audience. Hostility? Aggression? Another way of thinking about the child inside the adult?

What this is about, Slava explains – theoretically – is involving the audience. Not wanting them to see the stage, the act, as a flat picture. Slava sprays them with water 'to get their heavy heads up'.

My own view, already adumbrated – though not, of course, to Slava – is that water gets sloshed about in pantomimes and circuses as a substitute for urine. Hopi and Zuni clowns, less nice than ours, but closer to the original functions of clowning, do not bother with the substitute. Whatever their bodies manufacture, they fling. Not just liquids; solids too. For which, again, we have our substitutes. The custard pie. The wobbly jelly. Chocolate blancmange.

That there is as strong a desire to be the recipient of a custard pie as there is to throw one, is undeniable. Ritual humiliation has never wanted for takers. And the effect, on either side of the pie or the water pistol, may well be, in Slava's words, to raise a heavy head. But let's be a little bolder about the nature of the ancient impulses and satisfactions in play here. Unflattening the picture will hardly do as a description of the violent will to mortify in the one party, or the appetite for abasement in the other.

Mortification and abasement, though, are not words that figure much in Slava's philosophy of Clownade. He's on another mission. Romantic pantomime. And for an hour or so, as the light outside his window goes on dying through a succession of etiolated greys, and his own interior light goes on deepening from scarlet to crimson to umber, he sweeps up even me, kicking and fighting every inch of the way, into the poetry of his calling. 'Loneliness, death, love, freedom – each piece I make is based on some unchanging principle of our nature. Because clowning simplifies, we are talking about myth and fable. On stage a clown is like the essence of theatre, so every piece should be the essence of life of a human being. But unstated. I like things to be unpronounced, not spoken, secret, irrational – something you cannot grasp.' To make this idea come alive, as much to himself as to us, he crumples something in his hand as he speaks. 'I like the immaterial, the ideational. I like things to be subtle. Suggestive.' What he says reminds me of Théophile Gautier's praise of silent pantomime, the same French pantomime to which Slava acknowledges his allegiance – 'vague, indefinite, immense, obscure, and yet comprehensible to all'. But Slava seems to have ambitions beyond that form. 'Now I'm trying to broaden,' he tells us, 'to include tragedy in what I do.' (I hate to hear him say this. I hate to hear comedy making concessions to what isn't comedy. I hate the suggestion that comedy has to look outside for support, for breadth, for anything. 'Immense', Gautier called pantomime. How much bigger than immense can you get? I hate the common assumption that immensity resides in tragedy, not comedy. But I stay silent.) 'What I like,' Slava goes on – I hate; he likes – 'is trying to balance. Reversing and balancing. Just as it happens with us every day.'

It is absurd, but even as he is describing it, so it transpires – life reversing and balancing. Ros notices it before I do, the contrast between the warmth of our modest red-lit symposium and an unfolding drama outside in that rutted courtyard to which the world's whole sap has sunk, where boys are making fires, running with bits of flaming rag and twigs and cardboard which they light from a fiery canister held by the biggest of them, a sort of Molotov cocktail, a Roman candle spitting liquid fire, like golden rain. As though to combat the squeezing of the light, they drop conflagrations as they go, now stamping them out, now starting others, waving their flambeaus through the visible cold, like banished demons of the volcano and the grate, serving the command of the single Prometheus who ignites them individually, separate sparks of the one great blaze.

Back where we are, by Slava's transparent heart-throbbing telephone, under Slava's shaded lamp, within grasping range of Slava's red-handled stewing-pans, the talk continues quietly of mime. And of what Slava has learnt on his travels of different national expectations of comedy. In England humour is more intellectual. People like intricacy there. In France it's the fate of the character they go for. In the USA, where there are no traditions of theatre, it is the holiday that counts; there they go to the theatre simply to be distracted and to forget. For the Russians compassion is all that matters. They identify completely with the character they see on stage; they see themselves as suffering just as he does. But it is India that has impressed Slava the most. India is very special. They don't care about your art. When they hear you're coming they do nothing the whole day; they just wait for you to appear. You do not even have to perform. They just want you to be among them. You must touch them. Look into their eyes. At first they were cold to his act. So he improvised. Approached a beautiful girl. Soothed a crying baby. This they loved. They stayed on with him for another four hours. What's important to them is the state of their souls at the particular moment. If you can catch the spirit and appeal to it, then you are a great success. They will watch the same act repeated a thousand times. They are at that moment above time, as though in a frozen state. Whereas in the USA they respond only to what is new, and each second they demand a new action.

Out in the courtyard, where it looks like night though it is barely afternoon, the boys are still scorching the bog which Peter the Great filched from Finland to build a western city on. Peat burning, in the centre of town.

We rise from the bar to watch videos of some of Slava's old projects, caravans he has led across Europe, carnivals he has organized, feasts and festivals of folly. The television is so small we have to bang our foreheads against the screen to see anything. We gather in a tight semicircle, jerked forward like skinheads competing to see who can do more damage to a television set with his skull, Slava on a low stool, utterly fascinated by his own moving image. I don't think it's conceit or self-love, just reabsorption in whatever business it was that absorbed him in the first place. It is my impression that he would watch himself till Doomsday were there enough tapes of him to last that long.

Maybe he wouldn't admit the distinction, but it seems to me, watching all this stuff, that too much of Slava's creative energy has gone into entrepreneurial activity – kickstarting romantic pantomime in poor old denatured Mother Russia and the rest of it – and not enough into actual clowning. He tells us about his Crazy Women venture, of which he would like Barbra Streisand to be president; the folk and street theatre he has associated himself with; the first carnival in Russia since the Revolution, which he made happen in 1993 – three nights of devilry, angelry and eroticism. And his First All Union Congress of Fools – an elaborate Dadaist charade which delegates and guests were required to attend in formal dress, and where, from a rostrum resembling a political platform, clowns addressed the populace in the manner of the nation's leaders, saying utterly 'useless things'. Entrances to the theatre were boarded up; notices were posted advising roundabout ways for the audience to enter – down steps leading to a basement, through the basement to a shower-room where the showers were on – laugh! – then on through unlit corridors, past piles of coal and rubbish and other obstacles, until, having negotiated all this, you found yourself – guess where? – that's right, out in the street again. The next test of the sense of humour and nervous system of the audience, whose whereabouts I am now uncertain of, was a line of sailors, or rather a double row of sailors which you walked between like a visiting dignitary inspecting the fleet. After which the words CONGRESS OF FOOLS were rubber-stamped on your brow. Whoever refused to be stamped was not allowed entry. 'Remember,' Slava pauses to remind us, 'this was happening to dignified people.' And the stamp would not wash off for at least a week. So, given that there were five shows, each with an audience of more than 1,500 people, upwards of 8,000 respectable citizens were walking around St Petersburg – or Leningrad as it then was – with the words CONGRESS OF FOOLS stamped on their foreheads. (Smile!, I think. Say cheese, I think. Whatever the effect on the people of Leningrad/St Petersburg at the time, it hasn't lasted.) And that wasn't the end of it. After the stamp – which allowed you into the hall but not, not yet, into the theatre – came the questionnaire. And this questionnaire too had to be stamped, ratified, legitimized, before you could perform the simplest task, such as going to the toilet or the cloakroom or the bar. Finally, the hat you had been obliged to wear was tagged and ticketed to allow you into the auditorium, and once you were seated, an army of cleaners – clowns in disguise – swept up around your feet.

Maybe you needed to be there.

And that *was* the end of it? No, not quite. The congress coincided with the twentieth anniversary of Slava's theatre group, and Stanislawski had decreed that a theatre last only twenty years. So a funeral was in order. Black balloons. Black confetti. Black banners. Ros might have been right that red and yellow, signifying danger in nature, were Slava's colours; but he had as much trouble as any contemporary fashion victim getting black out of his system. Black-clad clowns lay in coffins. Speakers climbed on to a black-draped stage to deliver funeral orations. Then 4,000 mourners followed the black hearses . . .

I'm wondering how Sergei is taking all this. Absurdism can't be his bag. No interplanetary activity affects the electricity in his hair. He is trimmed, clipped, belted into his leather jacket, under which he wears a green pullover and a blue-striped shirt. He works on his vowels. He reads *The Times* and the *Telegraph*, not the Dadaist Manifesto.

Slava's newest scheme, about which he has written to CNN – and which Sergei might have been able to help him with had he known of it the week before, when Ted Turner was in town – is for a Ship of Fools. A 'Parade of Life' he calls it. Five hundred brides in white will line one side of Nevsky Prospekt. Five hundred grooms in black will line the other side. Black and white horses will be in attendance. Small girls in white tutus. Small boys in black tails. A bride on stilts, with a huge trailing veil, the length of Nevsky Prospekt, will open the ceremony. She will be accompanied by a groom, also on stilts. Couturiers from around the world will be invited to design the bridal gowns. From a huge bed, forty children of each sex will leap. The city's cleaning vehicles will disgorge the guests. The Patriarch of All Russia will officiate. After which there will be a parade of pregnant women. The Parade of Life.

The newlyweds and their guests will then be taken to an island. The sirens of the boats, having been tuned individually, will play Mendelssohn's *Wedding March*. The conductor will conduct them from a crane. From the island the assembly will embark upon the Ship of Fools. Where they will be joined by clowns. One clown to each nuptial principal. From here the ship will visit fourteen European countries. In the main harbour of each country the clowns will come ashore and perform their routines. Then the ship will sail on again. 'I want to combine the idea of a Ship of Fools,' Slava says, 'with the idea of Holiday in Real Life.'

I am scribbling all this down, religiously, when it occurs to me that Slava is making it up as he goes along, extemporizing, piling crazy detail upon crazy detail, getting wilder and wilder, out-Dadaing Dada, for the sheer exhilaration of inventing, and for the fun, maybe, of making a fool of me, the humourless conscientious scribe. I charge him with this, but he denies it. Disappointingly denies it, I think; or at least disappointingly fails to register the appreciation of his mischief that lies at the bottom of my charge. This is me being humorous by way of admiring his being humorous. Man to man. Clown to clown. But he shows me a dead bat.

I blame Sergei. For not translating me in the right spirit.

It would be too easy to conclude that you don't go looking for reciprocal amusement in a professional clown.

I have been out walking. Trying for a long take on Slava. As I left the Astoria I was accosted by a very small kid who wanted to sell me a pen. He and the pen were about the same size. And about the same colour. Green. The kid showed me that the pen wrote green by scrawling with it on the back of his hand. He wanted a dollar for it. A dollar for a Bic. It took me two blocks to shake him off. No sooner had I done so than I came upon another kid, a bigger kid, just about a teenager, standing crying in the cold. Stock still, consumed with grief. No tears. No tears left. Just two craters under his eyes. Frozen. Then, on Nevsky Prospekt, where no one knows how to say cheese, I almost fell over a dead man lying on the pavement with his leg gashed from the ankle to the knee, its works spilling just like those of Slava's telephone. After which I decided to return to the Astoria.

Ros is still in the lounge where I left her, intermittently writing her own diary, reading a newspaper and doing without tea. 'While you were away,' she tells me, 'the cruellest thing happened. Every thirty minutes exactly a young man of modest demeanour approached me, stood in front of me, said something in Russian, and waited to be interviewed. After a moment or two of confusion he realized his mistake, blushed, and retreated to the seats behind me, where he sat and waited for a further hour before getting up disconsolately, putting on his modest winter coat, picking up his plastic briefcase, and leaving.'

'The same young man?'

'Of course not the same young man. Just in the same condition. They come over, stand in front of me, wait, retreat, take a seat behind me, and finally, after an hour, pick up their plastic briefcases and leave. Having been interviewed by no one because no one is here to do the interviewing, except me. It's too upsetting. They leave as quietly as they came. One of them actually sat down at my table and waited for me to stop reading my newspaper and start to interview him. He just sat and watched me and waited, rigid in his chair. Eventually, I couldn't stave off my hunger any longer and took out the cheese and chocolate which I'd kept from the plane, peeled them, ate them, and crushed the wrappings on the table between us. Shortly afterwards he got up and went to sit on the seats behind me. And then an hour later he left. I fear he was quite prepared to be treated as though he didn't exist by one he took to be his potential employer.'

I shake my head. 'You don't think it could have been one of Slava's ruses?' I ask.

And become the recipient of a long, black, penetrating look. Am I still resisting Slava? Has my soul still not given up its struggle with the clown?

In fact I'm not resisting anything. Ros's experiences in the hotel, like mine out of it, explain and confirm all Slava's meanings. The best part of his stage act comes when a fantasy of domestic bliss is suddenly transformed into the howling storm of real unaccommodated existence. In an instant a backcloth swings and summer turns to winter. The wind rages, snow lashes the faces of the audience, the auditorium becomes Siberia, and Slava the clown is all but blown away into the obscurity of the blizzard. He is not Lear's Fool, braving the spitting fire and the spouting rain; he is Lear himself.

What you get for living in St Petersburg? What you get for dreaming of domestic quiet? Assuredly. But also simply what you get.

This is clown's business at its best. Here is who you are; here is what you get.

CHAPTER FIVE

The Priceless Gift

I

Are clowns aliens?

Not *alien*, in Thomas Mann's sense – monsters of preposterousness, world-renouncing monks of unreason – I mean, are they actually from another planet?

That's a question – I suppose it would be truer to say, that's a proposition – put baldly by *Killer Klowns from Outer Space*, a scary American B movie that appeared in 1987 to little even of that upside-down acclaim that can greet a B movie if it's B enough, but which for a while enjoyed some favour and, as we shall see, some influence in the video stores. *Killer Klowns from Outer Space* takes up where the Joker in *Batman* and the clown who inhabits the drains in Stephen King's *It!* leave off. Yes, the image of a clown *is* sinister, his laughter *is* menacing and deranging, and his merriment *is* nothing but a cover for malevolence; but why stop there? Why not release the terrors that inhabit all the paraphernalia of a kid's good time. Not just ventriloquism, either – we all know that's sinister. But popcorn, say. Let's make that capable of monstrous growth and virulent intent. And rubber balls. Let's have them bounce along in relentless violent pursuit of the innocent; let's have them kidnap people. And once they're caught, these nice blameless kids, let's have them wound around in candy-floss, and there let them deliquesce in spiky pink sugar until their innards are adequately softened, sufficiently confectionary, to be sucked out through fun-straws.

So far, so pleasurable. Good to see a B film having the courage of its

own B conceit. Where it goes still one better (B+) is in a final flight of backward-looking fancy – quite out-Danikening von Daniken – that has the clowns not as bad guys masquerading as clowns, but Klowns, the very things they seem, motleyed and white-face-painted not to mislead but because motley is their habitual day-wear and white is the natural colour of their faces, Klowns from outer space who visited our trembly planet in an earlier age, ancient astronauts who have been here before and treated us as badly then as they are doing now; and *that* is why we have feared all clowns ever since, even the sweet ones, even the ones who don't want to slurp our guts through rainbow-coloured straws, because they are modelled on our memory-traces of *them*, Klowns!

The idea that *ab ovo* they have been vicious bastards, clowns, is not without its appeal to someone who went through his childhood, and beyond it, dreading all contact with them.

And the suggestion that some ancient terror still clings to them – over and above their circus or children's party menace, quite removed from a circus context, in fact – seems to be borne out by the frequency with which schoolchildren report clown-associated dangers. In September 1991 Strathclyde Police issued a press release appealing for information regarding 'Lanarkshire clowns'.

Numerous reports have been received in the Blantyre/Cambuslang/Hamilton areas between Thursday afternoon and today of two persons dressed in clown outfits, using a blue coloured Ford Transit type van, approaching children and offering sweets . . . Anyone with any information about this vehicle and its occupants is asked to contact their nearest police office . . .

Despite there being not a single incidence of actual clown-related enticement, and not a single incidence even of attempted enticement either, the rumours persisted. Two months later the Glasgow *Guardian* reported that the 'Kill Klown Scare' had reached such proportions – 'mass hysteria' was the phrase – that attendance at the local discothèque was down seventy per cent among ten- to fourteen-year-olds. The Klowns were out there, in their van, waiting to spin the teeny-boppers into candy-floss.

It's an ill wind.

Killjoys that they are, the sleuths of the urban legend squad were not slow to attribute some of the specific details of this outbreak of

Klownophobia to *Killer Klowns from Outer Space*, the video thereof being easy enough to lay your hands on. Apart from anything else, those Ks looked pretty decisive. And then there was the coincidence of those red-nosed astronauts in the movie touring the fun-places where pulpy kids were likely to be found in a van that may well have been a Ford. But in an article updating their findings in DMT 31, a publication of the British Folk Studies Forum, David Cornwell and Sandy Hobbs also sound a precautionary note. 'Searching for single causes in such cases seems unlikely to be fruitful,' they remind us, mentioning similar fears and sightings of Phantom Clowns in other parts of the world at other times. 'The stories we picked up in the Glasgow area need to be seen as part of a much wider and older phenomenon.'

Back to aliens again?

Who needs them? Even as I write, a clown's face – an *Auguste*: red-nose, fright-wig, eyebrows independent of the eyes they're meant to arch – or rather a police reconstruction of a clown's face, an identi-clown, is stuttering out of my fax machine. A story in the *Daily Mail*, 6 October 1995: POLICE HUNT THE HITMAN DRESSED AS A CLOWN. 'Wearing a pink wig, red nose and false teeth, the attacker fired at his 26-year-old victim at point blank range with a gun hidden in a bouquet.' All the terrors that this story re-mobilizes are to do with deception. Murderousness hidden in a smile, cold purpose pretending to be fun, a weapon nestling in flowers. Not every clown has actual murder on his mind – not *every* clown – but even the smallest child sniffs a rat when a clown comes over innocuous. Who needs aliens? It is a perfectly terrestrial fear that we express both when we back away from clowns and when we laugh at them. Our laughter acknowledges that we find them alien only in the sense that they are excessively given over to being human. We fear them because they cannot conceal – there is no concealing – the pure aggression which is the secret of their vitality.

'The tale of his grievances', J. B. Priestley wrote of Little Tich, the diminutive English music-hall comedian – the 'tale of his grievances' being the very thing he acted out on stage, his material itself –

was illustrated by nothing less than a fury of movement and gestures. The energy of these minuscule characters, these infuriated and maddening gnomes, was astounding . . . He seemed to fill the stage with people like you, unable to face his burning indignation and furious gestures . . . If he said he would show us what he thought about some obstreperous fellow, his dumbshow would almost explode into wild careering round the stage, punching and kicking away, defying men of any weight to come near him. If, as it frequently happened, things themselves were hostile and got him all tangled up, he would release for himself and for us the raising fury of the human spirit dragged down into such a world as this.

Sacheverell Sitwell compared Little Tich to an engraving by Callot, to one of Hieronymus Bosch's demons, to Nellie Wallace, herself a music-hall grotesque, 'witch-like with her parrot beak', in Alec Guinness's memory of her, her voice 'hoarse and scratchy, her walk swift and aggressive . . . always bent forward from the waist, as if looking for someone to punch'.

Always looking for someone to punch, always looking for something to kick. Not the way they liked to see it at the Humor Convention in Saratoga Springs when I was there. And not the way the guardian-priestesses of our contemporary correctitudes like to see it either. 'To me comedy is inexplicably bound up with kindliness,' writes Athene Seyler in *The Craft of Comedy* (Banks and Swift). Inexplicable all right, since it isn't. 'As soon as a comment on character is inspired by contempt or anger it becomes tragic and loses the light of laughter. Irony, satire even, must all be charitable and compassionate at heart, or they stray into the realm of serious comment . . .' Which is about as weighty of thought as Lee Israel's defence, in American *Ms*, of the 'vulnerable human beings' – Elizabeth Taylor, Christina Onassis and the like – who are Joan Rivers' staple comic fodder. 'While Joan may argue that it is necessary to shock in order to amuse, I'm sometimes hearing a different kind of laughter coming from her audiences – the kind that derives not from what is being said but from the fact that it is being said at all. The laughter follows as a collective gasp and it is as much horrified as jollified.'

Has one actually ever *heard* jollified laughter? Does it exist in nature? Did it ever?

Look at the terracotta masks of the Greek New Comedy (itself a tepid version of the Old), of which you can find an example or two in most museums of antiquity. Nothing jollified about the lineaments of these faces. The eyes stare insistently under wildly up-arched brows, the mouths are deformed, seemingly pulled open by some foreign agency into a grimace more of horror than of merriment, resembling less the human mouth than a mollusc or a plant that survives by suction or the backside of a

Jacques Callot

Ven.

Cucorongna. *Pernoualla.*

baboon. Those Callot engravings in which Sacheverell Sitwell saw an analogue for Little Tich, though occasionally they prettify a stance or costume, are at their best when they twist and elongate the figures of the *commedia dell'arte*, extrude them until they look like demented insects, grasshoppers of malign intent, dragon-flies of tireless braggadocio. Still less kindly and compassionate at heart are the engravings of the *Recueil Fossard*, where Pantalon and Harlequin and assorted zanies fall upon one another with implements from the kitchen, with sausages, with clyster-pipes, with daggers even, frustrating one another's amours, scorning every beat of one another's hearts, their bodies bent and twanging like bows, their beards and mask noses thrust out horizontally, cleaving the air like instruments of belligerence themselves.

Of all interpretations of *commedia* characters the most demoniacally alive is Domenico Tiepolo's, done in a handful of Pulcinella frescos, some of which hang in the Ca'Rezzonico in Venice, and in a remarkable series of 104 pen and ink drawings which record the life and adventures of Pulcinella, now as a sequence of utterly prosaic Venetian activities – visiting the hairdresser, playing shuttlecock, preparing polenta, sawing wood – and now as a sort of *danse macabre* of crime and execution, fantastical exploit, death and even resurrection. Scarcely ever, throughout this extraordinary series, does Tiepolo's appetite for Pulcinella's mis-shapen vitality falter; he can't draw it often enough – the fearsome humped back, the hooked nose of the glutton and the drunkard, the contorted limber form, the agelessness, the eager quizzical curiosity about all things (as if each day is his first on earth), the crazed demandingness for life, and then for more life. Even dead he refuses to lie down, reappear-ing Christ-like at his tomb, slumped skeletally, see-through, but still wear-ing his high conical hat. I say Pulcinella, singular, but Tiepolo is so taken by the indomitable ferocity of the character that he draws him in mul-tiples; not one Pulcinella raids the orchard, a dozen do; while another six fight over a basket of apples. Ten of them cluster on the beach to stare at a giant crab; as many more dance the furlana, play the tambourines for performing dogs, gather for a game of bowls, visit the portrait painter, throw themselves into carnival, aim their rifles as a firing-squad, get shot by the firing-squad (for it is Pulcinella eat Pulcinella out there), bend their bodies to burying one of their dead, and then leap in terror – though it is still the terror of the quick – when he is discovered out of his sepulchre, a tumble of fleshless bones, hump and nose and belly gone, but not the greed for another day, another dance, another bite at the senses. And even to talk in multiples fails of justice to the invincible nature of these draw-ings. They teem with Pulcinellas. They riot with Pulcinellas. Pulcinella as everyman? How dull that sounds. And it is true only if you think of everyman as a sort of plague. For Tiepolo's drawings render no less than that – an infestation of Pulcinella life.

As any genealogist of clown blood-lines will tell you, from Pulcinella the English genetically engineered Mr Punch. In a Neapolitan scenario, *Pulcinella, Brigand-Chief*, Pulcinella finds himself up against the hangman. Where do I put my head again? The hangman shows him. Into here. Like this. Pulcinella does what someone who loves life as much as he does has to do. Tightens the noose and pulls the rope. Who's the fool now? A trick that Mr Punch returned to, and still returns to, again and again. Where do I put my head again? Show me. Who's the fool now?

And we laugh at such unrepentant murder? Of course we do. Our laughter secures our allegiance to the side of survival. The only one not laughing is the hangman, and he's dead.

II

You would think, reading comedians talking shop in William Cook's *Ha Bloody Ha: Comedians Talking*, that their business only ever takes them from the battlefield when it lands them in the morgue. 'We had about three hundred people in,' Bruce Morton remembers; 'the guy who was doing the support was hot. He killed, then I went out and killed, and then we did a bit together at the end.' A bit of what? Carpet bombing? 'I really hyped myself up,' recalls Mark Thomas, 'and went onstage and stormed it. I completely blew the place apart . . . I walked home – from the Comedy Store to Clapham. I was so happy. All the way home, I was replaying in my mind, thinking, "That was a great moment! You hit 'em just right!"' Operation Desert Storm. The comedian a sort of Biggles without compunction.

'Go out and kill the bastards!' Jerry Lewis tells his unfunny comedian son in *Funny Bones*. Las Vegas. A full house. Go out and kill for daddy. Meanwhile, just in case we have a mind to take that metaphorically, across the world in Blackpool Lee Evans, damaged by a fall, at the end of his rag familially, and the victim of one too many slaps himself, breaks open the skull of a fellow clown with an iron bar concealed in a newspaper. Not used to seeing real murders, the circus audience takes a minute or two to stop laughing.

But if it goes wrong, if your iron bar slips out of your hand or your bombs fall in the wrong place . . . 'You know that everybody knows you've died,' says Donna McPhail, 'and they're all creeping away from you in case it's catching.' Away from the contagion that there is in death. 'I did sixteen minutes,' admits Frank Skinner; 'after two I'd died. I did the other fourteen as a death rattle . . . I saw all the comedians' heads appear at the back. They'd all come out of the dressing room to watch.' To commiserate? Hardly. There's a hangman and a Pulcinella and only one noose. 'If someone dies before you' – Donna McPhail again – 'you feel quite relieved – because they're the one, they're the sacrifice, and that probably means you're going to be all right. I love following someone who's crap . . .'

Yes, it's Pulcinella eat Pulcinella out there. Always has been. Of a *commedia dell'arte* company in early seventeenth-century Mantua, the duke of that dukedom was advised, 'The whole of this company was in arms, although they fought each other more with sharp words than swords . . .

Thank God I managed to pacify them – but for who knows how long?'

'Indeede, lightly one foole cannot indure the sight of another,' observed Robert Armin, himself a professional comic actor in Shakespeare's company. By way of particularizing that generality, Armin tells of a certain Jack Oates, the fool of Sir William Hollis, who, when threatened with the introduction of another fool, his own fooling having turned dull and melancholy, 'burst out crying, flung away in a rage and vented his temper by breaking the bagpiper's head with his own bagpipes'. Where the merriment did not end yet. Out of loyalty to his bagpiper friend, one of the household minstrels disguised himself as that threatened other fool and turned up in some of Jack's old jester's clothes, 'making wry mouths, dauncing and looking asquint'. Upon which, 'Jack flew at him in a wild rage and knocked his eye out.'

There is, of course, a strong element of employment anxiety in rivalry of this sort. 'Comedians always compete,' noticed Mort Sahl, 'as if there were one job.' Only one noose to fill, and only one vacancy. Working close to an ageing Bert Lahr in *Foxy – Volpone*, with songs – the young actor Larry Blyden was well positioned to observe the common interests that bound laughter to a square meal. (Once again *Notes on a Cowardly Lion* is the source.)

Bert needs three things. One: he needs to be loved. Two: a thing he needs a little more than that is to be served. Three: he needs to be acclaimed. He doesn't need to love; but he needs to receive it. Laughter is that. Bert comes from a hungry time. When they laughed you were going to eat; when they didn't, you starved . . .

He has to have the biggest laugh in the scene; and he has to have the last line of the scene, and the biggest line that ends it. He has to have that . . . If you get a big laugh, it's okay; but he must have one to top that. He must. Otherwise, he's going to be hungry; and he's going to be fifteen and nobody's going to love him; and he's going to be looking for a job . . .

But that there may be some over-and-above brutality in the will with which you go about topping your co-star – 'I'm going to have to kill that laugh' – and then breaking his bagpipes over his head, and then putting his eye out; that from the grubbing exigencies of hunger may flower the wild voluptuousness of violence, now cultivated for its own sake, Blyden also learnt from watching Lahr. 'He came up in a school of butchers. They were killers those guys.'

They all are. Killer Klowns from Planet Earth. Even the cringing

Norman Wisdom. As reported by a Bob Monkhouse in an avowedly murderous mood himself:

The show [*Sauce Piquante*, 1950] folded after six weeks and I wasn't sorry. By that time, I wanted to kill Norman Wisdom. On the opening night the show had overrun by over an hour and his multiple appearances throughout

(wanting the biggest laugh, the last line, the biggest line, the last laugh . . .?)

had been drastically cut to three or four. His outrage was so intense that it still shines from his eyes today when he speaks about it. Working with him became a nightmare . . . I had to feed Norman in a scene that required him to kick me on the shin several times. Landau had overspent massively and so refused to pay for more than one shin pad. As Norman came onstage each evening, his eyes would glance at my legs and spot the padded leg. He vented his frustration on the other one. I tried switching the pad from shin to shin but Norman's foot always cracked me on the unguarded limb till both my legs were black and blue from knee to ankle. Today he says he can't remember doing this to me . . .

Mort Sahl, who has a more mordant memory than Norman Wisdom, and whose *Heartland* is a sort of silver treasury of remembered mordancy, remembers a guy coming to see Lenny Bruce and him in the club where they were working and saying that he was Shelley Berman's nephew. Lenny Bruce pretended to be impressed. Pretended he'd heard of the kid. Yeah? The kid said he worked a lot like Mort and Len did. 'I tell what's happened to me all day. I just sort of wing it.'

Lenny said, 'That's good, that's what we do.' Then he went out on the stage and said, 'I have a great surprise for you folks. We have a great comedian here tonight, Howie Berman.' And the kid said, 'I can't get up there.' And Lenny said, 'Sure you can.' Kid said, 'What'll I do?' Lenny said, 'Tell 'em what you did all day.' So the kid got on stage and we all cringed for half an hour while the kid told about going to the dry cleaner's and getting his car washed and getting change for the telephone. And Lenny just sat there ecstatically watching this guy drown. Sort of high gallows humour. I found Lenny to be a funny comedian, a great impersonator, and a very sentimental guy . . .

High gallows humour. Only one noose.

Only one noose between Lenny Bruce and Mort Sahl too. 'God, I love you,' Sahl reports Bruce saying to him once. 'But it's just as if we were in school. One person's going to get an A on the curve, and if there's a choice, I want it to be me, not you.' A favour Sahl returns right after those compliments to Bruce's gifts. A funny comedian, a great impersonator, a very sentimental guy, *but* – can't you just hear that but on a gallop – but, *but*, BUT, 'I did not find him profound, and I disagree with those who now put him on the cross. Even Lenny knew that only *you* can kill yourself.'

Right. But with a little help from your friends. Just as Howie did it all by himself with a little help from Lenny. Kill the other guy; then kill yourself. Out of the battlefield into the morgue. But don't expect your fellow killers to sanctify your memory. Only one noose, and only one cross.

Even though they go about their play in troupes, their bodies so convivially disposed that they can rest their humpbacks in the crooks of one another's arms, their hands about one another's waists, their noses on one another's shoulders, Tiepolo's diabolic Pulcinellas are always individualistic, ready to break from the pack to follow their single inclinations, attentive at the last to a clamour of the senses which is for their own ears only. The calling of the clown is not an altruistic one. In order for there to be a feast, there must be a killing. In order for one clown to succeed, a second must be sacrificed. So, if they cannot be kind to one another, how can we expect them to be considerate of us?

Playing Buttons in a pantomime of his own devising – *Sinderella*: the pun proclaiming it is for adults only – the rude but royalist comedian Jim Davidson first sprays the stage, then the front row of the audience, then as far back into the audience as he can reach, with apples. He doesn't throw the apples, he spits them, getting as close to his victims as the stage will allow, thrusting forward his face, bulging his cheeks, and spluttering out a cidery pulp of core and pip and skin. He cannot contain himself – that's how the gag works. The more you laugh at him, the more he laughs at you. And that means apple. Sprayed or not, on the night I watched *Sinderella* the audience shrieked with the pleasure of it. We laughed, he laughed, we copped it. Aspersion! Ah!

Sir Les Patterson does the same. Though with more attention to the social niceties. 'Good evening, ladies and gentlemen,' he says, advancing consularly downstage, a drink in one hand, attending to a monstrous appendage-related dressing problem with the other. 'Permit me to introduce myself . . .' The teeth don't work too well and that's the front row baptized with spittle. 'Permit me to introduce myself to you good people . . .' And that word 'people', soon to be joined by that word 'Patterson', ensures another bathing in what Barry Humphries himself has described as Les Patterson's 'copious expectorations'.

Spitting at the audience – well, it beats killing them. Storming them. Blowing them apart. Or at least it beats it for the audience. One way or another that's what we are all in it for – the comedian *and* the audience – abuse. That's what we've always been in it for. Great expectation of expectoration. Ridicule. And if we seem to be wanting more of it just this minute than we did, say, even twenty years ago, that might be because so many of the old forms of abuse – abusing your kids, abusing the other sex, abusing deviants, abusing foreigners – are closed to us. We are an indomitable species. By hook or by crook we'll get what we need, and that includes the almost religious sensation of deliverance that accompanies the expression of insult.

Quoting Semos of Delos, a first-century BC witness, the Greek scholar Athenaeus describes a performance of phallic singing – if not exactly Aristotle's phallic songs, then something pretty similar – in which the Phallophoroi, unmasked but ivy-clad, and so-called because one of their number, covered in soot, bore aloft the Phallus (the 'God . . . erect and in full vigour'), first entered the theatre by the side or central doors, then sang to the glory of Bacchus, promising not old but 'maiden' songs, then 'ran forward and satirized persons whom they had fixed on'. Not a discharge of apples or spittle, but insults. Derision. Words. Which, as we know, can be as murderous as any weapon. It is said that the iambic poet Archilochus, much revered by ancient writers for his 'raging invectives', was so scathing in his attacks on his enemy Lycambes, who would not take him for a son-in-law, that Lycambes hung himself, and his wife hung herself, and their two daughters hung themselves, for shame. After Archilochus's own death people were warned to tread softly by his tomb, lest the wasps that had settled there should be aroused. 'We are alike,' sings the hunchback jester Rigoletto, eyeing Sparafucile the assassin,

> I with my tongue, he with a dagger!
> I am the one who mocks.
> He is the one who slays!

The difference, in the instance of phallic singing described by Semos, being that the mocking words of the Phallophoroi do not slay as a dagger slays but on the contrary – this at least is the intention – somehow further the Phallophoroic promise of reinvigoration. *Fresh is our muse and virginal.* 'Maiden' will be the song they sing, and to ensure it is so, here comes a stream of freshly minted insults. New life, fertility, and abusive language – a complex of relations that bears comparison with expectancy, prognostication, and the Sibyl's cavern.

Let's not forget this is art we are talking about here. The Phallophoroi didn't just happen by. They were got up for performance. They'd booked the theatre. Put up the handbills. And the insultees, too, knew what they might be letting themselves in for by showing up. Think Bernard Manning's Embassy Club, Delos, circa one hundred BC.

But behind the formalized phallic singing were festivals such as the City Dionysia or the Lenaia (the feast of 'mad women'), where again the processioning of the phallus was accompanied by the improvising of hymns and the satirizing of individuals in the crowd. A Rural Dionysia must have been more knock-about and abusive still if what they say, or at least if what Aristophanes says, about country people is true. Leading his Rural Dionysia under a phallic banner, the peace-loving Dikaiopolis moves with that ease which is given only to the truly religious man from reverence to a god to pleasure in passing wind:

> Dionysos, Lord,
> Bless our procession, our sacrifice
> . . .
> Loaf-bearer, lift. Say cheese.
> Pussy-cat! What a lucky man he'll be,
> Who marries you, kittens you,
> Gives you a litter of lovelies,
> Fumbling and farting in the hay all day.
> So like their Mummy. Aah! Walk round.
> Show the audience. And you lot, watch it.
> No toying with her tassels.

If festive audience abuse in the *Acharnians* never quite gets beyond this ribald warning it is because Dikaiopolis' enemies break into the procession in order to abuse *him*.

You're twisted, bent.
Treaty-maker! Athens-hater!
Spartan-lover! Traitor!

Though the requirement to be abusive to *somebody* in the course of, or after a Dionysiac procession is eventually honoured by the chorus in an apparently gratuitous verbal assault on Antimachos, ex-supporter of Aristophanes and supposed splutterer after chorus-boys:

Ladies and gentlemen, an interlude.
Subject, Antimachos. What do you mean,
Antimachos Who? Old Spitface.
Our former backer. Our one-time angel. The man
With the petrified purse-strings,
Who takes you to dinner and leaves you to pay.

One way or another, it seems that no festival to Demeter or Dionysus, town or city, mixed or women-only, was free from the convention of invective. Wagons carrying jokesters travelled in the Dionysiac processions, for the purpose of deriding people they encountered along the way. Cultic clowns gathered on the bridge over the Kephissos in Athens to ridicule those who were heading for the shrine at Eleusis. At the Haloa of Eleusis the women themselves (shades of Demeter and Iambe) hurled obscenities and insults at one another. Noting in an aside that the Greeks learnt their festivals to the gods from the Egyptians (always blame the Egyptians), Herodotus tells of obscene doings in the city of Bubastis, home of the 'greatest and most piously honoured' Egyptian festival of all.

When they congregate at Bubastis, they go by river, men and women together, many of both in every boat; some of the women have rattles and rattle with them and some of the men play the flute all the way; the rest, both sexes alike, sing and clap their hands. At every city they find in their passage they bring their boats close to the bank, and some of the women continue with their music while others shout opprobrious language at the women of the place, some dance and some stand up and pull up their garments . . .

. . . but let's not return to Baubo and the Sibyl of Panzoust. We've raised enough garments. Let's stay with opprobrious language. Even though the one may just be the verbal equivalent of the other, and the two, anyway, go everywhere together. As in J. G. Frazer's account, repeating what he has heard of the harvest festival of the Hos of northeastern India:

At this time an evil spirit is supposed to infest the place, and to get rid of it men, women, and children go in procession round and through every part of the village with sticks in their hands, as if beating for game, singing a wild chant, and shouting vociferously . . . Usually the Hos are quiet and reserved in manner . . . but during this festival their natures appear to undergo a temporary change. Sons and daughters revile their parents in gross language, and parents their children; men and women become almost like animals in the indulgence of their amorous propensities . . .

Similarly with 'the negroes of Guinea' on the Gold Coast, during whose annual expulsion of devils 'a perfect lampooning liberty is allowed, and scandal so highly exalted, that they may freely sing of all the faults, villainies, and frauds of their superiors as well as inferiors, without punishment, or so much as the least interruption.' Similarly with . . . But why bother? Frazer's great unfashionable work groans with tales of demons being expelled, now with fires, now with sticks on cooking pots, now with muskets, but invariably, to boot, with invective. Nothing seems to work so well as cursing. Francis Cornford, whose *The Origin of Attic Comedy* is almost as out of favour as Frazer's *The Golden Bough* – the Edwardian English mind being too assured and Anglo-centric for current taste – is as clear as one needs to be about the ubiquitous efficacy of invective. 'The simplest of all methods of expelling . . . malign influences of any kind is to abuse them with the most violent language. No distinction is drawn between this and the custom of abusing, and even beating, the persons or things which are to be rid of them, as a carpet is beaten for no fault of its own, but to get the dust out of it.'

So the Phallophoroi clear the way for their 'maiden' verses by employing invective to expel what is not 'maiden'. 'The purpose of satire,' wrote Robert Graves, 'is to destroy whatever is overblown, faded and dull, and clear the soil for a new sowing.' For the duration of that particular procession or performance the individuals satirized have to accept that they are to the stale and the infertile what the carpet is to dust. And must take their beating. It could have been worse. The next stop on the processional route is the altar to Dionysus, and every god expects a sacrifice. Once upon a time the satirized might have suffered a more literal victimization; for burning flesh is another effective method of stimulating fertility and turning away bad influences. In this sense, then, we are back with the dagger Rigoletto carries in his speech. The abusive language does, after all, mean to kill. But just as a goat now lies upon the altar and not a man, so verbal violence replaces physical. Instead of murder, magic. Always remembering, from the example of Archilochus and Lycambes, that the magic itself was a strong brew. Archilochus would probably have sung his waspish verses at a festival to Demeter. In so far as he meant to clear the ground for a new sowing, he must be reckoned to have succeeded.

The Phallophoroi – Killer Klowns from the Aegean Basin.

And if there is sacred privilege in victimhood, then those suicidal people who risk the front row of an Edna Everage concert know something that the more cowardly of us, who cringe in an aisle seat in the gods, don't want to know. That to be torn apart by words is to be possessed by the divine spirit, that it is to become J. G. Frazer's 'man-god, slain to take away the sins and misfortunes of the people'.

III

And then, Cornford reminds us, 'when the serious purpose has died out' there is the 'inherent pleasurableness of obscenity' itself. This is a disappointing move. All 'inherent-in-themselves' arguments are unsatisfactory, and where comedy is concerned they bedevil as well as disappoint – funny is funny is funny in itself, why can't you leave it at that? But Cornford's descent into inherence is doubly disappointing, setting at each other's ears, as it does, pleasurableness and seriousness (nothing is ever not serious; even anti-serious is serious), and abandoning the admirable logic with which he came to understand the seriousness of obscenity in the first place.

I would be the last to argue that the obscenity we are concerned with here – invective and satire, cursing and swearing, the verbal dead spit of Baubo's shaved pudenda and the Sibyl's effrontuous arse – is *not* pleasurable. Outside of sex and food there is probably nothing *more* pleasurable. And even that proviso may be too cautious, given that cursing and swearing belong to food and sex as well, help give them savour, show them the way out of moderateness into excess, furnish the necessary vocabulary of congratulation, lover to lover, glutton to dish. Is there any pleasure *inside* sex and food that cannot be enhanced by the expression of profanities?

What I am unable to accept is the proposition that such pleasure in obscenity has now somehow broken loose, slipped its moorings, neither recalls its ancient function nor acknowledges a present one. My own first essay at unconstrained cursing is vivid to me to this day: the humpbacked approach to the local railway station where it happened, the friend I was fighting with, the woman who tried to separate us, the clearing of congestion in my chest and my throat when I abused her. It is not the profanities I uttered that I remember but the sensation of vehement release that accompanied them, release *from* my own previous inhibitions – fear of the functions, fear of naming the functions, loyalty to those who had named them timorously – and release *into* the power of wording parts, the devil-expelling ferocity which the shameless allusion to the entrances and exits of the body can unloose. I felt that I had murdered. Not only the interfering woman, who fell back from me outraged and terrified, as though aspersed, but also my parents, those who had taught me to word timorously. Orphaned, I felt like a god. No, I felt as unconfined as a god and then more powerful again because of my mortality, and because of the stink of it that I'd set free.

Whenever I next swore – whenever I next swear – it was, it will be, to recapture through base materiality this sensation of lordly exemption. What else would any curser bother expending the energy of cursing for? 'For a pure sense of being tumultuously alive,' exults Philip Roth's Mickey Sabbath – Philip Roth, that most crafty and purposeful of cursers; Mickey Sabbath, an anathema on two legs – 'you can't beat the nasty side of existence.'

And nothing exalts the nasty side of existence as triumphantly as cursing does.

Not single-godhead cursing. Not the appeal to monotheistic blight. *That* has only one ambition: to extinguish utterly. To annihilate. As in the story of Elisha and the little children (2 Kings, 2, 23–5):

And he went up from thence unto Beth-el: and as he was going up by the way, there came forth little children out of the city, and mocked him, and said unto him, Go up, thou bald head; go up, thou bald head.

And he turned back and looked on them, and cursed them in the name of the LORD. And there came forth two she bears out of the wood, and tare forty and two children of them.

And he went from thence to mount Carmel, and from thence he returned to Samaria.

That's what comes of cursing in the name of a Lord notorious both for his literal-mindedness and his deficiency in humour. An eye for an eye and a life for a joke. No mention of Elisha returning to Samaria irradiated with a pure sense of being tumultuously alive.

Cursing in the name of Dionysus, though, cursing in the name of a body that ruts and rots, in the name of the nasty side of existence, does not take life out of the world but puts it back, increases it by the degree to which the cursing itself invents and multiplies. 'All the charms of Sycorax – toads, beetles, bats light on you!' inveighs Caliban, just warming to his theme, which is nothing short of peopling the isle with Calibans. Maybe all the same creature, but lots of them. A *commedia* curse of Pantalone's, fished out as an exemplar by Andrea Perrucci, and to be imagined in its original broad Venetian dialect, seems to repopulate an already perilous sublunary existence with the threat of so many more hazards and misadventures that you can barely wait to hit the road and encounter them:

Oh son (I almost said of a randy old goat) how have you repaid all that I have done for you, the sleepless nights you have caused me, the bezants I have paid for you, the labours I have undertaken for you? With what ingratitude you repay a father who has done so much for you! . . .

But since you want to live like a beast, may all the beasts of the world be against you; may the cocks disturb your sleep, the dogs gnaw your bones, the cats scratch your hands, the crows peck out your eyes, the lice eat your flesh and shame you in your clothes; may the fleas, the bugs, the horseflies, give you no rest with their pricks, their bites, their stink and their puncturings. When you go out in the country may the snakes bite you, the wasps sting you, the oxen lacerate you, the bulls gore you; when you are in the city may the donkeys jostle you and the horses trample on you; should you travel by sea may the dog-fishes poison you, may the dolphins signal tempest for you; if you travel by land may the litters and the carriages break your collar-bone and, finally, may all the animals created for the service of man become for you toads, serpents, dragons, panthers, basilisks, hydras and Spanish flies.

The best curses are always swelling, hyperbolic, crawling with monstrous beasts, gorging on impossible torments, veritable circuses of acrobatic agonies. 'The Bastard from the Bush', that great Australian poem of scurrilous one-upmanship and high-toned indignation, attributed in part to Henry Lawson and in part to the national genius for profanity, climaxes in a crescendo of spluttering imprecations, some spectacularly convoluted, others magnificently feeble, but all tumbling out at such speed that the verse can scarcely catch up with itself. That, you might say, *is* the curse – the breathless vehemence of its delivery. The Bastard's such a bastard there's no time to pause to wish him all the ill you'd like to.

> 'You low polluted Bastard!' snarled the Captain of the Push,
> 'Get back where your sort belongs – that's somewhere in the bush.
> And I hope heaps of misfortunes may soon tumble down on you;
> may some lousy harlot dose you till your ballocks turn sky-blue!
>
> 'May the itching piles torment you; may corns grow on your feet!
> May crabs as big as spiders attack your balls a treat!
> And when you're down and outed, to a hopeless bloody wreck,
> may you slip back through your arsehole and break your fucking neck!'

There's a touch of the Rural Dionysia or the phallic songs about all this. *You low polluted bastard!* Something earth-mystical, taboo-laden. Isn't that the function of any good agrarian festival – to expel all low polluted bastards?

But there's something final about expulsion which is contrary to the spirit of ribald cursing. Those Phallophoroi belonged to the first century before Christ. Archilochus to the seventh. Things change over six centuries. Maybe the Lycambes family suicide cast a pall over the partying. Maybe there was a feeling that this was going a bit far, that Archilochus had overdone the invective somewhat (keep away from his tomb, lest you stir up the wasps) and that Lycambes and his women had taken it all a bit too much to heart. Certainly, by the time satire is in the hands of the Phallophoroi and Aristophanes you feel that everything's become festive again. Not kind, not humane, not innocuously 'pleasurable for its own sake', but not bent on annihilation either. You want the devils out but you also want them to return. Else no party next year. Yes, it is your fervent wish that that low polluted bastard, once reduced to a hopeless bloody wreck, should slip back through his arsehole and break his fucking neck, but that doesn't mean you want his fucking daughters to hang themselves, and it doesn't mean that you don't want the low polluted bastard back again. Not, come back all is forgiven; but come back so I can go on swearing at you.

The ambition of invective is plenitude. More it wants. More. More. When Prince Hal, now become King Henry, dismisses Falstaff – 'I know thee not, old man: fall to thy prayers' – it is language that's the loser. No more

thou clay-brained guts, thou knotty-pated fool, thou whoreson obscene greasy tallow-catch ... this bed-presser, this horse-back-breaker, this huge hill of flesh ...

And no more, by way of come-back,

'Sblood, you starveling, you eel-skin, you dried neat's-tongue, you bull's pizzle, you stock-fish – O for breath to utter what is like thee! – you tailor's-yard, you sheath, you bow-case, you vile standing tuck!

The come-back. Where would cursing be without it? Curse a silent person or one who walks away and invention dies on your lips. Your mouth becomes a grave. That's it; the party's over, the world's an empty place. A come-back, though ... It even sounds resurrectionary. A return from the dead. A living riposte. Don't put your daughters on a rope, Mrs Lycambes; put them on the stage. Have them slug it out. Here's yours, Archilochus, with interest.

Of all institutions, marriage, of course, is the most suited to retaliatory invective. The double act on which all subsequent double acts are modelled. Henry Fielding's *The Author's Farce* turns the reciprocal violence into a sort of conjugal carnival:

> PUNCH:
> Joan, Joan, Joan, has a thundering tongue,
> And Joan, Joan, Joan, is a bold one.
>   How happy is he,
>   Who from wedlock is free;
> For who'd have a wife to scold one?

(An old conundrum; but you can detect appreciation in his voice, companionableness in invective, even as he formulates it.)

JUDY:

Punch, Punch, Punch, pr'ythee think of your hunch
Pr'ythee look to your great strutting belly;
   Sirrah, if you dare
   War with me declare
I will beat your fat guts to a jelly.

[*They dance.*]

PUNCH:

Joan, you are the plague of my life,
   A rope would be welcomer than such a wife.

JUDY:

Punch, your merits had you but shar'd,
   Your neck had been longer by half a yard.

PUNCH:

Ugly witch.

JUDY:

Son of a bitch.

BOTH:

(ah, *both*!)

Would you were hang'd or drown'd in a ditch.

[*Dance again.*]

Whatever their prospects for the future, they are up to each other, blow for blow. Well-matched, we ordinarily call this, and what else is a couple so well-matched that they think as one on the question of the other hanging or drowning in a ditch to do, except dance and make more babies.

Outside of marriage, this hankering for a loving reciprocity of insult has long sought legitimacy. In his book *The Scurra* – a *scurra* being a Roman mime and jester – P. B. Corbett describes, courtesy of Horace, what you might have been given in the way of diversion had you kept consular company and been invited to Marcus Cocceius Nerva's villa for supper. 'An entertainment for the guests is provided by a contest of wit between a *scurra* named Sarmentus and one Messius who is called a *cicirrus*, a word meaning "cock" . . .'

'*Equi te esse feri similem dico,*' begins Sarmentus. 'You look like a wild horse to me.'

The guests laugh and Messius tosses his mane.

Sarmentus then goes on to rag Messius about his mutilation – a scar on his head, 'the relic of a growth known as the Campanian disease, probably consisting of horn-like excrescences.' I am able to find no help, in the guide to disability terms put out by the Royal Association for Disability and Rehabilitation, in the matter of what to call the scar left by horn-like excrescences. But I suspect that Sarmentus's jokes, alluding to the relationship between disfigurement and potency – broken horn; call yourself a man? – would not have found favour with that body. The callous Roman villa guests enjoyed them, though.

Then Messius gets his go. Weren't you once a slave, Sarmentus? And didn't you run away? Beats me why. Given how little of you there is, I'd have thought you'd have been more than contented with what they give a slave to eat.

Fatness, thinness; man, beast; wholeness, mutilation – the grand eternal opposites. Where else are these differences to go but into competing satires?

But as far as Marcus Cocceius Nerva's villa-party is concerned, that is where, with the two clowns just getting started, Horace leaves it. We get the hors-d'œuvre but not the meal.

Horace is prim in the matter of invective. Had there been an Imperial Association for Disability and Rehabilitation Guide to Terms he would have subscribed to it. He fears the present ferocity of jesting and laments the passing of its erstwhile charm. This is the weaker of the two recurring idealisms of comedy. Once it was savage now it's tame. Once it was kind now it's cruel. Horace sends his mind back on one of those 'golden-age' folk-journeys to the days when the old-time farmers,

hardy folk and content with little, at festival celebrations, after the corn was gathered in, relaxing their bodies and their spirits too, which had endured hard things in the hope of outcome, . . . made offering of a pig to Mother Earth and a sucking lamb to the Woodland God.

The Fescennine freedom of speech discovered in this way poured forth rustic abuse in alternating verses [jest and response]. This licence, becoming an accepted form through the running years, thus continued its amiable playfulness, until the jesting became cruel and turned into an open savagery and pursued its way with a threatening impunity into the very homes of decent citizens.

Ah, that amiable rustic playfulness. Antimachos libelled as a slurper of chorus-boys. Lycambes's daughters swinging from their cottage beam. Where are the jokes of yesteryear? Where are they now?

IV

The Fescennine Verses, whatever else they were, clearly owed something to the satires of the Phallophoroi and the opprobrious songs of the women on the way to Eleusis and Bubastis. We know enough about the temperament and requirements of Mother Earth to be sure she wouldn't have got up from the stone 'Unsmiling' to hear 'The Archers'. Abuse is abuse. It means to frighten and invigorate. But it is interesting to note that in a past remote enough for Horace to be nostalgic about it, abuse had already become formalized into competition – jest and response. Someone was answering the Phallophoroi back.

The Fescennini – from Fescennium in southern Etruria, is the guess – were rural festivals at which masked or painted men jousted insults in rough metre. The indecency of these insults, together with the dramatic form in which they were couched – men behaving badly, but to a pre-determined model, if not exactly to a script – made them especially suited to pre-nuptial festivities. A taste of structured combative indecency before you settled down into your own more chaotic version.

It's in another context, though, that the Fescennine Verses have come to intrigue us most: as mocking songs sung by soldiers accompanying the return of a triumphal hero, an emperor even, into Rome. In the midst of all the cheering and the adulation, their abuse. The greater the adulation, the more licentious and disparaging the abuse. A profound intuition, which must not be reduced to superstition, to touching wood or blowing kisses to a divinity, underlies all this. Yes, there is some supernatural envy out there, some cosmic will to pull down whatever has elevated itself above the common; and yes, maybe – since it is stupid, since all envy is stupefying – it can be fooled, by deriding the elevated thing, by increasing the volume of the insult until it drowns out the volume of the praise, into directing its malevolence elsewhere. But that's only the engineering of it, the staging, the sound effects. The profound intuition such a pageant is got up to serve is this: without the answering mockery of dispraise, praise giddies the mind; without the ballast of laughter, solemn grandeur topples into ridiculousness; every man is his own mirror image, alive only in so far as he is an argument. And ridicule is always the necessary other voice in his argument with conceit.

It was for this reason that rich men kept fools. And why fools are invariably garrulous. There is always much to say in answer to a rich man.

First the encomium, then the insult. First the blessing, then the cursing. With his customary masterful cunning, Rabelais pulls us into a complimentary embrace: 'Most illustrious and most valorous champions, noblemen, and others, who gladly devote yourselves to all gentle and honest pursuits' – only to cast us out now that we are jelly –

may St Anthony's fire burn you, the epilepsy throw you, the thunder-stroke and leg-ulcers rack you, dysentery seize you, and may the erysipelas, with its tiny cowhair rash, and quicksilver's pain on top, through your arse-hole enter up, and like Sodom and Gomorrah may you dissolve into sulphur, fire, and the bottomless pit, in case you do not firmly believe everything that I tell you in this present *Chronicle*!

Of course we enjoy the insults as much as we enjoyed the praise. The one is always latent in the other, anyway. I know of few social caresses to equal being called a bastard by an Australian *in situ*. 'You bastard, Jacobson. You low polluted bastard.' It's almost pillow talk. For his part the Australian is clearing out your demons. For yours, you are submitting to benign magic. In the alcoholic haze the categories slip and slide. We have another word for that slippage when we're feeling sentimental – we call it love.

At its heart, then, abuse is dialectic. Craves conversation. Is always in an argument. Even when it doesn't start out argumentatively. There's a passage of sublime swearing in the first Derek and Clive record Peter Cook and Dudley Moore made – not initially a cursing contest, though its rationale is an exchange of curses recalled – which by degrees becomes competitive, partly because that's the nature of the Pete and Dud relationship, but mainly because cursing won't sit still, can't ever resist replicating itself.

Dudley Moore starts it off, in an idle ruminating sort of way:

I tell you, the other day some bloke came up to me – I don't know who he was – and he said, 'You cunt.'
Yeah.
I said, 'What?' He said, 'You cunt.'

And you replied, 'You fucking cunt.'
Not straightaway. I said, 'You cunt.'
Yeah . . . Yeah . . . What did he come back with . . .?
He came back . . . He said, 'You fucking cunt.'
You're joking . . . He said 'You fucking cunt'?
He said, 'You call me a fucking cunt, you fucking –' I said, 'You fucking cunt.'
I should hope so . . . 'You fucking cunt'!!
I said, 'You fucking cunt . . . You come here and call me a fucking cunt.'
I should say so.
I said, 'You cunt,' I said, 'you fucking cunt,' I said, 'who are you fucking calling cunt, cunt?'
What'd he say to that?
He said, 'You fucking cunt.'

By this time a sort of perpetual motion of obscenity has been found. There is no reason for it ever to stop. Caliban's cursing sought to people the whole isle with Calibans. Derek and Clive's populates the entire universe with cunt. And in the course of the proliferation – one cunt breeding another breeding another – even the grammar becomes big with obscenity. The comma that separates the two cunts in 'who are you calling cunt, cunt' – a masterpiece of filthy punctuation – lights the way to infinity. The cunts can now go on backing into one another for ever and a day, without ever losing their strict grammatic causality.

But because of the insatiable hunger for a contest in the belly of invective (and in Peter Cook, who in this instance might be seen as invective personified), what was an abusive argument remembered quite out of the blue becomes an abusive argument reduplicated.

Well you fucking cunt,

Cook inexplicably explodes, suddenly taking the other bloke's side,

who are you to say to him that he was a fucking cunt?

And if we thought we were in a universe of cunt before . . .

The beauty of an insult contest is that there are no lengths to which it is not prepared to push this principle of argument. Off and away into the

Sibyl's cavern of infinity it goes. The ridiculer ridiculed in his own conceit. The curser cursed in his. Nothing safe from detraction. Not ever.

Wherever verbal skills are prized, competitions in insult become irresistible. The protean trickster-god Loki, whom we last saw tying his penis to the beard of a goat in order to make a giant's daughter laugh, gets his own invective epic – *The Lokasenna*, or *Loki's Wrangling* – in that collection of tenth-century Icelandic mythology we know as *The Elder Edda*. Here, the exhilarated Loki takes on all the assembled gods and goddesses, knocking them off verbally one by one, never more alive or more contemptuous than when they swell as in a chorus against him. 'Be silent, Tyr! for a son with me / Thy wife once chanced to win . . . Be silent, Byggvir! . . . What little creature goes crawling there, / Snuffling and snapping about? . . . Be silent, Ithun! . . . In thy seat art thou bold, not so are thy deeds / Bragi, adorner of benches! . . . Be silent, Heimdall! . . . Be silent, Othin! . . .' And so on and so on, shaking the vaults of heaven, until Thor threatens to quieten him with his hammer. Irish poets of the Middle Ages and earlier are said to have similarly satirized one another into exhaustion. Wilde was always looking for a worthy combatant. Shaw and Joyce, unable to find adversaries, soliloquized themselves to a standstill. The Scots called it 'flyting' (Anglo-Saxon *flytan*: to contend or scold). As in *The Flyting of Dunbar and Kennedie*, or the *Great Flyting betwixt Polwart and Montgomery*, which Montgomery kicks off with a 'Come kiss my Erse', and Polwart is still concluding, some thirty or more pages later, with 'kiss the Cunt of the Cow'. In our own dainty, missionized times we have to look to black cultures for an equivalent. Perhaps this means that insult contests thrive on grievance as much as on high valuation of eloquence. Or perhaps eloquence only becomes virulently scatological under the pressure of grievance. Whatever the reasons, the only live flyting we routinely encounter today – I say routinely, but in this country movies are our only access – is snapping or dissing, what in American black street jargon was previously known as sounding, signifying, toasting, joning and, most famously of all for historians of these things, 'The Dozens'.

Countless learned articles have been written on 'The Dozens' or 'The Dirty Dozens', comparing the way they played it in Harlem with the way they played it in South Philadelphia with the way they played it in St Louis; finding its origins now in slave culture, now in Africa, now in Scots flyting even, via the Scots-Irish immigrants of backwoods America; and tracing its influences on jazz, calypso, rap, or their influences on it. But the most

Jacques Callot

Smaraolo cornuto. Ratsa di Boio.

accessible account of 'The Dozens' comes in a sketch recorded in the early seventies by the American comedian George Carlin for his album *Occupation Foole*. 'The Dozens' was the black version of what all kids were doing in the street: putting one another down. Only with mothers thrown in. 'Where'd you go last night?' 'I was out with your mother, man!' The more squeamish white kids weren't always up to it. 'No mothers, man.' But Carlin comes up with a little rhyme, to show that he is up to anything:

> You wanna play the dozens, well the 'dozens' is a game;
> But the way I fuck your mother is a goddam shame!

No mother, no 'Dozens'. 'Ya Mama', I also heard it called when I was in America in 1995 on 'Dozens' hunt. And when I did, at last, find kids prepared to play it with me, it was my mother who copped it nine times out of ten. Occasionally my shirt, once or twice my accent, my nose, my low intelligence, my reverend age, but mainly my mother. Not that I was trying of course, but had I wanted to outwit these Harlem kids, some of them no higher than my knee, I would never have succeeded; even allowing for the ritual nature of the game, and for the necessarily abstract concept of the mama, I could not have insulted theirs. Not even in play.

Jacques Callot

The taboo which 'The Dozens' had taught them to break was still too much of a taboo for me. It's possible I have that sentence the wrong way round, and that it was they, members of a matriarchal society with a biblical overlay, who felt more protective of the taboo than I did. Hence the joyful release of playing it, but also the edginess with which it is played. If you lose, if you run out of steam first, it's not just you, it's you *and* your mama that look bad. This explains the tenacity of the game. Family honour compels you to compete.

Over fifty years ago the anthropologist A. R. Radcliffe-Brown wrote an article on the phenomenon of 'joking relationships' for the journal *Africa*. Although I suspect his article is no longer highly regarded – like all other scholars, anthropologists only came to see the light round about 1968, when something French happened to thought – I am not aware that the following spare description, *sans* interpretation, has been discredited.

The joking relationship is a peculiar combination of friendliness and antagonism. The behaviour is such that in any other social context it would express and arouse hostility; but it is not meant seriously and must not be taken seriously. There is a pretence of hostility and a real friendliness. To put it another way, the relationship is one of permitted disrespect . . .

. . . among the Dogon a man stands in a joking relationship to his wife's sisters and their daughters. Frequently the relationship holds between a man and both the brothers and sisters of his wife. But in some instances there is a distinction whereby a man is on joking terms with his wife's younger brothers and sisters but not with those who are older than she is . . .

Free of quite such subtle family distinctions though 'The Dozens' and 'Ya Mama' are – 'Your mother's so stupid she takes a ruler to bed to see how long she's slept' – they must have originated in similar systems for negotiating kinship tensions. And certainly the ubiquity of these systems in African societies gives credence to the argument that 'The Dozens' and 'Ya Mama' are more African than they are Scottish.

We are perverse creatures. We are able to be rude only where we feel reverence, and we cannot revere without being rude. But the rules of these perversities are particular and guarded with great jealousy by the communities which employ them. I did not for a moment feel comfortable playing 'The Dozens' with those Harlem kids, young as they were, and tickled by the presence of cameras. I did not feel I had a right to exchange permitted disrespect with them. Who had permitted *me*? I was glad when it was over and I was out of there. So my claim for the inexhaustibility of the insult contest has to be tempered. It doesn't have a chimney reaching to the skies. It is closed ultimately. Governed by a culture and therefore subject to its edicts. For members only.

The other thing that has to be said about 'The Dozens', in whatever form one finds it, is that it quickly becomes monotonous. The insults lack zest. Suffer, perhaps, from the weight of too much grievance.

Altogether more exuberant and inventive is Extempo War, a sort of competitive form of calypso which I watched and filmed in Trinidad not long after extricating my mama from the streets of Harlem. Behind Extempo War is Picong, an abuse ritual which is said to date from the arrival of French settlers in the Caribbean. Picong, piquant? Also *se piquer*? To prick but also to pride oneself. The story goes that the wealthiest of the French settlers had a slave by the name of Gros Jean who, having discovered a capacity in himself for praise-singing, went on to discover that he could heap insults rather niftily as well. That he should be good at both will come as no surprise to us, knowing what we do of the latency of each in each.

As an off-shoot of the Trinidad Carnival, Extempo War annually takes to the stage, where extemporizers compete, solo for solo, before a panel of judges, the subjects of their riffs being chosen by lot or taken from suggestions shouted out by the audience. But what I saw was staged only in the sense that the participants knew I was going to be there; and their subject was at all times one another. So it was considerably less sedate, I was assured, than in its public form. I'd let it be known that I hoped I was going to get insult. Nothing but, they told me. I'd let it be known that I hoped I was going to get obscenity. Wherever I went with these cameras I was asking for obscenity. Show me every phallus you can find me, I'd asked the Italian fixer in Pompeii. Don't hold anything back for me, I'd pleaded with the kids in Harlem. I'd rung up performers who'd sent me videos of themselves performing at the limits of decency; 'Don't you ever cross over?' I'd asked them. And now here I was in a waterside calypso club in the capital of Trinidad, a country about whose codes of morals I knew absolutely nothing, doing the same. Every now and then it occurred to me that I was running the risk of being deported by the blushing police force of some outraged nation-state, for being a depraver of morals. When all I really wanted was that people in the laugh and insult business shouldn't pull their punches for me, just because I was English, white, middle-aged, prim-looking, and in company with a television crew, half of whom were women. Yes, the Extempo Warriors told me, yes, yes, yes, it would be obscene.

And it was.

No accusation of zestlessness could be levelled at this group. They kept it up for three hours or more, inventing as they went, keeping to the rhyme scheme, keeping to the metre, keeping to the stanza form, some of them rising from the table as the spirit of comic invective moved them, or because the insult thrown at them by the last singer had to be countered right away, others working away at their guitars, threading words and strings in the more familiar calypso mode, not always looking as though they knew how the stanza was going to come out, but always getting there in the end, others again making jazz out of their traducements, coming in on the half-notes, scat-singing, but never watering themselves down.

There must have been eight or ten of them at the table at any one time. Others drifted by, shaped a mortification just the right number of beats to the bar, received one back, and drifted off again. This was a narrative for as many voices as were up to it, sometimes narrowing to a head to head on sexual or gender grounds – if he accused her of preferring women, she had to let him know that the first woman she would ever have was *him* – but always opening out again to let the chorus back in. Truth was not the issue, nor was vehemence; wit was the arbiter of everything. If you were well insulted you took it, you laughed. And found inspiration for your retort in the quality of the opposition.

I sat on the outside of their charmed circle, regretting my colour and my culture, wondering if I should try my hand, thinking better of it, swigging cold beer, and marvelling like a kid at his first Oxford Union debate. My defence is that this was much smarter than any Oxford Union debate, employed a richer and more robust vocabulary and was infinitely more musical. But as far as the sheer unalloyed joy that goes with be-smirching your fellow human beings is concerned, I guess there wasn't that much to choose between them.

V

'A joke,' as everyone knows that Freud said, 'will allow us to exploit something ridiculous in our enemy which we could not, on account of obstacles in the way, bring forward openly or consciously.' *Exploitation, enemy, ridiculous* – a moderate enough vocabulary by the side of some of the comedy-associated violence we've been considering in the course of this chapter. But the more we've looked at ceremonial insult contests, the fewer of those obstacles to open ridicule we've encountered. Of course the gloves are never off entirely. If we truly told our enemies – or our friends, come to that – the number of ways we found them ridiculous, only pistols would ever settle the matter. Something like Extempo War, though, by virtue of its acknowledged competitiveness and aggression, its temporary but formal abrogation of the rules of politeness which them-selves constitute the Freudian obstacle, largely excepts itself from Freud's accusation of covert hostility. If Freud is correct and a joke is a sort of social sabotage, then Extempo – like 'The Dozens', like Phallophoroic insults, like the Fescennine Verses, like the banter between a Dogon hus-band and his wife's older sister's younger brother's eldest daughters – is a healing rite.

But joke-telling too, when it is elevated to ceremony, when the audience (a better word might be congregation) is conversant with the ritual, on reverentially disrespectful terms with the priest, and *needy* – joke-telling too can staunch communal wounds.

If you don't normally think of Blackpool's South Pier as a temple, go there when Roy 'Chubby' Brown is in concert. I went in 1994, on what happened to be the last night of the illuminations, a night notoriously horrible because of the crush of families, because of the time it takes you to travel a mile, especially a golden mile, because you cannot get a hotel room (I found a broom-cupboard in St Anne's, the nearest city with a bed, and was grateful), and because of the weather. In my case a night notoriously horrible, as well, because it had taken me three trains to get here from Aberystwyth, each one of them late, the last late twice, leaking rain and without a seat that didn't have at least three children standing on it.

Over fish and chips in curry sauce on buttered white bread with pink tea and peas in ketchup I reminded myself that I was in a part of the world where the arts of human to human disrespect, all the nuances of discomfort and disregard, had been brought to the highest imaginable degree of sophistication. Blackpool, where the underclass comes year in and year out to have its identity confirmed through suffering. Bad transport in the getting here, bad food, bad accommodation, bad weather, shit in the shops, shit on the beach, shit in the amusement arcades, death on the big dipper.

Only the expression 'throwing it down' does justice to what the rain was doing that night. It was elemental abuse. A dare from the gods. How much more of this would we be prepared to take? To which the answer was, 'We are the poor – as much as you want to throw at us.' It was like an anti-carnival, riotous pleasure in misery. By the time I got to the South Pier the streets were packed. People skipping through puddles, streaming wet, buying umbrellas which you bandage to your skull so that you can keep your hands free to eat chips or carry your babies, holding them up to illuminations which were less electrically inventive than the dashboard of a Ford Escort.

Out on the South Pier, where the weather was even worse, the crowd for Chubby Brown was forming. Despite the rain, they would not let us in, nor would they simply leave us to queue the way we wanted to. Instead, we were badgered into getting our tickets out, deciphering the numbers, deciding whether we were odd or even, over thirty-three or under thirty-three, and then joining that line instead of this. To our left the big dipper seemed to be leaping out of the sea, arching its phosphorescent back above the elements; to our right the tower, painted gold and saying PEPSI, rose like one of the spires of Atlantis. Or was it sinking, the last memorial of a once great civilization? The grey water sucked at the poles of the pier beneath us. Utterly without seduction, the bingo-caller beckoned us inside. 'Press the yellow button to light the cards. All four corners, any line. Just ten pence. Any more? Eyes down. White 70 – blind seven O.'

Press the yellow button to blow the world apart.

But at last we were moving Chubbywards. For some reason, the women among us had to enter with their bags open. A bouncer in a dinner suit frisked me. I tried to remember whether I had ever been frisked going into a theatre before. I would have liked to know what I was being frisked for – camera, tape-recorder, bomb, bottle, Bible? – but I didn't ask: I didn't want the bond of language between us.

It was rough inside. Like a game at Millwall. Stamping, shouting, drunkenness, funny hats, Valkyrie plaits attached to boaters. You could tell, somehow, that you were at the end of a pier, virtually at sea, on the edge. I *thought* I felt safe, but I was not entirely sure. What was the swearing going to do to the women, whose eyes were already swimming bacchically? To what dangerous heights was it going to raise the testosterone level of the men, already playing sexually ambiguous games with one another in the stalls, squealing, sitting on one another's laps, grabbing one another's members?

But now here's Chubby, appearing through coloured smoke, in his patchwork tails and his First World War pilot's goggles and his little boy's white socks, telling us to shut the fuck up. And that – once we've shouted 'You fat bastard!' back at him a few times – is exactly what we do. We shut the fuck up. We turn to putty in his hands. We couldn't be a more compliant or a more appreciative audience. We laugh – no, we roar – at every rank joke he tells us. 'Somebody told me not to go and see *Schindler's List* without taking a box of tissues . . . *Schindler's List*? I couldn't find anything to wank over in *Schindler's List*.' We adore that. 'I love wanking, me; I wank so often that when I do get a fuck I feel I'm cheating on my wrist.' We go mad for that. 'My wife's always complaining: "I suppose I'm expected to sleep on the wet bit again." I say there wouldn't be a wet bit if you fuckin' swallowed it.' We cheer that. Cheated of our immemorial rights to fellatio we cheer it to the roof.

His favourite word for the female pudendum is minge. It manages to be disgusting but somehow companionable at the same time. You can hear mean and fringe in it, and also singe and whinge, but there's mink there too, and mine – something both desirable and not desirable, depending how you tell it. And he tells it . . . well, ambiguously but with an extraordinary lightness of spirit, a big child, a great bungling boy spitting out mouthfuls of what turns out, in a tale of cunnilingus gone awry, to be bedspread and not minge at all. What that does to his audience has to be seen to be believed.

But by now we are not the sodden disrespected and disrespecting mass that queued with brimming violence in our hearts in the driving rain. Some transformation has taken place. Our aggression and frustration have been thrown back at us, not a jot of what is base and mechanical about us spared, and yet what is returned to us of ourselves has been purified somehow by high spirits, by a common and communicable cheerfulness, by the lordly exulting that there is in the obscene.

Baudelaire talks about laughter slipping in between divine intention and human actuality. Here on the South Pier, Blackpool, where the divide between what God wanted us to be and what we are could not be greater, comedy finds its grandest purpose and fulfils its highest function.

After an hour and a half of unremitting filth we go back out quietly into the rain and vinegar and bingo calls, touched miraculously by a beneficence.

In hostility and aggression is our beginning. Comedy cannot hope to change that. But by making play of our incorrigible combativeness, it propitiates it, harmonizes us with it. And more than that, reminds us of our inexhaustible capacity to evade the burden of sympathy and the compulsion to suffer.

Which is why, when Dame Edna Everage tells her infamous story of the little jest she and the hospital staff once played on her husband Norm –

It's not easy, is it, playing jokes on institutionalized loved ones? But every April the First we play some little April Fool's joke. I remember last April the First we pretended to Norm that he was going to be discharged from the hospital. Isn't that a lovely idea? You could do that to a loved one, too; you could. Of course the matron helped. She packed his little case. So he could see her doing it out of a corner of the mirror above his page-turning machine . . . Anyway, they got him into his dressing gown and he shuffled down to the front of the hossie where I had an ambulance ticking over, and just as Norm was about to fall into the ambulance . . . it whizzed off down the road. He fell flat on his face in the gravel, and all the doctors and nurses leant out of the hossie window and said, 'April Fool!'

– we laugh like drains.

Drains.

And why, when she makes her confession of supreme inhuman humanness –

I'm a lucky woman – because I was born with a priceless gift . . . the ability to laugh at the misfortunes of others

– our spirits are raised, not lowered.

CHAPTER SIX

A Brief Digression into Sado-masochism

Whoever has put his mind to the operation of a sense of humour in himself, and to what makes him laugh in others, knows there is something wrong with jokes. Not something wrong in the liturgical joke as told

ceremonially by comedian/priests, but in those jokes which are pitched at what relationship-counsellors call an inter-personal level. Something in the transaction between joke teller and . . . well, what do we call him? joke hearer? joke interlocutor? joke victim? . . . that works against precisely that deliverance from anxiety which comedy is meant to vouchsafe.

Listening to jokes can be a living hell.

In *Mr Saturday Night* – another of those rancidly intelligent American films which you wonder how a business dedicated to schlock ever had the nerve to make, and which come and go in the twinkling of an eye, proving to the business that it should never have departed from schlock in the first place – Billy Crystal plays a jokester past his best, but still in possession of all the skills that made him loathsome. His catchphrase, especially in conversation with his brother, whose loyalty he's exploited and whose life he's ruined, is 'Did you see what I did then? Did you see what I did?' An allusion to the parabola of a joke and the deviousness of a comic routine (for Mr Saturday Night loves nothing better than gags that disappoint expectation), but also an expression of a Gargantuan greed to go over it all again, to take the victim of the joke back through everything that's been done to him. 'You know I gotta tell you, Stan,' he tells his brother, after a bitter separation, 'seeing you walk into the back of that room today

. . . it just made me feel . . .' The music is getting misty here. Brothers. Time. Feelings. '. . . sick to my stomach. I thought I'd lose my lunch right on the stage . . . See what I did there? You thought I was going to say that I was overjoyed to see you again, but I took you the other way . . .'

'I saw,' Stan says.

The *other way*. Whichever way feeling isn't. Jokes in the service of sub-version of sentiment. Only play, of course. 'I'm only playin' here.' The sentiment's still in there if you listen for it. Only a joke. As when Stan, in a rare risk of confidence, announces, 'I'm seeing a woman.' And the com-edian, quick as night, comes back with, 'What – like through a window?'

'What's the sense in talking to you?' Stan asks, punch-drunk.

There is none.

Freud's 'hostile purpose' has always seemed to me a tame description of the cargo most person-to-person joking business carries. When you have been taken hostage by alien forces, locked up in a darkened room and kept in interminable suspense, not knowing when your release will be negotiated or the final blow will fall, you don't call it hostile purpose, you call it terrorism. I take it that no one will deny the analogousness of the experience of waiting for a jokesmith stranger to release you from the waiting and hit you with his punchline. Will you know when it's been delivered? Will you manage a spontaneous response? Will you have suf-ficient power over the muscles of your eyes and mouth to fake one?

In part, one is in fear of the agelast, the party-pooper in oneself. It is a failure of manners not to get a joke; it breaches the social contract. Society is harsh on those who don't collaborate with mirth. In medieval festivities whoever wouldn't wear green or wouldn't stop working for the day found himself in the ducking stool. Malvolio is bated to the point of madness because he failed to see the point of a fool. In Rabelais' story of Master Villon and Fliptail, the latter's refusal to support the 'people's amusement' leads to his skull being broken open, his brains being spilt, his arms and legs being snapped off, and his bowels being left as a gift to the crows. The lesson is the same at all times and in all places: if you can possibly get the joke, get the joke.

But there is fear for one's intelligence as well. Fear of not measuring up to the joke, of not being intellectually adequate to it. And this fear can ring so loud in your ears that you hear nothing else, only 'Will I get it, will I get it?' in which eventuality you definitely won't. In this, the experience of listening frequently mirrors the substance of the joke itself, for jokes love nothing better than instances of incomprehension. Jewish jokes, especially – on account of Jewish over-valuation of cleverness – delight in the torture of a slow mind by a quick one. I do not know how many stories of would-be converts to Judaism I have been forced to hear, in which the tortuous subtlety of the examining rabbi in the joke merges with the tortuous subtlety of the teller of it, and the poor gentile's metaphysical bafflement becomes indistinguishable from mine. But a sufficient number to make a pagan of me.

Indubitably, there is risk on both sides. The examining rabbi can return to his *yeshiva*, but where does the examining comedian go when he can't raise a laugh? Out of your house, if you're lucky. On to somebody else's. Or else, if he's a professional, out the back door of the theatre, as Lee Evans reports in *Ha Bloody Ha*, where he might just find the pathologically unamused waiting for him, shouting, 'We'll fucking kill him', or making off with his motor.

They'd got my piano out of the car, and they were running down the road with it – then they decided to take the handbrake off and roll my car down the hill. I was chasing them down the hill shouting, 'You've got my car! You've got my life!' And they went, 'Your fucking life is shite!' And they pissed off with the car. I came home on the train – without my car or my piano.

Who's the lucky one? At a late-night fringe show at the 1993 Edinburgh Festival I watched a comedian who called himself the Rapping Rebbe doing everything in his power to get his tiny audience to tell him that his life was shite. He got half the way there, and even gave them the vocabu-lary, with the joke, 'What's the difference between a German and a bucket of shit? The bucket.' Unwilling to sit through jokes of a racial complexion – though it's hard to imagine what else he thought he was going to get from a show called *Shalom, Motherfuckers* – a pious little lilting Irishman, who'd been having no trouble with Jewish jokes about Jewish mothers up until that point, raised a pious little lilting riot in the theatre and led a party of outraged kids out into the street where, incidentally, they were still to be found an hour later, trying to interest the Edinburgh police in what the Rebbe had been saying about the people of the Federal Republic of Germany. Back inside the theatre, meanwhile, the Rebbe was hauling another righteous heckler on to the stage, shoving a microphone in his face, daring him to tell a joke if he thought he was funnier, and then ejecting him from the hall, screaming, 'Get out of my fucking gig!' Not a

Jacques Callot

thing you say – according to the usual conventions – unless you want to do a Samson and bring the lot down on yourself. Which was, without question, the Rapping Rebbe's devoutest wish.

Scratch a sadist . . .

'You stand alone and just do it,' Phyllis Diller has said. 'You either make it or you die alone.' Death is always just round the corner. 'Disaster', is Steve Martin's word. 'In general I think every comedian knows that you're only an inch away from disaster all the time.' If these were mountaineers talking we would know at once what they were in it for. The fall no less than the climb.

A story bearing on both these ambitions is told of the domestic fool Jack Oates, whom we last heard of breaking a bagpiper's bagpipes over his head, and shortly afterwards putting out a rival jester's eye, the cause of his displeasure this time being the cook. A pie of out-of-season quinces has been prepared at immense expense. The guests are gathered in the great hall. It is to be a night of entertainment, but especially a night for eating out-of-season quince pie. Seeing his opportunity to avenge himself on the hated cook, Oates seizes the pie, though it is scalding hot, leaps into the moat with it, and there, with the icy water up to his armpits, and all the guests and fellow-servants at the windows, he sets about

Jacques Callot

devouring it, burning his mouth with every bite. 'To the wonder of the beholders.'

How to separate, in this instance, damaging another from damaging oneself? Wherein lies the satisfaction for the fool – being seen to win a domestic argument or being seen to submit to pain?

Some time before his sense of himself had developed even to the stage where he knew that his penis belonged to him, was his to carry in a box or send scudding across the water to lodge in the vagina of a chief's daughter, Wakdjunkaga, trickster-hero of the Winnebago, put a burning brand to his anus and was surprised to discover that it hurt. The action was intended to be punitive. Wakdjunkaga had turned over to go to sleep, leaving his anus in charge of the evening meal, a couple of 'scabby-mouthed' ducks, cooking on the fire. When he woke he found that the foxes had come in the night and stolen the ducks. A clear failure of vigilance on his anus's part. 'Did I not tell you to watch this fire? You shall remember this! As a punishment for your remissness, I will burn your mouth so that you will not be able to use it.'

Seconds later he is dancing with pain.

Wakdjunkaga slowly piecing himself together, discovering what in the world is him and what isn't, is a myth of individuation not a metaphor for the arrested learning curve of a professional fool. But the confused condition he is in, not knowing where the outside ends and he begins, seeking to wound but hurting only himself, mirrors exactly that of quintessential clowning. You take a swing at somebody and you fall over. You aim a punch and knock yourself out. You steal a pie to spite a cook and burn your mouth. Mouth/anus, why split hairs? The applause you thrive on – wishing to be 'the wonder of the beholders' – is applause for your having successfully made a victim of yourself. Norman Wisdom was unremitting in his pursuit of this pleasurable pain. But then so was Tony Hancock, if we think of it as a moral no less than a physical condition. Similarly John Cleese as Basil Fawlty, if we think of it psychically.

Jesting and self-murder – the pairing has a long lineage.

Sweetest love, I do not go,

sang John Donne,

> For weariness of thee,
> Nor in hope the world can show
> A fitter Love for me;
> But since that I
> Must die at last, 'tis best,
> To use myself in jest,
> Thus by feign'd deaths to die.

Using oneself in it; using oneself up in it; abusing oneself by it; keeping oneself to oneself through it. Grant the conceit all its slithery meanings, it comes back to the jester jesting himself to death.

Shakespeare, too, knew the feeling and the strategy.

> Alas 'tis true, I have gone here and there,
> And made myself a motley to the view,
> Gor'd mine own thoughts, sold cheap what is most dear . . .

Whoever clowns, wounds himself, holds himself at no estimation, attacks his own tranquillity. Gor'd is arrestingly reflexive. As though the clown's horn turns upon the brow that bears it. Back at Marcus Cocceius Nerva's villa, the *scurra* Sarmentus would have seen his opportunity in that. 'Gor'd your own thoughts, Messius?'

But that's sadism, and we've moved on to masochism. Masochism before there was a Masoch to name it after. Call it algolagnia, then. Psychoanalysts do. And the psychoanalysts must be right about the chronologies of making oneself foolish. It must begin this way: first the pain finds you, then, to effect a perverse victory, you go in seek of it. Sweetest love, I do not go . . .

In an article 'On Teasing and Being Teased', Margaret Brenman, Ph.D. (Stockbridge, Mass.), tells of how a certain Allerton W ('so named by her wealthy, snobbish mother who had expected her to be a boy') progresses from 'teasee' to jester.

Her parents who set great store by decorous manners did not permit her to enter the living room while there were guests present until she had mastered the art of curtsying properly. The patient, much later in therapy,

– (from 'teasee' to jester to sanitarium, I should have said) –

recalled her debut as a young curtsy-er when she bowed so low that she fell flat on her face arousing much consternation in her parents and merriment in the assembled guests. It seemed quite clear in the context of this later discussion that while her conscious wish had been to produce the most perfect curtsy ever seen, she was at the same time teasing (or better here, mocking) her parents by producing a live caricature of the behaviour they were demanding and directing attention to herself as an awkward but lovable buffoon.

Sit a comedian down opposite a chat-show host, ask him, or her, how it all began, and the answer is always the same. You inadvertently (or *apparently* inadvertently) fall flat on your face, you hear the laughter, you like it, you want to go on hearing it, so you fall flat on your face again. In that way you please the class, outwit the bully, and find love.

'The production of laughter is a special means of masochistic gratification for the comical person,' notes the American Freudian Theodor Reik in his classic study of self-help through self-hurt, *Masochism in Modern Man*. But the gratification comprehends a pay-off as well as an indulgence: 'That he makes a fool of himself, does not mean that he is a fool.' In fact, it proves he isn't.

Where, maybe, we ought to leave it. Psychologically interesting, no doubt; but the strategy of self-repair ought to command the respect of silence – why take a person back through the process whereby he has turned a failure into a success? We know better than to torment the princess with the reminder that her prince was just a frog when she first kissed him. And what is comedy, after all, but the comedian's faery kiss, transforming the ugly into the beautiful, the inadvertent into the controlled?

We have been here before. Face to face with the 'ordinary bad taste', in Thomas Mann's words, of supposing that we can coax back into our everyday comprehension those who have taught themselves to renounce the everyday. But the masochistic process by which a 'teasee' becomes a jester is interesting, I think, for reasons that aren't only pruriently intrusive. Never mind the consequences of the masochistic strategy to the masochist comedian individually, what are they to the material? Margaret Brenman, Ph.D. (Stockbridge, Mass.) offers another little twist to her interpretation of Allerton W's circus curtsy. 'Thus, while we may suppose she provoked a barrage of benevolent teasing from her parents' friends, she was hostilely unmasking her parents as shallow, pretentious people.'

Lovable buffoonery as withering satire. The pratfall as a means to make a prat of someone else. By this token, Jack Oates knew exactly what he was about. In order to seriously damage the cook he had first to seriously damage himself.

No one traces the intimate connections between the desire to expose the buttocks and the decision to shape a joke, more persuasively than Reik. And no one pursues more conscientiously the 'peculiar detour' which the masochist makes in order to conceal his 'rebellion' behind 'his obsequiousness', his 'opposition' behind his 'submissiveness'.

If analysis did not enable us to peep behind the silhouettes of conscious proceedings, who would be able to recognize defiance, vengeance, sarcasm and derision, altogether a murderous satire, in masochism?

. . . But how is this defiance, this sullen derision, expressed? It is only in this way that the masochist succeeds by preserving his personality even in surrender, by remaining stubborn while yielding, by staying haughty in humility. By giving in on petty details he maintains his claim to his existence and to his peculiar kind of pleasure. The derision represents a step beyond defiance. Having become prouder through humiliation, more courageous through pressure, the masochist becomes a spiteful scoffer.

One man's spiteful scoffing, of course, is another's comic genius. Sarcasm, derision, murderous satire – where would our national literature be without such qualities? No Donne, no Jonson, no Pope, no Swift, no Byron, no Peacock, no Austen . . . And where would Jewish jokes be . . .?

'There are nations,' Reik goes on – the Jewish joke is already clamouring for attention in his analysis: *pride in humiliation*? . . . me, me – 'who in such a masochistic manner produce the most malicious and most biting jokes against their own national peculiarities and weaknesses.' But following the pattern of the individual masochist's devious victory, they too proffer self-abnegation only to revel in haughty exclusivity.

You can see why the strategy might have appealed to Chaplin, who was forever claiming (and then denying) that he was Jewish. Or to Hancock, who often said that he'd have liked to be Jewish. Or to Dame Edna Everage, who begins her autobiography with the frank confession, 'I am probably Jewish.'

Barry Humphries himself – important to make the distinction – told John Lahr of his memories 'of Jews coming to Melbourne, a group with whom I've always sympathized and identified. I felt envious of that kind of hermetic culture. Community. Family. Even persecution.'

Even persecution! How about, *particularly* persecution?

Ah, 'the euphoria,' admits the comedian Jenny Eclair, 'of being hated so much by so many people'.

As Leopold Bloom, Jewish masochist hero of the century's greatest comic novel, stood persecuted by unnotice beside the girl buying sausages at the pork butcher's counter, 'the sting of disregard glowed to weak pleasure within his breast'. Only *weak* pleasure. But it's early in the day. It will glow a lot brighter than that before Bloom's back in his abused bed with his nose in his wandering wife's wandering rump. James Joyce, another not-Jew who got to defiance vengeance sarcasm derision among others by thinking Jewishly.

You can't be the centre of a great comic novel – however passive your nature – and not yourself be something of a comedian. Bloom has this in common with Don Quixote and Tony Hancock – he arranges his own disgrace.

A manoeuvre which proves and ensures, in Theodor Reik's words, that 'The masochist has made himself the master of his destiny.'

Small wonder then, if a joke or a comic routine contains the whole history of this progress from humiliation to hauteur, that it can be exacting to follow. Small wonder, if laughter represents shame transubstantiated into triumph, that we are not always willing, or able, to part with it. Hating waiting for the joke to unravel, fearing to sit within a comic's sight lines in a club, dreading an encounter with a clown in the street – they all come down to the same terror: will he embroil me in the heaven and hell drama that is his act?

You could also call it dog-in-a-manger. 'The crowd around me seethed with joy and merriment,' recalls Thomas Mann's Felix Krull of his days attending the Stoudebecker Circus. 'I, however, in some measure shut myself off from their seething and yearning, coolly, like someone who was a member of the profession, who "belonged" to the performers. Not as a member of the circus profession or a performer of the *salto mortale*, of course; I could not feel myself that, but as a member of a more general profession, as an entertainer and illusionist.'

In other words, why should one masochist put his hands together for another?

CHAPTER SEVEN

How the Devil Became a Holy Fool

I

The first opera I ever saw was *I Pagliacci*. In truth I must have seen it as half of the usual double-bill with *Cavalleria Rusticana*, but it was *Pagliacci* that made the impression on me, in particular the clown-troupe leader

Canio's aria, 'Vesti la giubba'. In English, 'On with the motley'. Unacquainted as yet with Shakespeare's Sonnet 109 – 'alas 'tis true, motley to the view' etc. – I took motley to mean a dirge or lamentation. So, 'On with the motley' meant 'On with the dirge'; an exhortation to go on being miserable. And that was how I sang it in my darkened room, dirgefully, imitating the sobs, the jealous heartbreak, the bitter recognition that the show had to go on, whatever was tearing me apart. '*Ridi, Pagliaccio!*' – 'So laugh, Pagliaccio!' Laughter as dirgeful as death.

'*La commedia è finita,*' Canio sings when it is all over, his wife and her lover dead by his hand – 'The comedy is ended.' In my version the comedy had never begun.

I must have been eleven or twelve. In Pagliaccio I saw a reflection of my own condition. A tragic clown. In fact the phrase was tautologous. What was a *non*-tragic clown? You sat in front of a mirror, you painted your face, and you sobbed in a high tenor voice. That was what you did if you were a clown; and, apart from the face painting, that was what you did if you were eleven or twelve. I make no apologies for the anguished assumptions of my boyhood. Or for the contradictions that supported them (where was the actual malign circus clown I blenched from in all this?). But what are we doing as grown-ups sentimentalizing buffoonery,

imagining there is some holiness in simplicity, that red noses are benign, that there is a tear in the eye of every Pierrot? A popular song has only to send in a clown and we are, immediately, in lachrymose collusion with him, heroically falsifying gaiety, bleeding inside.

Who would ever guess from so much sad-clowning and hollow-masquerading that when we address laughter it is the devil's business we are on?

In a wonderful passage of aerial speculation in *The Book of Laughter and Forgetting*, Milan Kundera imagines an hour, an actual moment in real and metaphysical time, when an angel first heard the devil's laughter and understood its danger.

The angel was all too aware that the laughter was aimed against God and the wonder of His works. He knew he had to act fast, but felt weak and defenceless. And unable to fabricate anything of his own, he simply turned his enemy's tactics on him. He opened his mouth and let out a wobbly, breathy sound in the upper reaches of his vocal register ... and endowed it with the opposite meaning. Whereas the Devil's laughter pointed up the meaninglessness of things, the angel's shout rejoiced in how rationally organized, well conceived, beautiful, good, and sensible everything on earth was.

For the angel's mirthless wobbly rationality, in the context of this novel, read Czech Communism. But read any other optimistic political or religious ideology as well. Read Humor Conventions too, come to that. Read Christian clowning. Read the *Reader's Digest*. Read laughter the best medicine. Read the extraordinary American doctor-clown, Patch Adams, with whom I shared a pig-trough lunch in 1995 on a visit to 'Gesundheit!', the Utopian infirmary he is building in West Virginia, but whose book on joy and health, also called *Gesundheit!*, determinedly renounces the pig in us in favour of the angel – an angel much given to aphorizing, at that: 'Laughter is the white noise of happiness'; 'To the happy . . . nature is the sandbox of life'; 'In a healthier world, humor would be a way of life'. A healthier world, well-conceived, beautiful, good . . . In short, read whatever dogma supposes that the devil and his meaningless mocking laughter must be forever expelled.

Devil expulsion has always been the name of the game. Pointing the phallus. Frightening with bad language. Raising the skirts. Repelling with rudery. If there were no devils to expel there would be no comedy to enjoy. Not comedy to enjoy *after* the expulsion – that's the angel's position: joy in rational organization – but comedy to enjoy *during*. Which is another way of saying that we have never really wanted the demons to turn their backs on us for ever. If Demeter didn't lose her daughter to the netherworld each winter, what justification would there be for Iambe's ribald routine? Or Baubo's piggy-shaven pudenda show?

Another year, another contest. The seasonableness of comedy, whether it's theatrical or popular-festive, a play or a procession, is something we take for granted. Come winter we go to a circus or a pantomime. Come spring, we carnival. Come summer, we sit on the beach and watch Punch beat his wife and cheat the hangman. And in all those activities, so long as the healthy-minded or the angelic have not got their hands on them, traces of that first diabolic tussle remain. Even when the devil is no longer in there as a character, you smell the sulphur of his presence, detect some trace of his costume and physiognomy, hear the virulence of his mockery.

How to tell the dancer from the dance, the demons from the clowns who defy them, in this account of the way the basketmaking Pomos of California clean up their community every seven years? (J. G. Frazer again the disseminator of the information.)

Twenty or thirty men array themselves in harlequin rig and barbaric paint, and put vessels of pitch on their heads; then they secretly go out into the surrounding mountains. These are to personify the devils ... At a signal agreed upon in the evening the masqueraders come in from the mountains, with the vessels of pitch flaming on their heads, and with all the frightful accessories of noise, motion and costume which the savage mind can devise in representation of demons.

We shouldn't rest too much on that word harlequin. It's unlikely that the Pomos of California would have ransacked the iconography of the *commedia dell'arte* for ideas for their costumes. All 'harlequin rig' tells us is that the witness to this ritual – a 'farce', he calls it later – has had to ransack his own pantomimic memories to find the appropriate vocabulary for what he saw. But that doesn't mean he invented the confusion between clown and devil. The moment those twenty or thirty men painted themselves up and set about their personification, they slipped categories, now becoming the things expelled, now becoming the force that expels them.

If this or that clown frequently resembles this or that devil, the explanation is not to be found in contiguousness. Clowns and devils look alike because they perform identical functions. The only difference is that the clown is the devil of our own making. Think of him as a figure necessary to our communal masochism, the means whereby we get in first (since we can't get *out* of diablerie) and make ourselves masters of our destiny.

In her book about her travels with a Mexican circus, *A Trip to the Light Fantastic*, Katie Hickman describes 'the demon army' – naked, fantastically painted, hundreds strong – got up by the Cora Indians of Mexico during the *dias prohibidos*, the forbidden days. The 'Judea' they are also called. The Jews. No need to stress the diabolic significance of Jews to a Holy Week ceremonial in an agitatedly Catholic country. Even if there's nothing specifically or recognizably Jew*ish* about what the army gets up to.

All day the demon army cavorted through the town, appearing and disappearing out of the dust like a fantastic mirage from the hills ... They ran in and out of the crowd at will, nicking cigarettes, *refrescos* and lighters, knocking off the men's sombreros; doing anything, in fact, which took their pixie-like fancy. They threw water and urine and burning straw; they ran races and staged mock fights with their swords. Their movements were gleeful, Puck-like; and they made strange little crowing sounds as they pounced.

It was not dangerous to be around them but it was never exactly safe, either ...

As far as the individual ingredients go – the licence, the petty larceny, the piss-taking, the piss-throwing, the animality – we are on familiar territory. We could be with the Zuni. Or we could be at a circus. Or we could be at a carnival.

During the *dias prohibidos* all civil authority is suspended, and the *Judea* alone rule. All the rules of the real world are turned on their heads. Everything which symbolizes real life is forbidden; everything which is forbidden in real life is courted, magnified, driven to its most extreme limits.

Our old friends the policemen clowns, violating the very taboos they police, policing the very taboos they violate. But also being the very community demons the community wants to be rid of.

Courting what is forbidden; materializing what is dreaded.

Watching the demon army tracking from house to house a child dressed up as Jesus – they are a pretend Jew-army, remember – 'beating the door with their fists, digging in the ground around it with their bare hands, scratching, snuffling, howling for blood . . . hissing and hooping and sniffing the ground', Katie Hickman puts it to herself that this is not a masque after all, but reality. 'These were no longer just men in papier-mâché masks, but real coyotes, real wolves, real demons . . .'

'Your divell' – meaning, one must suppose, your English divell – 'doeth alwayes leade the daunce,' complained Christopher Fetherston, an early Festival-of-Lighter, a man known only for his authorship of *Dialogue Against Light, Lewd and Lascivious Dauncing* in 1582. We might read that metaphorically if we choose – whoever dances is on his way to hell – but 'your divell' did, in person and in body, frequently gatecrash public merrymaking. A black-faced bent-backed figure variously known as Little Devil Dout and Jack Devil Doubt employed his broom to sweep space for the first lines of a St George play, and then swept the play away again when it was finished. One Beelzebub, whose longevity is recognized even by the folklore-doubting Ronald Hutton in his *The Rise and Fall of Merry England*, regularly turned up in popular drama, carrying a club and a frying-pan. And how to tell the devil from the fool in the morris dance (a fool whom Fetherston castigated for abusing the divine gift of reason, and a dance which Philip Stubbes castigated for being the 'Devil's Dance'), when that latter – the fool, not Stubbes – might appear with a black face, or a humpback, or dressed in animal skins, and with a tail?

You always know the devil's never far away when the animal skins come out. What else is the devil in the end, but the animal in us? And in so far as clowns and comedians exist so that we may go on dancing to the devil's tunes while not acknowledging that we are ungodly, their animal costumery is a tactful affirmation of their lineage. Zebra-striped or tiger-spotted, Katie Hickman's demons sniff the ground through their jungle masks, like real coyotes, real wolves. The savage dismemberment of Fliptail for failing to support the 'people's amusement', is effected by Master Villon's actor-devils, 'all dressed up,' according to Rabelais, 'in wolves-, calves-, and ram-skins, surmounted by sheeps' heads, bulls' horns . . .'

Think of the Bacchae, followers of Dionysus with fawn skins on their backs, pulling apart Pentheus, limb by limb.

And how come Master Villon has this bestiary of little devils to hand? Well, he is putting on a Passion Play, is he not? For the people's amusement. And what's a Passion Play without devils?

'You'll play your parts well, my dear devils,' says Villon proudly, when he sees how complete a job they have made of separating Fliptail's feet from his legs, his legs from his trunk, his bowels from his body, his brains from his head. 'You'll act splendidly, I promise you . . . I defy the team of devils of Saumur, Doué, Montmorillon, Langeais, Saint-Épain, Angers, and even the Poitiers troupe in their great hall, by God, to put on as good a show.'

That's one hell of a lot of devils.

But the following stage directions to the twelfth-century *Play of Adam*, unearthed by Chambers, give an idea of why their services, and why so many of them, were in demand.

Adam and Eve walk about Paradise in honest delight. Meanwhile the demons are to run about the stage, with suitable gestures ... Then shall come the devil and three or four devils with him, carrying in their hands chains and iron fetters, which they shall put on the necks of Adam and Eve. And some shall push and others pull them to hell; and hard by hell shall be other devils ready to meet them who shall hold high revel at their fall ... there [in hell] shall they make a great smoke arise, and call aloud to each other with glee in their hell, and clash their pots and kettles, that they may be heard without. And after a little delay the devils shall come out and run about the stage.

Given the clownish violence required of them, you can see why Villon felt that his actors had proved their theatrical mettle in their escapade with Fliptail. For our part, we may feel that this high revelry, with its clashing pots and kettles, its pushing and pulling, its special effects, its ceaseless frenzy, its delight in all the pleasures that are *not* 'honest', reminds us of nothing so much as the circus.

How often, in late medieval painting, do the damned resemble acrobats and tumblers. As though the descent into hell necessitates or teaches particular big-top skills, balance, prestidigitation, adroitness on the high wire. The devils in Bosch's *Study of Devils* look like whippers-in of recalcitrant audience members, tutors at a circus school. Parenzano *The Temptation of St Anthony* shows mental torment as a sort of dream of panto.

The circus which was a *Play of Adam* was a circus in a church, at that. For in the twelfth century, mystery plays had still not moved out into the streets. When they did, hell remained a locus for hilarity. Bakhtin describes the gaping jaws of a mechanical hell – mechanical because it was required to open and close – 'located in the very centre of the stage and at the level of the spectators' eyes'. And it was on these jaws, Bakhtin argues, that the medieval audience concentrated its curiosity, 'expecting the most amusing and comic protagonists to emerge from them'.

To the medieval public, a comedian from hell was not a term of disapprobation. Hell was where comedy came from.

And the hellish comedian's get-up was that mixture of demonic, bestial and popular-festive with which we are familiar. 'The ordinary equipment of the devil,' in the words of the nineteenth-century historian of theatre, Mantzius,

consisted of a tight-fitting skin, which covered the whole of the body except the head, and was generally made of the shaggy hides of wolves or calves . . . Sometimes a kind of feather-dress covered the devil's body, or a green-painted, reptile-like skin. [They] either had their faces grotesquely painted . . . or they wore different masks, for the most part heads of animals, for example rams or goats, or, occasionally, of birds. As a rule they had big horns of oxen or rams. Their feet ended in long claws of beasts or birds of prey; hoofs appear less frequently. In their hand they generally held a cudgel of stuffed cloth for beating the refractory souls; later . . . hollow staves filled with combustible explosives or burning torches.

All we know of the paraphernalia of comedy is here. The grotesque physical distortions we associate with Aristophanic farce; the bodily exaggeration and animal attributes of the satyr play, to say nothing of the resemblance to satyrs themselves; the slapstick beatings of the *commedia dell'arte* and silent cinema; the gunpowder and fireworks of the circus; the phallic weaponry of the jester, the tickling stick of Ken Dodd.

By 1600 religious drama had for the most part been suppressed across Europe. A new efficacy in morals put paid to the high revelry, and a new efficacy in reason to the low superstition. So far the devil had sung all the best songs and told all the best jokes; the best way to deprive him of both was to internalize him. Mix him up with all the solemnities of personal guilt. No more pantos to test St Anthony's resolve. And no more tumbling into hell. The angels had taken over.

Elsewhere another transmutation of devil into clown had been progressing quietly.

Harlequin, with his 'monkey's mug and serpent's body', in Gautier's words, 'his black mask, his particoloured lozenges, his shower of spangles', incarnating 'wit, mobility, audacity, all the brilliant qualities and vices'; Harlequin, whose name sprang to the mind of the witness to those Californian Pomo diableries, and whose strangeness helped Conrad's Marlow to define the nature of the uncouth, inexplicable Russian gesturing to him, 'thoughtlessly alive', from Kurtz's dark shore: 'His aspect reminded me of . . . something funny I had seen somewhere. As I manoeuvred to get alongside, I was asking myself, "What does this fellow look like?" Suddenly I got it. He looked like a harlequin'; – Harlequin, too – Harlequin, especially – had diabolic antecedents.

From the early Middle Ages we glimpse him, hell-smoked, as one of a band of tormenting devils or even as the leader of a troupe known as

Erhard Schön

la chasse Arlequin. A medieval chronicle reports a priest of St Aubin de Bonneval witnessing a procession of devils – armed, dwarfed, sooty, scattering fire: the 'family of the Herlechini' – leading the souls of the damned in the direction of the eternal fires. 'They come by night with tumult, warring with themselves.' In Adam de la Halle's *Jeu de la Feuillée* (1262), Hellequin is a devil-prince in cahoots with faeries and attended by a comic demon, Croquesots – eater of fools. A minor tormentor called Alichino is alluded to briefly in Dante's *Inferno*. And the fourteenth-century Herlequini were street revellers, instigators of bridal ribaldry and the like, 'troops of grotesque figures,' according to K. M. Lea's *Italian Popular Comedy*, 'half-naked or wearing skins, lions' manes or ox-horns'. Part devil, part beast, and therefore part clown.

By the late sixteenth century Harlequin had begun to establish himself as an indispensable member of the *commedia*. But the clowning didn't alienate him from his earlier associations, any more than it disabled him from many of his early duties. Once accept that expelling demons and personifying demons are only *apparently* contradictory activities, and Harlequin's assault upon hell, in a piece for stage recitation, written in 1585, is absolutely in character. His descent is from first to last acrobatic, a bounding, somersaulting journey to the underworld. Charon he jumps on like a monkey, entertaining him with 'mille gambades/ Mille saults, mille bonds et mille bonnetardes,/ En reculant tousiours'. Pluto he entertains by dancing a Bergamesque, and when that's through he pokes his tongue out at him to show how little he is afraid. Christ himself scarcely harrowed hell with more address.

Duchartre notices that scarcely any change was made to Harlequin's mask from the Renaissance to the eighteenth century. The eyebrows and beard remained 'bushy and covered with stiff bristles'. The forehead

strongly lined with wrinkles which accentuated the slightly quizzical arch of the eyebrows. The eyes were tiny holes beneath, and the *ensemble* gave a curious expression of craftiness, sensuality, and astonishment which was both disturbing and alluring. The huge wen under the eye, the wart, and the black colour completed the impression of something savage and fiendish. The mask suggested a cat, a satyr, and the sort of negro that the Renaissance painters portrayed.

Almost too many influences seem to be converging on Harlequin here. Not only was he a devil, he was also a satyr, and his face was black. Early engravings show him as phallic. A tail frequently hung from his soft cap,

Barthel Beham

otherwise a tuft of feathers protruded from it. Michelangelo was said to have found and restored an ancient satyr mask, with the purpose of turning it into a mask for Harlequin. Black. Why black? Duchartre has a thought about that. Perhaps because 'the ancient Harlequin was a phallophore', and a phallophore, as we know, made himself up sootily in order to sing his phallic songs.

Is this what the witness to the fearful yelling and whooping of the normally peaceful basketmaking Pomos of California was remembering when he spoke of their 'harlequin rig' – Harlequin's ancient origins in riotousness and invective?

II

A word about horns.

That's to say a word about satyrs and devils. We shouldn't, after all, go on being surprised when a figure that recalls the one recalls the other. Any natural history of the Judaeo-Christian devil must take it as axiomatic that the cloven-hoofed one with his horns and hairy skin has his iconographic origins in the pagan bull and goat-gods. If A is going to part company theologically from B, it stands to reason that A will quickly turn B's gods into A's devils. Satan did not spring unparented into the Christian imagination; Satan's grandfather was a satyr.

'Wild beasts of the forest shall lie there,' warns Isaiah, according to the Authorized translation – 'there' being Babylon once it's laid waste. 'And owls shall dwell there, and satyrs shall dance there.' In St Jerome's version the dancing satyr has become 'the hairy one'.

And since we are on St Jerome, his *Life of St Paul the Hermit* tells of a desert encounter between St Anthony, the panto-dreamer, and a mournful and repentant satyr who delivers himself thus:

A mortall creature I am, and one of the inhabitants of the desart, whome the Pagans being deluded with variety of errours are wont to worship, by the name of Fawnes, Satyres, and Incubus's, I performe the office of an Embassadour for the rest of the flock wherof I am. And our suit is, that thou wilt pray for us to our common God, whome we know to be come for the salvation of the world, and the sound of him is extended all over the earth.

Hearing this, St Anthony weeps tears of joy 'in the glory of Christ and the destruction of Sathan'. And you can see why. It's a big catch. If that's not Satan himself who's come begging for salvation, it is at least his kin.

The Greek geographer Strabo, born about 60 BC, reported on satyrs as though they were actual individuals he had encountered on his travels:

... a kind of inspired people ... subject to Bacchic frenzy, and, in the guise of ministers ... inspiring terror at the celebration of the sacred rites by means of war dances, accompanied by uproar and noise and cymbals and drums and arms, and also by flute and outcry.

A performance scarcely to be distinguished, in noise and fearfulness, from that of the devils in the *Play of Adam*.

So if we wonder how come the devil and the clown look so alike to the eye of the medieval dramaturge and painter, here's part of the answer. The devil originates in the satyr-gods who are themselves already possessed of that vitality, phallic and holy-cacophonous, that we associate with comedy. As the romantics would rediscover, the devil always was a bit of a comedian.

Oh, and the horn . . .

Remember the horseshoe, which Thomas Wright believed to have been nailed up on barn-doors erroneously, in a graphic confusion with the female generative organs; well, an alternative superstition was to hang a piece of horn to the stable, or to couple it with a cowhouse key, in order to protect the animals from night-fright or other terrors. A similar superstition, clearly, to that practised by my Italian fixer at Pompeii, who carried a horn in his car to protect himself from day-fright. We know that a horn is a phallus, that a satyr was ithyphallic, that the devil is horned, that a jester was often ithyphallic *and* horned, that the badge of the cuckold is a horn, that the sign of virility (the bull, the cuckolder) is a horn, that a horn shaken at the heavens is a curse on God, that a horn is a hex and a promise (may you be cuckolded!), that the horn, therefore, is both subject and object, protagonist and victim, curser and cursed, evil and good . . . The satyr, the devil, the clown, the phallophor, the cuckold, the lecher, the fooled, the fooler – back and forth the transference goes. All have a horn about them, all have a horn showing, somewhere.

All except the holy fool.

III

An alternative history of fooling.

1 Corinthians – lowered already? Funny how holy fooling always has a lowering effect, except on the holy – 1 Corinthians, 3, 18–19:

Let no man deceive himself. If any man among you seemeth to be wise in this world, let him become a fool, that he may be wise.

For the wisdom of this world is foolishness with God.

For the implications of which see 1 Corinthians – and funny how of all lowering New Testament citations 1 Corinthians is the loweringest of all; but be brave, it's brief – 1 Corinthians, 4, 10:

We are fools for Christ's sake.

The idea took a while to catch on. Despite St Paul's encouragement, early Christian heroes were more inclined to *abjure* foolishness for Christ's sake. As in the story of St Genesius the Comedian, for example, in so far as we can track it through the usual minefield of martyrology. (If, as some think, St Genesius the Comedian is a western Christian variant of an eastern St Gelasius the Comedian who met a similar fate, that just proves the dogged persistence of this particular variety of humourlessness.)

This, anyway, is how the tale is told.

The Emperor Diocletian is paying a visit to Rome. Entertainments fit for an emperor are prepared for him. Among them a stage revue in which, as part of the fun, the comic actor Genesius is to burlesque the rites of Christian baptism. Come the performance, Genesius moves into his part. Lies down on the boards and complains that there is a great weight upon him. Fellow actors throw up their hands. What would he have them do to reduce this weight? Plane him like a plank, ho ho? No, fools! He wishes to die like a Christian. He must receive the grace of Jesus Christ and be delivered from his sins. Enter clown priests bearing baptismal water. Slosh slosh. Water all over the audience too. Hilarity. You can never throw too much water. Enter clown soldiers. Cur of a Christian, off to the Emperor with you. Hello, hello, says Diocletian, playing himself. What have we here then? Time for the examination. As in life, so in the parody. What does the

Christian have to say for himself? 'Hear! O Emperor,' declares Genesius. 'And hear! all you doubters. Time was when I too reviled even the sound of the word, Christian. Loathed those of my relatives who professed that religion. Learned its rites and mysteries only in order to ridicule them. And to encourage you in your contempt of them. But a company of angels appeared over my head while water was being splashed over me, reciting from the book of sins I had committed from my childhood. And lo! the book was cleaner now than snow!'

One minute dirty, one minute clean. Dirty, clean. Just like that.

What a gift he possesses, this Genesius. What a talent for mimicry. What timing . . . But wait. He is not pausing for his laughs. He is not coughing into his wrists. He is not slyly looking out from under his humbled Christian gaze to boldly meet the laughing pagan eyes of the ladies in the front stalls. 'Wherefore I advise you, O great and mighty emperor,' he continues, 'and all people here present who have mocked these mysteries, to believe with me that Jesus Christ is the true Lord, that it is through Him only that you may obtain forgiveness of your sins, as I have', and oh, my eye, he is not acting any more, he is not pretending, but by Bacchus he means it – he has seen the light, he has become a Christian!

The fooler fooled in his own foolery. Comicry converted in its own despite.

Given the chance to repent of his repentance and remember where the joke once was, Genesius refuses. He is put upon an iron rack, stretched, burnt with torches, and finally beheaded. A martyr to mirthlessness.

Once Christianity is able to feel more secure of itself, foolery for Christ's sake comes juggling out of the closet. After a career marked by rigorous abstinence, St Simeon took to eating sausages on Good Friday and dancing in the streets with prostitutes. A life of lunacy, he argued, was the natural consummation of a life of prayer. St Basil the Blessed walked naked through the streets of Moscow, throwing stones at the houses of respectable citizens. St Philip Neri divided himself down the middle like a court-jester, shaved off half his beard, and wore his coat inside out, over his cassock. According to Cardinal Newman he sought not to be persecuted, but despised. To act the fool that he may find wisdom. St Procopius of Ustyug kept company only with the poor, slept in church porches, devoted his nights to prayer and his days to insanity. '*Ioculatores Domini*', was how St Francis of Assisi described his own order – jokers and jesters of God. And so much good entertainment could be expected from a

J. J. Grandville

Franciscan friar that upwards of 15,000 people would gather in the market-place to hear the best of them.

That the popularity of knockabout preaching may have been something of an embarrassment to the church authorities, St Paul's incitement to holy folly notwithstanding, is borne out by a ruling of the Council of Salzburg in 1291, not long after Francis's canonization:

We order that the clergy must not be jesters, goliards or buffoons; if they pursue such disgraceful accomplishments for a whole year, they are to be stripped of all ecclesiastical privileges.

But once a man has been applauded for being wise in his foolishness it is hard for him to return to being foolish in his wisdom. St Paul understood that much about public speaking. And competition between clerics and actual comedians was still burning fiercely enough in 1762 for Diderot to write of 'a single square' in Venice where

you can see on one side a stage with mountebanks performing merry but monstrously indecent farces, and on the other, another stage with priests performing farces of a different complexion and shouting out: 'Take no notice of those wretches, gentlemen; the Pulcinella you are flocking to is a feeble fool; here (displaying the crucifix) is the genuine Pulcinella!'

From being a fool for Christ's sake, to being a fool *like* Christ. Our Saviour the Pulcinella. So when Tiepolo let his Venetian Pulcinella out of the grave, all bones but ready to party, he was only returning the favour.

But we must be careful not to run over ourselves here. Trails of opposing ideas of foolery are crossing. Pulcinella's feverish love of temporal life – so great that he will return to it even when the spirit has left his body and of his fleshly vitality only the conical hat remains – can hardly be considered Christlike. Christ courts the grave, as the Sibyl's cavern entrance into a new tomorrow. And it is certainly not in order to celebrate the here and now that he briefly rises from it. Nor was St Paul envisaging a noisy patterer of a priest capable of competing with indecency on its own terms when he spoke of renouncing what passes for wisdom in this world. Somewhere along this track the devil had seen his opportunity and devilishly re-substituted the original meaningless mocking thing for the counterfeit. The Feast of Fools was his. The drunken, fornicating friar was his. The mystery plays were his. The farceur prelate of 1760s Venice was his. But the idea of folly located in Christ himself – 'Here is the genuine Pulcinella!' – is still in harmony with Paul's first conception. The fool as inviolable innocent. The Christ as mock-king riding into Jerusalem on an ass, to be displayed in purple, beaten and laughed at, and finally revered, as his pagan predecessor Dionysus never was, for his divine purity and unworldliness. Christ and the fool as one in simplicity.

Not only not devilish but devil-proof. 'In children and in fools the devil has no influence,' wrote the author of *Piers Plowman*, concerned to distinguish between the artificial professional fool who is the 'fiend's disciple' (our horned chum), and the true fool, childish, witless, guileless and safe. Hence the crush of meanings that jostle in that word 'natural' – of nature, but also a fool, an idiot, 'one whom,' in Johnson's definition, 'nature debars from understanding'. *Understanding* always was problematic; proof of God's givingness to us, but at the same time our disobedience to him. *Understanding* was what we bit into with the apple, bought at the cost of our sempiternal garden felicity. So whoever lacks understanding has made no bargain with the serpent or with God; ergo is without sin. 'Where God gyveth no dyscerninge' – Thomas Heywood – 'God taketh none accownte.'

The ancients played it rougher with their 'naturals'. In general, half-wittedness afforded them the same entertainment as other deformities; whatever luck dwarfs and humpbacks brought, however talismanic their misshapenness, the main reason for having them about was still menagerie curiosity. And because curiosity always comes at a price, an idiot was worth money. To his owner, that is. It wasn't the beautiful youth or the perfectly proportioned bond-maid that attracted the most attention at the slave-market in Rome, Plutarch reckoned, but the freak. You bought him – much as you might a rare breed of dog – you took him home, and you had him run around your dinner table. Martial expressed a keen distaste for this practice of having monsters charging about whenever you went out to dine. Monsters such as the *morio* – 'a creature with pointed head and large ears which move just as a donkey's ears are wont'. And ideally with no more than donkey-intelligence in between them. Martial tells the story of a dissatisfied purchaser, angry that he'd been palmed off with something whole when he'd forked out for a deficiency. 'He was sold to me as a cretin. I paid 200,000 sesterces for him. Give me my money back, Gargilianus, he has all his wits about him.'

This may seem no better than human zoo-keeping to us. As far, at least, as humane treatment of deformity goes, we believe we have made

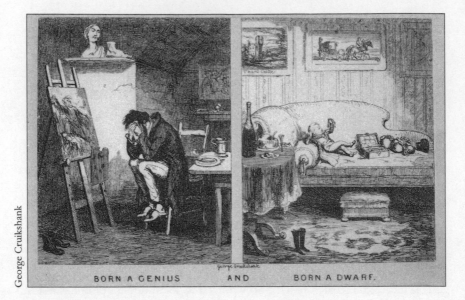

George Cruikshank

BORN A GENIUS   AND   BORN A DWARF.

progress since this Roman market-place in missing parts. But there's another way of looking at it. The ancients attached a high value to the buffoon who wasn't 'a natural' but who had all his marbles. Who could burst into a gathering of philosophers and out-sophisticate the sophists. Slug it out with Socrates. Or, like Aristophanes' Sausage-seller, out-rhetoric the highest, and the mightiest, in the city. Who was possessed in the highest degree, in short, of *understanding*. If such a valuation of mind meant that lack of it made you more than ever a freak, at least that insult to human intelligence implicit in the fetishism of *mindlessness* (Forrest Gump with all his Oscars, for example) never surfaced. The Greek buffoon and the Roman *scurra* were not moral outcasts, abandoned by God to a sphere of sacred vacancy, incorruptible because unaccountable. Their gifts were all of the human kind; their merits heightened *us*.

Another way of putting it is that the 'naturalness' the cretin-merchant believed he had been cheated of, the 200,000 sesterces' worth of genuine unwitted fool he had supposed he was buying, was not a pretext for moralizing. When the 'natural' leapt around the supper table no criticism of *unnaturalness* was implied. Once Christianize him, though, and morality becomes his medium; his role to be a permanent reproach to the short-comings of wisdom as the worldly-wise understand it. Even the artificial fool – the 'allowed fool', to borrow Olivia's phrase for Feste; the profes-

168

sional – sees a vindication of his function in this: his nonsense is not oppositional in a burlesque way now, it has become a superior *sense*. In place of the cartwheel a modest *bouleversement* – hardly carnivalesque at all; a matter, merely, of paradoxes and casuistry – by which the wise are shown to be foolish, and vice versa. At its most tedious, as say in Shakespeare, the strategy declines into routine exercises in chop-logic. Predictably topsy-turvy catechisms. The fool examining the master; the simpleton outwitting the sage. 'Good madonna, give me leave to prove you a fool.' 'Can you do it?' 'Dexteriously, good madonna.' 'Make your proof.' And by God he does, he does . . .

The exhaustion of foolery that we often feel in Shakespeare is, it is true, partly a reflection (Christ save us all) of sociological fact. A profession is running out of steam. We are at the end of the court-fool tradition, and the fools are beginning to look melancholy and vulnerable. I'll answer you, agrees Olivia, allowing Feste to make his proof, 'for want of other idleness'. She expects scant entertainment from her fool. Anything remotely better to do and you feel she'd be off. And even when she defends him against Malvolio she can drum up nothing more laudatory to say for his calling than that it has 'no slander' in it. No slander? We're a long way now from the Horace-hurting Roman *scurra*, who was *all* slander. Had you only an easier disposition, Malvolio, Olivia rebukes him, you would 'take those things for bird-bolts that you deem cannon-bullets'. Some praise for the subversive powers of the clown – bird-bolts! Blunt arrows for shooting wrens out of the sky.

Nothing is taken for granted about Feste. His point, his value, his whereabouts, his function, are all up for discussion. Only the Puritan sees anything definite to fear from him. So it is only against the Puritan that he is effective. Otherwise he is impotent and idle, more a soother than a subversive, more an emollient than a mocker, coming to the close of a 400-year institutional career that domesticated him from the uncouth itinerant entertainer of the Middle Ages into a friend and confidant of the great. Steadily throughout Europe during this time, the fool had been acquiring official status as *domini regis ioculator* or *fou en titre d'office*. Pope Leo X's Fra Mariano had a special apartment in the Papal Palace and, as formally appointed *offizio dei Piombi*, sealed all the Pope's correspondence. We hear of court fools retiring to comfortable houses with pensions and of kings consulting their fools on political affairs and taking their advice. The ex-soldier Chicot, who became fool to Henri IV, was on 'monsieur mon ami' terms with the king, as Henry VIII was 'Harry' to Will Somers. Antoine

Godeau (born 1605), a dwarf of Princess Julie d'Angennes, ended up (highly conscious of his fortune and his duties) as the Bishop of Grasse and Vence. In fifteenth-century Lille the office of Fool became a civic institution – 'Fou de la ville'. One of the first holders of the office was a lad 'mad out of his senses'; 300 years later a city banker assumed the position.

Allowed fools, all of them. So how, then, could they have ever shot anything but bird-bolts? One does not need to be cynical about human nature in general, or the nature of clowns in particular, to see that the ioculators and demi-demon comedians of the Middle Ages, who hung about monasteries and fairgrounds for their living, could not retain the vigour of their eccentricity once they were drawn into the static structures of power. They had foraged wildly about the edges, now they were comfortable and clothed in the centre. Hard to be a devil in a feather bed.

He suffers personally for his presumption in the end, discovers to his cost that you can always make even a tame cat scratch, yet Malvolio's criticism of Olivia's fool, that unless you 'minister occasion to him, he is gagged', is not wide of the mark. Yes, Feste pays him out for that sneer; but the disproportionate violence of that pay-out, the spectacle of Feste stung to the quick, the length of time Feste goes on festering, whirligigging his revenge, essentially proves Malvolio's charge. The clown is only good now for prosecuting a private quarrel.

Behind the very idea of the allowed fool, to whom one must 'minister occasion', you can still detect the old reverence for the 'natural'. In 1454 Duke Philip of Burgundy extended a special privilege to the members of his chapel in the matter of their New Year's Day revels – *allowing* their folly:

all gay fools [*joyeux fous*] clad in the habit of our Chapel shall hold their revels safely, without suffering any kind of outrage or scorn. And let no one, not even the wisest, contradict this order. But let the fools caper, gently, one or two days, as long as their money lasts . . . we command our subjects not to interfere with them but to allow them to go peacefully about their pleasure.

Let the fools caper *gently*. Let them go *peacefully*. Let them be unmolested. Unmistakable, the paternal, the pastoral note, as though this is a command guaranteeing safe passage to the innocent, the harmless, the simple. Suffer the little children . . .

Feste himself knows he has to slip into 'natural' mode to cover his tracks. Find, as New Agers put it, the child in himself. 'When that I was and a little tiny boy . . .' A song that Lear's Fool picks up – 'He that has a little tiny wit, / With hey, ho, the wind and the rain, / Must make content with his fortune's fit, / For the rain it raineth every day.' 'True, my good boy,' assents the maddened Lear. Assenting to his own witlessness as much as to the Fool's. Which is what his Fool wants from him. Admit it, Lear, admit it: you too have only a little tiny wit. You too, though a king, are just a child.

True, my good boy. The Fool is always a sort of quixotic, whimsical son to him. 'Boy', 'my boy', 'my poor fool', 'my good boy'. A strange wayward riddling child, more natural to him than his real children are. Play the Fool as aged, as Jonathan Miller directed it for the BBC's complete Shakespeare, and the effect is doubly poignant: two fatherless, childless, child-like old men, each futilely protective of the other. But play it how you like, Lear's Fool – for generations of Shakespearean critics the very apotheosis of the Fool – is like a last gasp of folly, all the wildness gone, a thing of sorrow, and of sanctity, of falling cadences and ineffective paradox, his naughtiness reduced to quibbles on a stormy night. Whose ineffectiveness is built into his performance. Whose exasperations know their own futility. Whose heart breaks. Who passes out of the action like a dream . . .

IV

So what was the devil doing meanwhile?

Well, *he* was more or less where he always had been, wedded to the earth and mocking it. It wasn't he who had moved, it was the clown. And it wasn't as though the clown had taken clownery away with him, either. There it all still was, the old cursing and swearing, the love of being flesh, the flesh-flaying derision, the libidinousness, the disarranged laughter. The only thing was, it couldn't quite be called comedy any more. With the exception of Falstaff, all Shakespeare's great clowns turn up, unmotleyed, in his tragedies. Iago, Hamlet, Richard III, Cleopatra. And in *King Lear*, not the Fool, no not the Fool, but the ugly sisters and their bastard lover. Elsewhere, too, the savageries continue, but not as the patrimony of clowns. Middleton's De Flores, Webster's whited devils, Volpone, Mosca. 'I fear I shall begin to grow in love / With my dear self,' proclaims the latter, fearing in fact nothing, masterful in his pretend amazement at his own self, infatuated with his own blood and too smart to be infatuated with anything, all at the same time. 'I could skip / Out of my skin, now, like a subtle snake, / I am so limber.'

It is this tradition of jubilant self-esteem, vitality as sleek-fitting as a glove, not the wind-and-the-rain doldrums of the allowed or the natural fool, that gets passed on to Mr Punch, and thence to English pantomime. Writing within the shadow of the Funambules and the recollected influence of Deburau, Baudelaire paid tribute to the vitality of the first English pantomime he ever saw.

In the first place, Pierrot was not the personage of pallor and silent mystery . . . to whom the much-to-be-regretted Deburau had accustomed us. This English Pierrot came onto the stage like a hurricane, and tumbled like a buffoon. When he laughed, the whole theatre appeared to rock on its foundations . . . Fundamentally, his character was the same as that of the Pierrot with whom we are all familiar, its distinguishing marks being jauntiness and irresponsibility which find expression in gluttonous and rapacious whimsicalities . . . There was this difference, however, for where Deburau would have just moistened the tip of his finger and then licked it, the English actor plunged hands and feet into the dainties which he proposed to filch.

The whole action of this extraordinary piece was played on a sustained note of fury. The atmosphere was one of dizzy and bewildering exaggeration.

How this English Pierrot then went on to cheat the gallows, not as Punch does, by hanging the hangman, but by sheer force 'of the creature's irresistible thievish monomania', the actual decapitated trunk making off with its own head which it stuffed into its pocket as though it were 'a ham or a bottle of wine', is the business of a later chapter. The death-defiance of the comedian we must leave till last. But it must be plain that he has not inherited this force of thievish monomania – the will to stay alive at all costs – from the court-clown of Shakespearean comedy or the *faux-naïf* of Pauline exhortation.

V

Robustness will always have its enemies. Long after it would not have been practicable for an enthusiast like Fetherston to inveigh against light, lewd and lascivious dauncing, and the divell's part therein, plain middle-class respectability was making an assault on Mr Punch. The issue – family values. 'The present age,' declares the puppet-master whose 'very grave and solemn entertainment' Tom Jones pauses on his journey just long enough to watch and fail to be amused by, 'was not improved in any thing so much as in their puppet-shows; which, by throwing out Punch and his wife Joan, and such idle trumpery, were at last brought to a rational entertainment . . . I remember . . . when I first took to the business, there was a great deal of low stuff that did very well to make folks laugh; but was never calculated to improve the morals of young people.'

Tom Jones' response to this is all you would expect it to be. 'I would by no means degrade the ingenuity of your profession,' he answers; 'but I should have been glad to have seen my old acquaintance Master Punch, for all that; and so far from improving, I think, by leaving out him and his merry wife Joan, you have spoiled your puppet-show.'

I recall being involved in a similar disputation myself, in the grounds of the Actors' Church in Covent Garden, where a group concerned about the rising incidence of domestic violence had set up a little stall to protest against the amount of it in Mr Punch's domicile. The occasion was Mr Punch's birthday, solemnized annually in the church with a succession of Punch and Judy shows and a service in which Mr Punch, swozzle and all, reads the lesson and leads the hymn singing. A singularly ambiguous and even self-contradictory event, given the un-Christian ruthlessness with which Punch pursues his rights to all the conveniences of an earthly existence. But then again, accommodating in a peculiarly and admirably English way. The presence of the little anti-family-violence stall therefore struck me as both literal-minded and haranguing. The fact that the Actors' Church was hosting Punch was sufficient acknowledgement, wasn't it, that what you see on a stage is at a remove from real life, and illuminates it in ways that don't remotely invite civic disapprobation or emulation. I found myself saying something of that kind, anyway, to a young person on the stall who had every right to take his time answering given that I had cameras with me. It's my memory that he was not against Mr Punch *per se* (he might not have said *per se*), only the braining of his wife and child. So he differed from the puppet-master who engaged Tom Jones in conversation only thus far: he didn't care about the lowness, just the blood.

But it all comes back to how we understand the moral bargain that is struck when we agree to a dramatic structure – the ancient benefits of ritual blood-letting. It wasn't many years ago that comedians calling themselves 'alternative' would turn up on chat-show sofas fulminating against mother-in-law jokes. There must be no sexism, grated Ben Elton, the first of the anti-comedic red-brick ranters. Jim Davidson saw nothing wrong with sexism but thought there should be no jokes against the Royal Family. Both positions equally preposterous, though at least we know what the Royal Family *is*. Myself, I think you can't proceed in any business that bears on the whys and hows of communality, but least of all in the up-for-grabs business of comedy, with words that have made-their-minds-up in the way that 'sexism' has made-its-mind-up in your vocabulary. In *Playboys and Killjoys*, a slim volume based on lectures delivered in Oxford in the early eighties, the American critic Harry Levin falls foul of his subject in exactly the same manner. 'For any study of comedy in its historic development,' he argues, unexceptionally if not quite Englishly at first, 'Aristophanes is primordial.' After which it's downhill all the way. 'Not, by any means, that he is primitive, though his cloacal and homophobic snickers may seem adolescent to grown-up tastes.' Even allowing for what an old boy has to say to a young audience to prove that he's still on the planet, 'homophobic' is not permissible. By begging the question, it misrepresents Aristophanes in particular, the workings of sexual insult in general, and comedy altogether.

Whoever is averse to meat should not go shopping in a butcher's.

In fact, this latest insistence on correct attitudes to sexual and social matters in jokes is nothing but Tom Jones' puppet-master's politics regurgitated; his substitution of 'rational entertainment' for 'low stuff', of 'improvement' for 'idle trumpery', in a different guise. In both cases the improver offers to be superior to the laughter ('the snicker') which the earlier incorrect attitudes provoked. And in both cases the motive force is mistrust of the disordering power of laughter itself.

'Funnier!' exclaims Mrs Jarley, owner of JARLEY'S WAX-WORK, when Little Nell wonders whether wax-works are funnier than Mr Punch. 'It isn't funny at all . . . It's calm and classical. No low beatings and knockings about, no jokings and squeakings like your precious Punches, but always the same, with a constantly unchanging air of coldness and gentility . . .'

Salting the devil's tail. Some do it openly, others in the dark. While pretending to be a friend of laughter, parodying the pious man who is startled by 'an innocent jest' as though by 'a blasphemy', who looks on 'a sudden fit of laughter as a breach of his baptismal vow', Addison was all the while looking to lure it into a safe place, to coop it up where he could keep an eye on it. Somewhere within that circle of pleasures which rational religion kept narrow all right, but still 'wide enough for her votaries to expatiate in'. Laughter was to be coaxed back into Christianity, where it could be kept Christian. A contract of sorts. The deal being, that

the true spirit of religion cheers, as well as composes, the soul; it banishes indeed all levity of behaviour, all vicious and dissolute mirth; but in the exchange fills the mind with a perpetual serenity, uninterrupted cheerfulness, and an habitual inclination to please others as well as to be pleased in itself.

If perpetual serenity reminds us of the idiot we failed to buy in Rome, that is because we can only imagine an idiot experiencing it. Addison does not mean to be recommending the equanimity of the simpleton to the readers of the *Spectator*, but cheerfulness in this account – 'uninterrupted cheerfulness' at that, uninterrupted especially by 'vicious and dissolute mirth' – feels like St Paul's foolery for Christ put into social action. It is the spiritual condition of the 'natural' let loose in society, a pattern for neighbourly behaviour, definitely of this world, but modelled on the unworldly fool's state of mind.

Decidedly unmystical though Addison's cheerfulness is, it keeps the idea of the 'natural', the holy fool, warm for mysticism until mysticism comes along. From serenity to 'seeing' may not be a short journey but it is a direct one. A hundred years after Addison, Lamb is celebrating All Fools' Day, and the direction in which foolery is progressing remains the same – not there yet, but steadily etherwards. Or do I mean etherialwards?

I have never made an acquaintance . . . that lasted: or a friendship, that answered; with any that had not some tincture of the absurd in their characters. I venerate an honest obliquity of understanding. The more laughable blunders a man shall commit in your company, the more tests he giveth you, that he will not betray or overreach you. I love the safety, which a palpable hallucination warrants; the security which a word out of season ratifies. And take my word for this, reader, and say a fool told it you, if you please, that he who hath not a dram of folly in his mixture, hath pounds of much worse in his composition.

The emphasis is less on spiritual imperturbability; for Lamb's was a far more troubled nature than Addison's. But the refusal of the antic and the untoward is comparable; as is the affectation of simplicity; as is the air of going out on a limb for jesting – though the limb is no more than a foot off the ground; as is the conviction of the benignity which controlled mirth (all viciousness banished; only some *tincture* of the absurd) bestows on social commerce. Gradually, though – 'and what are commonly the world's received fools,' he goes on to wonder, 'but such whereof the world is not worthy?' – Lamb slips the tether. Other worlds are in sight. Other worlds that *are* worthy of the fool.

Meanwhile, chugging along the rails kept clear for him by these Laodiceans of laughter, the long line of lukewarm apologist for offence-less comedy and toothless clowns, is a figure we last saw passing out of the action of *King Lear* like a dream . . .

The truth-telling fool. Sometimes buffeted for his pains, sometimes not; but always puckishly wan, not quite all there as the world judges all thereness, always listening to voices speaking to him from some other place. The voices of angels. Or fish. The visionary fool, no more of this planet than the Killer Klowns from Outer Space, but here on a mission to open our hearts to the divine, not slurp them out through coloured straws. And to do whatever else visionaries are meant to do. Give witness?

Having fallen overboard the *Pequod* in its mad pursuit of Moby Dick, and then, by the merest chance, having been picked up again, Melville's little negro shipboy, Pip, 'from that hour . . . went about the deck an idiot;' – a long pause, a mighty hiatus in comprehension, signalled by that single semi-colon; – 'such at least they said he was'.

Said he was. Such at least *they* said he was. They being, taking the long view, well . . . us. As for the truth of the matter –

The sea had jeeringly kept his finite body up, but drowned the infinite of his soul. Not drowned entirely, though. Rather carried down alive to wondrous depths, where strange shapes of the unwarped primal world glided to and fro before his passive eyes; and the miser-merman, Wisdom, revealed his hoarded heaps; and among the joyous, heartless, ever-juvenile eternities, Pip saw the multitudinous, God-omnipresent, coral insects, that out of the firmament of waters heaved the colossal orbs. He saw God's foot upon the treadle of the loom, and spoke it;

(thus, fool talk = God's foot talk)

and therefore his shipmates called him mad. So man's insanity is heaven's sense; and wandering from all mortal reason, man comes at last to that celestial thought, which, to reason is absurd and frantic; and weal or woe, feels then uncompromised, indifferent as his God.

And so, thanks to time's whirligig, the idiot that was worth 200,000 sesterces on a good market-day at Rome, and would have earned his keep making faces at a rich man's table, has now washed up on a distant shore to find himself a hero of romanticism, proof that God the underwater weaver weaves unreason. A vicious circle indeed, since it was something like the presence of the divine in the absence of the idiot's wits – something having to be there to explain what wasn't – that was cause of his being valued at 200,000 sesterces in the first place.

VI

A circular return, too, it might seem, taking account of the shipboy's new spiritual state – 'uncompromised, indifferent' – to the insouciance of Hippoclides. All one to Hippoclides. And all one to the sea-maddened Pip. But there's indifference and indifference. Hippoclides may have danced goodbye to a wife and a dynasty, caring nothing for the loss of either, but his was a peculiarly worldly act of unworldliness; a celebration of his fleshly self, not an abnegation of it; an extroverted performance, liberating and comic precisely because it was communal, for everybody, except his father-in-law elect, to enjoy. The little shipboy's indifference is of an entirely different order. It is the indifference of self-sufficient interiority. And is to the blitheness of Hippoclides what pornography is to obscenity. What a darkened room is to an open stage.

Any history of comedy and the fool, like any history of metaphysics and gods, is bound to be, above all, a history of our relentless progress indoors. Onwards and inwards we march, bringing everything in out of the storm, swapping our weather deities for household ones, steadily closing our eyes to the external world, drowning ourselves if we must, until the only voices we hear and trust are those we hear inside our own heads.

Even the satyr, embodiment of all that is unconfined and wayward about us, our very own animal self run wild, has had to suffer the ignominy of being brought within four walls. The Romans started it, making curlicues of his horns, shortening his tail, abbreviating his penis, luring him out of his savage haunts into pastures where he might the more sculpturally graze – a faun. Half-way to being a garden ornament. Soon Jerome would have him whimpering to be baptized. And if he found a second lease of life as the wild man of medieval and Renaissance northern European imaginings – now feared, now idealized, in proportion as the age felt the benefits or the burdens of ordered society – he wasn't left free to nibble trees for long. The religious wanted him for a Christian. The respectable for a family-man. Soon there was a satyress to legitimize his appetites. Then satyr-babies. By the beginning of the sixteenth century Dürer and Altdorfer had made a caring husband and a doting father of him. A householder and burgher. *Heimatlich*. But quite useless now as a clown or acrobat. However else the new satyr would entertain his loved ones as the woodland shadows gathered in the evening, and the chill from their cottage chimneys winnowed their pelts, he would not be making them laugh by balancing a goblet on the tip of his dick.

After the confinement, the sadness. In Mallarmé's hands, and then Debussy's, the satyr who had never known stillness or repose, who had never once come upon a phallic challenge he was not equal to, falls prey at last to the melancholy longueurs of the faun's *Après-Midi* – an afternoon of introspection, *vaine, sonore et monotone*.

French fatigue, as we have seen Baudelaire attest, spread through the pantomime as well. To this day our idea of the *commedia* remains definitively coloured – French, not Italian – by Watteau's poeticization of the principal characters. His saintly Pierrots. His famously donkey-witted but innocent Gilles, elevated, in Anita Brookner's words, to 'quasi-tragic status'. Some reversal: the comic figure become tragic by virtue of the degree to which he is perceived as comic. She goes on: '[Watteau's] Gilles belongs to a more contemplative setting than that of knockabout farce. The impassivity of the face suggests that the ability to survive continuous if light-hearted cruelty is not only potentially tragic but at all times heroic.' Something quintessentially Brooknerish, perhaps, in that '*at all times*'. No let up in the quiet struggle between the gross world and the trembling but obdurate individual soul. But then the Goncourt brothers, writing a century earlier, had already gone much further than that in their appropriation of Watteau's wistfulness. 'Yes, at the heart of W.'s work, a slow vague harmony informs the laughing words; a musical and imperceptibly contagious sadness steals through his *fêtes galantes*.' Wistfulness and morbidity – 'You come to see [Watteau's] works as the game and distraction of a suffering mind, like the toys of a sick child, now dead.'

A description of unbalance and debility that would very nearly do to characterize nineteenth-century French pantomime in general. We have already made allusion to Deburau's Pierrot, both as he came to be reinterpreted by Jean-Louis Barrault in *Les Enfants du Paradis*, and as

Albrecht Dürer

Jacques Callot

Baudelaire originally described him, a 'personage of moonlit pallor and silent mystery, supple and mute as a snake, tall and rigid as a gallows, that mechanical man operated by strange springs'. Deburau's successor at the Funambules, Paul Legrand, took Pierrot still further in the direction of the static white-face of ceramic kitsch. Reviewing Legrand's performance in *Pierrot Dandin* in 1854, Gautier could barely keep pace with his own sentiment:

But where he is superb is in the scene in which, returning home with a dress, a little shawl, and an apple turnover he has bought for his wife, he finds the conjugal nest deserted and, in place of the unfaithful spouse, a letter revealing that Madame Pierrot has left with the seducer Léandre. It must indeed be difficult to make people cry when one is wearing a little black skullcap, when one is sporting a face plastered with flour and a ridiculous costume. Well! Paul Legrand expresses his sadness in such a naïve, true, touching, and profoundly heartfelt manner that the puppet disappears, leaving only the man . . .

Only the man, the individual man . . . One can't put all the blame on the French. Goldoni, too, a hundred years before, had been ridding the *commedia* of the mask in order to render more truthfully the individual man. Which invariably means the inner man. (Onwards and inwards.) Which, in

Jacques Callot

turn, invariably means the sentimental man. Much loved by the sentimental spectator, as Gautier goes on to marvel:

In the stage-boxes, the giddiest madcaps forgot to run their tongues over their
green barley-sugar sticks and smothered their sobs behind their lace
handkerchiefs.

Deburau may have substituted silence and supple mime for the robust
antics of earlier Pierrots, but he seems never to have been the unambiguous domestic tear-jerker Legrand became. It's not impossible that that
shadow of the gibbet which Baudelaire causes to fall across Deburau's
pallor is a reference to the virulence of Deburau's own character. On one
occasion when he was out taking the Paris air with his wife, a street boy
taunted him; I don't know that there is any record of what the boy said or
did, only that Deburau raised his stick in retaliation and struck the boy
dead, returning to the Funambules a few hours later where he performed,
as usual, and without any perceptible diminution of authority or variation
of style, the part of Pierrot. But even if Baudelaire did not have his eye on
this homicidal episode, there was sinister material enough in Deburau's
interpretation of Pierrot to justify the imputation of frigid malignity. In *Le
Marrrchand d'habits*, famously re-enacted in *Les Enfants du Paradis*, his

Pierrot murders an old clothes-seller in order to steal the finery necessary for him to enter the glittering world of a wealthy woman with whom he has fallen desperately in love. On Pierrot's wedding day (the stolen clothes having done the trick) the ghost of the old man rises from the cellar and asks for a dance. Not with the bride but with the bridegroom. The sword with which Pierrot killed him still protrudes from his belly. And as they dance what Gautier calls 'this hellish waltz', that very same sword retributively 'enters Pierrot's chest, piercing him through and through'.

In other pantomimes, according to his biographer, Tristan Rémy, Deburau's 'face and gestures . . . showed, each time a scene gave him occasion, that he was reckoning with a world that he made laugh at will, he whom the world had never made laugh . . . When he powdered his face his nature, in fact, took the upper hand. He stood then at the measure of his life – bitter, vindictive, and unhappy.'

Couple Legrand's lonely vulnerability – only the outcast palpitating man now visible behind the mask, behind the powder, behind the puppet – with Deburau's moonstruck and macabre vindictiveness, and you can see why the French romantics were regular attendants at the Funambules: they came to see, and in turn to fashion in Pierrot, a mirror image of themselves. In the white unsmiling face of Pierrot, the fevered pallor of the consumptive poet. Gautier's investment in Pierrot as 'the ancient slave, the modern proletarian, the pariah, the passive and disinherited being' is all of a piece with his sympathy for the febrile interpretations of Deburau and Legrand. Yet even Baudelaire, who 'regretted' Deburau and was so ardent in his praise for the more robust English pantomime, was not able to resist sounding the pathos in the resemblance between rejected entertainer and neglected artist. In this case, the entertainer being that most pitiful of all cast-offs, the old acrobat, 'stooped, obsolete, decrepit, a human ruin'.

He was not laughing, the wretched man. He was not crying, he was not dancing, he was not gesturing, he was not shouting; he was singing no song, neither jolly nor woeful, he was not beseeching. He was mute and motionless. He had given up, he had abdicated. His destiny was done . . .

Turning around, obsessed by that vision, I tried to analyse my sudden sorrow, and I told myself: I have just seen the image of the old writer who has survived the generation whose brilliant entertainer he was; of the old poet without friends, without family, without children, debased by his wretchedness and the public's ingratitude, and whose booth the forgetful world no longer wants to enter.

The other side of romantic self-pity is always the satanic snarl. He whom the world rejects, rejects the world. Fallen, the Prince of Light puts out the light. World, I banish *thee*. And the other side of Pierrot pitiful – the white face who could make the giddiest madcaps sob into their silk handkerchiefs – is Pierrot pitiless: Pierrot who can kill a baby and put a doll in its place, Pierrot who decapitates a rival for the hand of Columbine, Pierrot who tickles the soles of his wife's feet until she dies of laughter. Pierrot whose 'sinister buffoonery ... ferociously comic in its excess' inspired Huysmans and Hennique to come up with a little *fin-de-siècle* pantomimic necrophiliac nasty of their own – a madly murderous, newly widowed Pierrot who develops a passion for a wigmaker's manikin, assaults whoever gets in his way, kills the manikin when she remains unresponsive to his overtures, sets fire to the evidence, burns the whole world, and finally breaks into a dressmaker's shop from which he steals a dummy and makes off with her in high excitement, hell-bent on rape.

So devils are back, you might say, though without the diablerie. The laughter they are generating now – if you can quite call it laughter at all – is of the bitter, inward, highly strung, solitary sort. The laughter of a sick and sorry satanism. Performing no communal function, it is a condition of desolation and damnation; splenetic and vengeful; cruel – and therefore of morose satisfaction – only to itself. Tracing its lineage back to that quintessential Romantic hero, the 'bored and pallid' Melmoth the Wanderer, Baudelaire at once anatomizes and gives vent to it – laughter which is 'the perpetual explosion' of 'anger' and 'agony'. For Melmoth is

a walking contradiction. He has turned his back upon the fundamental conditions of life. His organs can no longer endure the pressure of his thoughts. That is why his laughter freezes and torments the bowels of mercy and of love. It is a laughter that never sleeps, but is like a malady endlessly pursuing its destined way . . .

Laughter not a cure for malady but the malady itself.

VII

As far as any history of laughter is concerned, this dandified diabolism of fraught nerves and freeze-dried mirth – *the toys of a sick child, now dead* – has had its day. Stripped of its vindictiveness, though, it has bequeathed us the debilitated fool; not just the holy and the innocent fool, but the fool unsteady on his pins. Another way of putting it is that by interiorizing laughter to the degree it did, the *fin-de-siècle* French pantomime helped change our sense of the topography of mirth; made it soulful; subjected the antics of the body to the promptings of the heart.

'Fool is hurt,' sighs the simple Gelsomina in Fellini's *La Strada*. Fool is more than hurt. Fool – Il Matto, the Madman – played angelically by Richard Basehart – is dead. In a rage that is part jealousy, part pique, and part nothing but idle rancour, Gelsomina's strongman lover has killed him. Nobody has ever been kinder to Gelsomina than Il Matto. He has played with her, fool to fool, and touched her with his wings. Not real wings; circus props. But then again . . . 'Fool is dead,' she says, forgetting to bang the drum as the strongman prepares to burst the chains fastened about his chest. He touches his forehead – she is not well, 'up here'. But whether she is well up there or not, the hurt *she* is referring to is in another place. 'Fool is hurt.' The Fool Il Matto and the fool her feelings. Destitute now of the vigour of actual fooling, the fool has become synonymous with the affections, devotion, simplicity, love, the human heart itself. The wounded human heart, at that.

'The Fool,' wrote the visionary artist, Cecil Collins, painter of angels, 'rejects modern society, because the Fool represents that profound fertile innocence, down from which we have fallen, into the dirt and filth of mechanical existence.' A rejection made from a position of weakness – dirt and filth, I banish *thee* – if ever there was one. Collins' fools are enervated, introspective beings, glowing with an inner conviction of worldlessness (and guilty therefore of the sin of self-righteousness), whose bodies look incapable of any function, and whose spirits are never raised by mirth. They are fools only in the sense that they are unfitted for a corporeal existence. A gouache *Feast of Fools*, painted in 1979, shows three simpletons in dunces' hats sitting vacantly at an all but empty board. There is a wan defiance about the work. Everything that we associate with the Feast of Fools – its cacophony, its bawdiness, its blasphemy, its violent reversals of hierarchy – is wilfully excluded. But so is everything we associate with simply sitting down to dinner. All pleasure in food is gone. All pleasure in drink. All pleasure in conviviality. Truly the fool is now an invalid entire. Maimed in the heart. Blind to everything except his inner vision. And lacking a stomach.

Debilitated himself, the angelic fool exquisitely gauges the debility of others. 'A golden rule of clowning,' writes the ordained Anglican priest-clown, Roly Bains, in *A Call to Christian Clowning*, 'is that the clown, like love, must always allow the other person space.' The aptly named school for circus arts, Circus Space, does not go quite so far as to equate clowning and love, but in a leaflet advertising its course on clowning – 'The Art of Play with Commotion' – it is similarly attuned to modern nervous systems, and similarly concerned to respect distance.

Playfulness is the starting point for the clown. A performance that is based on playfulness builds a direct relationship with the audience in which there is no room for dishonesty. Tricks – yes. Mischief – yes. Lying – no.

Some commotion!
La commedia è finita.
Except that it isn't. 'Nothing is ever lost,' Jung assures us in his famous essay 'On the Psychology of the Trickster-Figure', 'not even the blood pact with the devil.'
Exactly in proportion as we proliferate social boundaries beyond which we dare not step, careful of class, cautious of race, fearful of sex, each one of us a nurse to the other's crippled spirit, so does our hunger for the contrary consolations of comedy grow. The extraordinary burgeoning of comedy is now a regular item of Sunday paper tittle-tattle: the phenomenon of comedians enjoying rock-star status, the mushrooming of the provincial and suburban comedy club, the fierce competition around comedy scheduling on television, comedy conferences, comedy festivals, the emergence of the specialized comedy reviewer. And there can be no question that the comedy that is burgeoning the most – whether it's a sit-com like 'Roseanne' or a game-show such as 'Have I Got News For You', or anti-chat-shows such as 'Mrs Merton' or 'Clive Anderson Talks Back' – is unkind, cruel, confrontational, and not at all a respecter of distances and feelings. It would seem that the more we school ourselves, against our natures, in the arts of putting up with people's differences, the more we require the ancient relief of seeing them pitilessly put down. Call it a hunger for community. For as every primitive and unchristianized clown and demon teaches us, it is not by respecting space that we celebrate communality, but by invading it.

CHAPTER EIGHT

Everyman in His Humour

.

I

Monday morning on the U-Bahn. Oktoberfest. Munich. Six plump she-revellers of the night before, each wearing a William Tell hat, roll to the motion of the U-train. Their feathers are broken. As is their suspension.

They haven't slept, though they may well have been slept on. They are drinking cans of Diet Lilt. Something about their hands is suggestive of the tearing of human flesh. Their fingers have been where Maenads' fingers go. Their fingernails are black and bloody, like the fingernails of Bacchantes. I fold the English newspaper I have brought with me from Heathrow and fill my lungs with thin Teutonic U-Bahn air. Normally, I come to Munich as a pilgrim, for Dachau. This time I am here as a celebrant, for the Dionysia.

The origins of the Oktoberfest, at least as currently explained in guide-books and brochures, are disappointingly unmythological. In 1810, Crown Prince Ludwig marries Princess Thérèse von Sachsen-Hildburghausen, the huge wedding party – to which the whole of Munich is invited – proving so successful that it is repeated every year thereafter on the same field, now named Theresienwiese in honour of the bride. Believe that, believe that a beer-driven bacchanal held at harvest time dates back no further than 1810 and honours not the old gods and goddesses of grain but a mortal royal couple, however much in love, and you may as well believe that the Di in Dionysia signifies the debt we revellers owe to the (once) bulimic English Princess of that name.

My instincts are right. In the first beer tent I enter an ox is being roasted. The spit may be modern, turned by electricity, the ox skewered with stainless-steel plates and wing-nuts, but the crowds who stand and stare at it, regardless of the cries of waitresses whose path they're blocking, the trance they're in, their submission to the mesmeric revolutions of the flaming beast, all testify to the ancient agrarian emotions which have been loosed. We are watching dinner cooking, but we are also at a sacrifice. That's a deity being barbecued.

A waitress – a temple virgin, rather – drives a dozen tankards into my back. Another flattens my hair with a tray of chicken halves. It's only when I relinquish my place in the ritual slaughter reminiscence queue that I see what a vast hall I am in, how many thousands of people are jammed into it, how much beer and meat is going down. A gasp escapes me. It could be the noise stress makes when it has found somewhere to run to; it could be the music of the isolated soul, acknowledging its membership of the tribal horde.

The impulse to communality runs deep in Munich. Even when the city is not officially Oktoberfeasting it takes itself to drinking palaces each the size of all the pubs in Glasgow put together, or to beer gardens in which you could lose Richmond Park. And having given itself all this room, it then compresses itself, packing twenty on to tables built for ten. Maybe this is what eating and drinking should be, an activity so dense and cramped and fleshly that you do not have the space to distinguish your own individuality and cannot tell whether it's your stomach or your neighbour's you are feeding. It's certainly what a carnival should be – the abandonment of the self you've been stuck with for the rest of the year, submission to the exhilaration of numbers . . .

Careful. The end of the twentieth century is not a good time to be extolling the virtues of crowds. We know about crowds, we children of the last years of the second millennium. We're up to here with crowds. Crowds become mobs become rallies become armies become you-know-what. And you don't have to be much of a sociologist or historian to detect affinities between Munich's togetherness-carousing-houses and the architecture of its long broad inflexible marching streets. A beer hall putsch one day, a mass meeting of brown shirts in Marienplatz the next.

But a military parade and a carnival are not the same, however important the exhilaration of numbers is to each. Parades move strictly in straight lines; carnivals spill over. What's intriguing and even, I think, affecting about Munich is that it's a place of straight lines trying hard to be a place of bendy ones. Architecturally it hasn't made it. Leo Von

Klenze, the mastermind of Königsplatz, hoped to bring something Greek and poetical to the capital of Bavaria, but the Propylaeum and the Glypothek and the Staatliche Antikensammlungen stare out at one another, dumb, disciplined and Doric, across a draughty square. Von Klenze didn't intend Königsplatz to be a parade ground for Nazis; his paintings of Pisa and La Spezia and the Acropolis, all hanging in the Neue Pinakothek, show an imagination that would be romantic if only it could learn how not to be rigid. Aesthetics teach the same lesson as history: whoever is inflexible by nature but would leap to uninhibitedness by an act of the mind, exposes himself to credulousness. Nazism answers to the cravings of the rational mind for ecstasy.

Carnival, though – community giving itself up, however temporarily, to play – is pre-rational, is determined by the seasons not the will, admits necessities of irreverence and disorder that no marching culture can accommodate with comfort.

Now that I've got my exhilaration, I'm stuck with it anyway. I'm excited by what I see and by what I hear. Put enough people in a room this big and they raise a din that makes you think of graves opening on Judgement Day. A mist seems to settle over them as well, a shimmer or a mirage that may just be an effect of body-heat but which is dangerously suggestive of a communal halo. Then again, it may simply be cigarette and cigar smoke, for no dainty rules of consideration for the sensitivities of others obtain here: you smoke, you sing, you elbow, you embrace. There are boxes around the hall, where you can reserve family or company tables and withdraw a little from the central mass, but these, giving you greater access to the waists of waitresses, are doubly riotous, being simultaneously private and public parties. There is no place to escape to from the inconsiderateness and incorrectness of it all, because no one wants to escape.

I cling to mirth – the private stuff: irony, ridicule, all that – to stop myself from swooning and to still the marching anthems and Zarathustrian Odes to Joy which jostle in my brain. I count the number of ways there are of wearing lace if you're a Bavarian barmaid – lace at the bosom, lace at the elbows, lace at the knees, lace at the ankles. Agrarian again: flesh and handicrafts. And I count the number of ways there are of wearing a bib and codpiece if you're a Bavarian man and going in for being Bavarianly *männlich*. I hadn't, I confess, expected quite so much national costume. There is enough chamois leather in this single beer tent to clean all the windows in Christendom.

Another thing I count – charm bracelets. And not on the women but the men. And not where either sex would normally wear a charm bracelet, either. For these charm bracelets are strung low around the waist as an adornment to the *Lederhosen*. They draw attention the groin area, in other words. They jiggle and jingle there. And among the charms sported thus suggestively by these husbands and fathers, out with their respectable families, their wives and daughters and mothers-in-law, are phalluses, little silver twists of cornucopian chilli, identical to the bottom half of my Pompeian fixer's key-ring. Think of that. Upright Catholic family-men, patriotically attired citizens of this most rigidly rectangular city, getting about with little penises hanging from their belts.

Because something tells me that the beer tents will hot up still more when the sun goes down, I spend what's left of the afternoon exploring the fairground. The Oktoberfest boasts rides which are so dangerous that only Germans have the courage to try them. I marvel, reluctantly, at the technology, the marriage of space-age design to Bavarian kitsch, the ingenuity which is put at the service of turning people upside down. One ride specializes in long-term inversion, concealing the bodies of the victims from the spectators below, so that all you can see as they hang there is the hair of their heads, fluttering like the fringes of an over-upholstered pelmet. Another spins a couple of dozen people at a time, locking them in rows and securing them with identical purple harnesses which make them look as though they're in uniform, a Mormon Tabernacle Choir undergoing torture.

Topsy-turviness – the great cliché of carnival historiography. The world upside down. Not a modern critical text to be found that doesn't carnivalize its subject and turn something the wrong way up. Perhaps because that's all that's left of Marxist criticism – Bakhtin on carnival, and the infinite multiplicity of inversions. When it comes to carnival at least, you can still talk about 'the people', let alone conjure revolution (the real, not the figurative thing) – the substitution, if only by licence and for a day or two, of one class by another. But whether they've read Bakhtin or not, the people of Munich certainly want nothing so much as to topsy-turvy themselves. They cannot hang upside down often enough or long enough. Every machine capable of reversing you has a queue outside it. And there are dozens of these machines. Round and round's had it. Up and down is over. Ditto side to side. It's a holiday for your body – head where your feet normally are, feet where your head is – or it's nothing.

I don't count, but it feels as though these rides are more attractive to

women. Not for me to wonder why. The men are more comfortable –
that's to say more comfortable being uncomfortable – around the trial-of-
strength machines. You raise a hammer, hit a peg, and send a chuck racing
towards a bell. Because you're German your chuck reaches the bell more
often than it doesn't. If you ring it three times out of three you get a key-
ring. Otherwise you get a plastic rose. '*Scheiss Blume!*' I hear one giant
boy complain, as he tosses it in a bin.

The phrase is destined to stay with me for the rest of the fest. Shit
flower! It catches something about opposites necessary to the understanding of ritual.

It is getting dark. The bands are beginning to strike up in the beer tents.
In one, a group called Municum – not for me to wonder why – alternates
local yodelling songs with '*If I Said You had a Beautiful Body Would You Hold
it Against Me?*' People are dancing on the tables. The communal halo is
fugged with smoke, the way the shafts of light that give you moving
pictures used to be in cinemas in the good old days when we were all
happy to go to hell together. Municum proposes the toast – *Ein Prosit! Ein
Prosit!* – and the tankards clash like cymbals.

If you pace yourself right you can go from beer tent to beer tent and
get nothing but *Ein Prosits!* Skip the rest of it and go only for the human
connection, glass to glass, spume to spume. But I wind up in the Pschorr-
Brausrosl tent which is less tacky than the Löwenbrau and less touristical
than the Hofbrauhaus, and which I like because it is Italianately garlanded
in blues and golds, and because the band is spirited, and because the
atmosphere manages to be at once wild and familial, somehow more
universal because it's more local. And it's here, although I am only an
observer, although I cannot possibly break in and join them, and although
I am hemmed in with cautions and provisos, that I finally go at the knees,
surrender, suddenly and once and for all *get* it, while they're singing
Funiculi Funicula in German, get what this festive thing all means, get how
grand, how necessitous and how tragic it is to celebrate a communal
vitality. For they are vital, these four or five thousand swaying celebrants,
they are fearsome in their pleasures, singing out of the fulness of life, not
with the maudlin we-shall-overcome feebleness of English kids support-
ing a losing side again, not with the frustrated irascibility of any under-
privileged football crowd, locked into another match that's not worth
watching. They leap the tables, they dance in the passageways, they applaud the band, they applaud the life in themselves, and that life is so
strong now – and strength of life always brings to mind its opposite, its

necessary opposite – that I'm brought to tears, have trouble with my breathing, fear for my appearance and my dignity.

On my way out, a drunk falls violently into me. He's out of tune with the spirit of the tent. Out of kilter. That's what's wrong with getting *so* drunk – you fall out, you break rank, you lapse into individuality, you are delivered back into the misery of your isolated self, your Cecil Collins fool self, your Deburau's Pierrot self. But this is the way it's going to end, before the night is out, for many of us. So perhaps there is only a brief moment between the isolation of complete sobriety and the isolation of complete drunkenness when we can enjoy communality, and perhaps that is why we seek it so urgently, and why it is ultimately so upsetting in its short hour of achievement.

Here is why multitudes upset us. Now we see ourselves happy and united, now we don't.

I mean, though, to give it another go. It is raining on the Theresienwiese when I return to it the next day. More pressure on the beer tents. I decide to skip the scene of the previous night's epiphany and plunge into one of the tents where you don't have to be a member of an extended Bavarian family or wear a chain of penises round your waist, but can stand up to your ears in strangers' tankards. This turns out to be a mistake, but now I'm in there's no getting out. I am walled about by English kids who cannot deal with that moment in the progress of an intoxication when you fall in love with everybody. They confuse the feeling and think it's hate.

A New Zealand girl takes advantage of an *Ein Prosit!* to smash my glass and stumble into conversation with me. She has erupting spots and the red cheeks which come from having prematurely made yourself the companion of men who drink. She tells me she's been nannying in Turkey but is now in Brixton. Great place, great people. But she begs my pardon, she hates the English hierarchy. They're fuckwits. 'Fuckwots.'

On the other side of me an English boy is drawing a map of Britain with pretzel crumbs so as to show a couple of Romanians where he lives. 'Manchester . . . London . . . Devon!'

They look bemused. 'Devon?'

He doesn't know what to say. Then he thinks of something. 'Exeter City . . . yeah!'

The New Zealand girl is telling me her blood type and her blood lines. She's got German, Scottish, Irish, French and Jewish in her.

I suppose she must be very proud.

'Proud? What of?'

'Well . . . all that blood.'

She moves in close again, but she is no longer steady. 'The French . . .' she says. 'You know what the French are?'

I should, but I don't. I shake my head.

She waves two fingers under my nose, a V-sign of unusual flexuousness. If she had water on her fingers I would consider myself blessed.

'Fuckwots!' she confides.

An Australian boy, who must have seen the V-sign, falls instantaneously in love with her. He wins her with bird calls: crows, kookaburras, cassowaries. '*Caw*,' he says, '*kraaark, ehrgnk.*'

Relieved not to have me to talk to, she edges her erupting skin towards him. '*Quock, quock*,' she answers.

A space forms around me. Suddenly I can use my elbows, don't have to drink my beer back-handed. Only when the space does not refill, only when I see that even the girls in the Chunder Club T-shirts have backed off, do I look down and discover that someone has thrown up on my shoes. *Scheiss Blume*!

I leave the tent, the party, the fairground, the Dionysia, and pack for home. My own fault. I should have quit when I was ahead. I should have quit when I was crying.

II

The three-cornered argument mankind is always having with itself on the question of holidays, festivities, public mirth:

On the side of release, pure and simple, Mr Sleary, proprietor of the circus horse-riding in *Hard Times* – 'People mutht be amuthed. They can't be alwayth a-learnin', nor yet they can't be alwayth a-working, they ain't made for it. You *mutht* have uth, thquire. Do the withe thing, and the kind thing too, and make the betht of uth . . .'

On the side of restraint – 'your divell doeth alwayes leade the daunce' . . . well, take your pick: Sabbatarians, agelasts, puritans, utilitarians, Festival of Lighters, upholders of the family, anti-rockers like myself.

And somewhere subtly in between, fully conversant with the Sleary doctrine but fearing that the powerful have appropriated it and always will appropriate it for their own ends, Flote, the clown-monk protagonist of Peter Barnes' *Red Noses*, reneguing on his own philosophy of good times:

'In the days of pestilence we could be funny but now we're back to normal, life is too serious to be funny ... I tried to lift Creation from bondage with mirth. Wrong. Our humour was a way of evading truth, avoiding responsibility. Our mirth was used to divert attention whilst the strong ones slunk back to their thrones and palaces ...'

Little by little, position three invariably ends up siding with position two; better the people should be denied amusement altogether than that someone not of the people should profit by it.

And position two does enjoy this advantage over position one: it recognizes the powers which festivity looses. In the end, amuthement for those who can't alwayth be a-working, does sound more like intelligent provision on the part of a benignly despotic management than the main-spring of a Saturnalia or a carnival. Accounts differ as to the wildness of the Roman Saturnalia. Did it begin moderately and grow to be excessive later? Did the Romans ever really know how to let their hair down? 'Let's Greek-it-up like mad,' proposes one of Plautus' slaves, implying that you had to be Athenian to be able to enjoy yourself. And Shakespeare's reading told him that the Romans were as stiff as boards, needed the spectacle of Alexandrian indulgence, including Cleopatra in her love-sick barge, before they could unbend sufficiently even to fall over. Whereas Seneca, who at least was there (though in that supposed more intemperate later evolution of the Saturnalia), wrote of it as a time 'when excess has a general dispensation ... when all the world's engrossed in sensual pleasure ... when every one else is either in liquor or throwing it up'. But however one judges it, the Saturnalia seems to have answered to deeper and more various impulses than Sleary's horse-riding and the principle of innothent amuthement therein.

For a start, it was – to borrow a terrible term from self-help groups (my point being that you only need a self-help group when you don't have a Saturnalia) – *pro-active*. You didn't sit and watch. You didn't buy a ticket. And you didn't go back to work again at six the following morning. By the end of the first century AD the Saturnalia was a five-day affair. Schools closed, business activity stopped, and the usual routines and hierarchies of Roman life were halted and reversed. No way of avoiding it, we're back to the World Turned Upside Down. Laws lost their force. Masters served their slaves and otherwise exchanged roles. And a mock-king, selected by a roll of the dice, presided over the *bouleversement*. Flote would doubtless argue that this was merely a five-day diversion, a temporary avoidance of responsibility, after which the strong ones were able to slink back to their thrones and palaces. And we don't need to have been there ourselves to know that that's exactly what would have happened. On the last day of every summer term at the grammar school I attended the teachers served us our dinners, then dressed up in unbecoming costumes and put on a revue or panto for us. Come the first day of autumn term they were back in their black gowns, slippering us for the slightest departure from legality, expecting us to clear away their plates, not a pinpoint of memory of looser times showing in their lowered eyes. But that there *had been* a looser time – albeit only for a day or an hour – made a difference to our sense of the possible, shook out all our restrictive patterns of deference and fear, introduced us, in a way that we would never forget, to latitudes we would otherwise have known nothing of, unless dreamt up in sullen schemes of retribution.

'When the ceremony was over,' reflects Black Elk, holy man of the Oglala Sioux, 'everybody felt a great deal better, for it had been a day of fun. They were better able now to see the greenness of the world, the wideness of the sacred day, the colours of the earth, and to set these in their minds.' And what was this ceremony that had such power to reconcile people to the material world they lived in, its vividness, its expanse, and to fix this renewed perception of it in their minds? A Heyoka ceremony. In which, in Black Elk's words, 'everything is backwards'. Yep, the World Turned Upside Down again. For Heyoka clowns are contraries, sacred fools divided down the middle, the right sides of their heads shaved, the hair on their left sides left hanging, in their hands bows too long and too crooked to be serviceable. Whatever is normally done, the Heyokas do otherwise. They shiver when it's hot, and remove their clothes when it's freezing. They pronounce their words backwards. They dive into dried-up river beds and pretend to swim. 'One would then plunge into the shallow puddle head first, getting his face in the mud and fighting the water wildly as though he were drowning. Then the other one would plunge in to save his comrade, and there would be more funny antics in the water to make the people laugh.'

The laughter which contrariness releases is too common, is mobilized by too many cultures, for us to pass over it lightly. The Sioux laugh and feel better. Every delegate at the Saratoga Springs Humor Convention could, with quick recourse to the jogging model, have explained that. *Laughter accelerates breathing, raises blood pressure, increases pulse rates, improves ventilation. It can increase adrenalin which in turn may activate the release of endorphins and enkephalins . . .* But Black Elk is a mystic, not a physiologist. His

20. *Pulcinella on a Swing* by Giovanni
Domenico Tiepolo (*Ca' Rezzonico, Venice*)

21. *Pulcinella and the Acrobats*
by Giovanni Domenico
Tiepolo (*Ca' Rezzonico, Venice*)

*Gurning then and now –
the art of showing the body's
lewd construction in the face*

22. *Christ Crowned with Thorns* by
Lucas Cranach

23. Gurning competitor

24. Mental torment looking like a dream of panto. *The Temptation of St Anthony* by Bernardino Paranzano (*Galleria Doria Pamphili, Rome*)

25. Detail from *The Struggle between Carnival and Lent* by Pieter Breughel the Elder (*Akademie der Bildenden Künste*)

30. The comedian as victim of comedy. *Gilles* by Antoine Watteau (*Musée du Louvre, Paris*)

31. Cecil Collins's Fool – 'symbol of the lost ones of this world'. *The Sleeping Fool* by Cecil Collins (*Tate Gallery, London*)

32. The great Russian clown Slava Polunin dying protractedly, like the human spirit on Nevsky Prospekt

33. Death and the Fool – old friends with much to talk about. 'The Pantomime' by Thomas Rowlandson from *The English Dance of Death*, London, 1815

34. The comedian Bernard Manning, honouring his origins

claim for the curative properties of laughter extends beyond the body's production of narcotic happy-dust to a revivification of the senses, a re-confirmation of belief, to nothing less than a restoration of glory to the earth. And it is not simply the physical activity of laughter that has achieved this, but the occasion of the laughter – the putting of the world into reverse. Things are not now to the Sioux what they were *before* they'd laughed at clowns drowning where there is no water to drown in, because they have played briefly with the obstinacy of things, entertained the fancy of a universe governed by entirely different laws, and have returned from this comic dream of an alternative existence – backwards, contrary, upside down – with a shadow earth superimposed upon the actual one, ringing it like a penumbra, or a halo.

If tragedy briefly puts out the sun, emptying the sky at afternoon, comedy proliferates our own planet, like Caliban filling the whole isle with his likeness. In the deranging, disarranging communal laughter occasioned by the contrary clown – a laughter which has something of the devil's unmeaning *and* the angel's reconciliation in it – we see what isn't possible and thereby make it possible. Like Black Elk, we become visionaries, putting life into a spin and remaking it.

Hence the persistence of ceremonies and holidays in which violation of all the usual religious and civic taboos, and disregard for all the prevailing hierarchies, is not just an associated pleasure but the commanding justification. The medieval church wasn't uniformly comfortable with such periodic evaginations of reverence as the Feast of Fools, but it went on allowing them. Accounts dating from as early as the ninth century tell of organized sacrilegious roistering in Constantinople – the mime and buffoon, Theophilus, acting the part of the patriarch, riding the streets on a white ass, burlesquing the sacred mysteries with vinegar and mustard, while the real patriarch had to suffer the insults and mockery of the revellers. In the west the disorder had hardened into ritual by about the twelfth century. Specific dates in the church calendar were set aside for it: in some countries, Holy Innocents' Day, in others, Circumcision or Epiphany or St Stephen's Day, now our Boxing Day. If we put all the information we have about the Feast of Fools together, remembering that the luridness may in some measure be due to the denunciatory nature of many of the descriptions (actual participants being far too busy having a good time to take notes), the following composite picture assembles itself:

At the singing of the Magnificat at Vespers, the line 'He hath put down the mighty from their seat and hath exalted the humble and meek' acts as a signal: now is the time for some lowly cleric to be elected Bishop, Prelate, Abbot, Archbishop, Cardinal, or even Pope of Fools. The *baculus*, or staff of office of the precentor of a cathedral, might be handed over here. This transference of authority sets the full reversal into motion. Clerics in masks or blackened faces, perhaps wreathed with flowers, yahoo around the church. During the mass, perhaps dressed as dancers or women or with their clothes turned inside out, they dance in the choir, riot, sing dissonant and scurrilous songs, and instead of blessing the congregation, curse them. Others eat sausages on the high altar, play cards or dice in front of the celebrant. Alcohol flows. Celebrants light torches in preference to candles and cense with black puddings and sausages, or with incense-kettles in which old clothes or the soles of shoes are burnt; some resort to burning dung ... and to throwing it. Given which infectious sequence of inversions you can hardly expect even the most modest to keep their clothes on. 'They run and leap through the church,' observed Eustace de Mesnil of the Paris School of Theology, in 1445, 'without a blush at their own shame.' Mass is recited at top voice and punctuated with brays and howls. Especially at Circumcision, when the delivery of, Mary and the Christchild into Egypt is supposed to be celebrated, an ass is led into the church, sometimes ridden by a man facing backwards, while a 'Prose of the Ass' is chanted:

> Orientis partibus
> Adventavit Assinus,
> Pulcher et fortissimus,
> Sarcinis aptissimus

ending with the braying refrain starting: 'Hez, Sire Asnes ...' The Introit, Kyrie, Gloria and Credo all end with braying; the rubrics of the 'office' directing that, instead of saying '*Ite missa Est*', the celebrant 'shall bray three times and people shall respond in the similar fashion'. After high mass a procession takes off from the church through the town. People sit up on carts full of dung and pelt the crowd with it. Clergy 'drive about the town and its theatres' (this is Eustace again) 'in shabby traps and carts; and rouse the laughter of their fellows and the bystanders in infamous performances, with indecent gestures and verses scurrilous and unchaste'.

That carnival obeyed – and in some places still vestigially obeys – these same anti-rules, is evident from every description and assessment of it, whether anthropological, religious, political, or plain prurient. In the Feast

Attributed to Albrecht Dürer

of Fools it was the clergy who wore masks or blacked their faces or dressed as women; in a Heyoka ceremony it was the clowns who played the fool; in carnival the masquerade is universal. No distinction between watchers and watched is recognized; everyone participates. And the logic of reversal is universal too: what is holy is profaned, what is elevated is lowered, where there has been respect and awe there is now travesty, where modesty, lewdness. The crowned are uncrowned; fools become kings; those who have nothing are suddenly the recipient of plenty; staple foods are left to rot, while luxuries are given away or sold for a pittance. Nothing stays still; nothing is as it was; every possible fantasy of social revolution and retroversion is realized ... until the renunciations and restitutions of Lent.

After the Sioux have laughed at the Heyokas' backwards pantomime, the earth is refreshed for them, a brief tremble of time and season has been effected. But European carnival is in a sense already out of time, at the point of transition from the solar time of the normal calendar to the lunar time by which Lent and Easter are calculated. The French historian, Emmanuel Le Roy Ladurie, talks about 'the delicate, central nerve impulse of Carnival which sent time flowing backwards and rendered everything topsy-turvy': from 2 February, Candlemas, when the bear traditionally came out of hibernation to test the sun for the end of winter, until Mardi Gras, the Tuesday after the new moon preceding Ash Wednesday, things are in volatile transition. In this seasonal and interplanetary sense, carnival is a nudge at what is already in flux of its own accord. This fly-spring delicacy of carnival's timing is presumably what Bakhtin has in mind when he speaks of 'the pathos of change and renewal'. For time asserts its forward flow at last, to the hour of reconstitution, king to kingship, poor man to poverty.

If Frazer is right in his guess that the Roman Saturnalia contained the memory, and even sometimes sought to continue the practice, of putting the mock-king to death once the fires of revelry had burnt down, and that such is the ritual explanation for the universal recourse to an annual festival of inversion with its temporary Lords of Misrule and comic monarchs – 'the long array of similar figures, ludicrous yet tragic, who in other ages and in other lands, wearing mock crowns and wrapped in sceptred palls, have played their little pranks for a few brief hours or days, then passed before their time to a violent death' – then the pathos of change which in one sense is no change, and of renewal bought at the highest human price, is of the essence of carnival.

Es brennt manch baum inn hellen glut
der nit wolt tragen gütte frucht.

Vom lon der Weißheit.

Zür rechten handt findt man die kron/
Zür lincken handt die kappen stohn/
Den selben weg all Narren gohn/
Vnnd finden entlich bösen lohn.

NACH grosser kunst stellt mancher dor
Wie er bald werdt meyster / Doctor /
Vnd man ihn halt / der welt ein liecht/
der kan doch das betrachten nicht/
Wie er die rechte kunst erler/
Mitt der er zü dem himel ker/
Vnnd das all weißheit dieser welt
Ist gegen Gott ein dorheit gzelt.
Vil meynen sein auff rechtem weg
die doch verirten an dem stäg/
Der zü dem waren leben fürt/
wol dem / der auff dem weg nit jrrt

l   Wann

This is the progress, from affliction to revelry to consolation to the reassumption of power, that Peter Barnes' *Red Noses* re-enacts. 'Please the populace with passing shows,' orders Pope Clement VI, who had offered to be a friend of Flote's revelries when they were expedient, and is friendly to them still, so long as they aim at nothing beyond sedation; 'relax them with culinary delights – meringues, jellies and whipped cream. But give them no meat to chew on.' The carnival is over. It's Lent.

So has there been no change at all? Has it all been illusion and passing show? That 'breath of an imaginary freedom' which Charles Lamb reckoned was just the ticket for getting men to return contentedly to their 'shackles'?

After an almighty struggle with the agelastic half of his nature – 'How happy I shall be when Tuesday is over and the fools are silenced. Nothing is more boring than to watch others go mad when one has not caught the infection oneself' – Goethe braces himself for a more considered assessment of the Roman Carnival of 1788. The temper of his lucubrations is, as you would expect, late-Shakespearean melancholic. When it comes to revels and their ending, what other model but Prospero is there? He does not, though, permit the pageant to dissolve into baseless insubstantiality . . .

And so the exuberant revelry has passed like a dream or a fairy tale . . .

In the course of all these follies our attention is drawn to the most important stages of human life: a vulgar Pulcinella recalls to us the pleasures of love to which we owe our existence; a Baubo profanes in a public place the mysteries of birth and motherhood, and the many lighted candles remind us of the ultimate ceremony . . .

If I may continue to speak more seriously than my subject may seem to warrant, let me remark that the most lively and exquisite delights are, like horses racing past, the experience of an instant only, which leaves scarcely a trace on our soul; that liberty and equality can be enjoyed only in the intoxication of madness, and desire reaches its highest pitch of excitement only in the presence of danger.

. . . knowing that life, taken as a whole, is like the Roman Carnival, unpredictable, unsatisfactory and problematic, I hope that this carefree crowd of maskers will make [my readers] remember how valuable is every moment of joy, however fleeting and trivial it may seem to be.

Yes, the hour has been and gone. But then transience, too, has been carnival's subject. The old sad paradox: in the giddy hilarity that accompanies our attempts to make the sun stand still, we do not stop to notice that we have only made it run faster forwards yet.

No one but the preacher, though, would argue that it has therefore all been vanity. If the most lively and exquisite delights are experiences of the instant only, how can it be vain to have grasped them for that instant?

III

But what about the other case that is often made against the essential conservatism of carnivals and Saturnalia and the like? Nothing to do with planets or the powerful, this is a charge levelled at the cautiousness which huddles in communality itself. For all its escapades at the edges of our reverence and decency, is it not the first ambition of festive laughter (and maybe of all laughter) to corral the wayward back into conformity? To draw the eccentric back into the circle? 'Laughter is, above all, a corrective thing,' Bergson is saddened to have to concede at last. 'By laughter, society avenges itself for the liberties taken with it . . . Always rather humiliating for the one against whom it is directed, laughter is really and truly a kind of social "ragging".'

And even the term 'ragging' is a touch innocuous for some of the carnivalesque ways – ducking and pillorying, tarring and feathering – in which groups have always loved to mobilize laughter against errant individuals. Take charivari – the cacophonous processional burlesque, got up to mock or chide a married couple. At the level of pre-nuptial knock-about rudery, reminiscent of the rural Fescenni, a charivari may have been possessed of a certain rough charm, provided that you were not the bride or groom, that it was not your wedding that was obscenely interrupted, not your house that was looted, and not your bodies that were thrown into the river and then carted along – lest you should value sacred love above carnal – to the local brothel. But once a charivari had actual marital 'irregularities' in its sight, once it meant to have its say in the matter of one partner's shrewishness or unchastity, of a wife being older than her husband, of a spouse being imported from foreign parts, of a widow remarrying above her station, or a widower remarrying beneath his, to say nothing of the decency of either remarrying at all, then it could become a violent and fearful thing. The crowd would gather, setting up a terrible racket beating pots, pans and kettles, clashing ironmongery, banging kettledrums, shouting insults. The victim or victims might be made to ride backwards on an ass and paraded through the streets, if not in their own persons then in cruel effigy. And as to what might follow . . . Well, as the infamous skimmington-ride in *The Mayor of Casterbridge* plays it out, a paroxysm of epilepsy ending in death itself was not out of the question:

Lucetta's eyes were straight upon the spectacle of the uncanny revel, now advancing rapidly. The numerous lights around the two effigies threw them up into lurid distinctness; it was impossible to mistake the pair for other than the intended victims.

'Come in, come in,' implored Elizabeth; 'and let me shut the window.'

'She's me – she's me – even to the parasol – my green parasol!' cried Lucetta with a wild laugh as she stepped in. She stood motionless for one second – then fell heavily to the floor.

Almost at the instant of her fall the rude music of the skimmington ceased. The roars of sarcastic laughter went off in ripples, and the tramping died out like the rustle of a spent wind.

To the man who knows how to look at it from a proper perspective, Thomas Hardy once remarked, life offers not a single occasion for mirth. So you would hardly expect him to see the best in a skimmington-ride. All that vitality and unruliness; the skills of the effigy-maker; the extemporized orchestra; the community coming together to express opprobrium

William Hogarth

and enact solidarity; the seizure of authority; the joys of burlesque . . .
No?

No. Whoever has lived for any period of time in a rural community
knows how many skimmington-rides are forever on the point of being
nearly got up; what ugliness of mind and erroneousness of judgement are
the mainsprings; what mild or imaginary offences are the cause. It is less
than twenty years since a man in a red wig was kettledrummed out of a
Cornish village of my acquaintance, the local women coming out of their
old-world whitewashed cottages to bang their pots and pans in his ears as
he left. His offence? Being from other parts and waving his willy on the
cliffs.

It would be convenient if we could exclude charivaris and skimmingtons from our definition of the carnivalesque. Such censorious antics
hardly topsy-turvy the prevailing structures of power, anyway; they don't
loosen screws, they tighten them; they don't replace the high with the low;
nor do they burlesque the unknowing cuckold or the ageing lecher in
anything of that true carnival spirit – enacting the very licentiousness they
mock – such as we find, say, in the Pulcinella 'cuckold' Goethe observed
in Rome, fitted out with movable horns,

so that he could protrude and retract them like a snail. He would stop under the
window of some newly married couple, and show just the tip of one horn, then
. . . shoot out both horns to their full length. Little bells were attached to their
tips, which twinkled merrily whenever he did this.

Compare trial by skimmington, furthermore, with the Court of Fools
held in the German market town of Grosselfingen every Shrovetide,
where the townsfolk are called to answer for their misdemeanours of the
previous year by black-robed *Butzen* (or bogeymen) and white-clad whip-
crackers, redeeming their mock-punishments (which might have been a
ducking 500 years ago) by payment of token sums of money. Or compare
it with the castigation ritual played out by the Bambara clowns of Mali, in
West Africa, after harvesting is over. First a hymn to the sun. Then a re-
enactment of the main tasks of the agricultural year, danced by men in
dog's-head masks. Then, as the music of the flute and drum quickens, the
year's malefactions of every villager or visitor to the village are brought
alive in jokes, riddling references and lewd allusions, to which the *sogi* – the
fools of the festival – mime grotesquely, suiting the dance to the
infraction.

Why do little Gaoussou's ears look so like those of Tjemoko from Douga? Because Fanta [his mother] collected them there. Tjemoko stuck them in her belly so that she wouldn't lose them.

Why is Mamdou so fat? Well, if you eat someone else's chickens, fear drives away digestion.

[On a homosexual merchant who visited the village] Diop from Djenne came and ate up the cowrie shells [money]; when he went on his way, the shells wanted to stay here, so they hid themselves in the backsides of the *n'domo* [a ritual grouping of young men in the village].

After which, at nightfall, the ceremony ends with a great feast around the fire – beer and wine, appeasement for those castigated. And no personal ignominy of the sort that parted Lucetta from her senses.

Now customs such as these, although they too elevate the fool – the community's representative of its conjoined mirth – to the role of judge and executioner, are carnivalesque in the sense we most like to think of carnival. Ribald *and* democratic; with restoration not expulsion as the aim; the expression of the community's generosity, not its narrowness. Its confident repletion, not its touchy exclusivity.

If the community must employ its laughter to rid itself of something, we would prefer, we carnivalesque types, that it laughed only to rid itself of evil. Isn't that what laughter has always been for? To shoo away the demons. As witness, in Bruce Kapferer's vivid accounts in his *A Celebration of Demons*, the Sinhalese exorcism ceremony. Not exactly carnival, but utilizing many of carnival's tricks, the Sinhalese exorcism rites empower comedy to dispossess the patient, jeering the diabolic out of his system, literally laughing him back into health.

Demons are shown to be out of place in the everyday world of human beings. Moreover, they are demonstrated as victims of their own illusion of dominance and control, tricked by their own artifice. The demons as tricksters are revealed as subject to the trick and, therefore, subordinate to those whom they sought to delude . . . The comic discourse involves the drummer's ensnaring the demons in clever wit and repartee and making them the butt of the comedy. The drummer plays tricks on the demons . . . and caught on a rise, the demons reveal themselves as pathetic figures, and they howl and cry at the insults and obscenities hurled at them.

The comedy whittles away at the demons' supernatural agency, at their claims to invulnerability and infinity, reduces them to recognizable and manageable proportions, makes clowns of them just as the Feast of Fools for a day made jesters of the clerisy. They shit and piss in holy places, they fart and eat excrement, they stumble and confuse their words, they get stomach pains, they whinge and wheedle; and this '*play* destroys any sense of awe which may have surrounded the demonic in the earlier episodes'. In debasing their 'symbolic articles of divine and human power', they 'divest themselves of power' and at the end of each act they 'shuffle absurdly away'.

The patient himself, having been first submerged in an isolated subjective trance-like state, under the dominion of the demonic, is thus drawn, through laughter, into a dimension of shared awareness – understanding 'appropriateness and inappropriateness according to common-sense everyday knowledge'.

During the morning watch the exorcists and the audience exhort the patient to laugh, or show other signs of amusement in other words, symbolically to express that he or she shares in their attitude towards the world. The laughter of human beings, particularly laughter as shared enjoyment in a community of others, is culturally viewed by the Sinhalese, in the context of exorcisms, as the laughter of order and of a full attention to and awareness of life in the everyday world. It indicates a stability of mind and body.

But there's a catch in 'laughter as shared enjoyment in the community of others'. The skimmity-catch. The-what-happens-if-you-just-happen-to-be-the-one-who's-been-skimmitied-catch. Because you never know who or what the community is going to decide is the evil in its midst. The Sinhalese have this worked out nicely. There's Mahasona and his subsidiary demons. If you're possessed, they're the regulation cast of characters who have possessed you. But where the mythology has worn thin and the culture grown jumpy, evil may come in the form of a henpecked younger husband, or an adulterous French woman, or an old maid – getting a spinster to pull a plough through the streets was someone's idea of carnival fun – or a Jew. In Lithuania, where Communism kept the lid on such activities for half a century, they have just rediscovered an old Shrovetide festival. They put on witch and devil masks, wear articles of clothing inside out, gather in the squares, play music on rural instruments, and dance. So far so carnivalesque. They also call it Going Jew. Check out the devil masks and you see why. Bent noses, cringing features, the age-old caricature of international banker's avidity. The World Turned Upside Down. Think of inversions of the usual, things back-to-front, things the wrong way round, and your mind may just turn – if you come from Lithuania – to Jews. More than a few carnivals over the years have given Jews a hard time. To this day, if you wander off the beaten track a little, you may still find a carnival or two that can't make it to a climax until there's been a ritual burning of Judas. Ethnically speaking, there's nothing here to get too het up about. Jews are just a manner of speaking. The inverts could just as easily be gypsies or Huguenots. My point is only that when a community celebrates its shared pleasure in the ordinary, *something* perceived as extraordinary has to get it in the neck.

'In this sense' – Bergson driving towards his pessimistic conclusion – 'laughter cannot be absolutely just. Nor should it be kind-hearted either. Its function is to intimidate by humiliating.'

Well, I've been arguing all along for the invigoration inherent in that unkindness and injustice; the necessity of a periodic release from our compulsion to overdo the sympathy and suffering; the divinity we take upon ourselves when we allow comedy to lower us on to the sacrificial stone. How can I backtrack on it all now, just because, here and there, I see a gross travesty of my antecedent self fuelling the fun?

Erhard Schön

An episode I left out of my account of my last night at the Munich Beer Festival:

I am in the Spaten tent, lumpy-throated again, indulging the existential throb of my isolation from the chamois hordes swaying on their benches. I walk round and round the inner perimeter of the tent, looking on, looking over, listening in. The exquisite pain of someone else's party. Suddenly, I am aware that a blonde German woman, preposterously provocative in a crackling leather suit, sheathed in it (ox hide, for sure) from the spikes of her black boots to her thonged and studded throat, is heading towards me, not accidentally – because I just happen to be between her and where she's going – but actually making *for* me. That she has strong teeth and a firm jaw, that her corn-husk hair is cut severely and yet falls lightly upon her shoulders, that those shoulders are powerful although overall she is sleek, that her eyes are ironical, cruel but willing to play, goes without saying. This woman has figured in the pornographic fantasies of men of my persuasion since the destruction of the Second Temple brought us wandering to this land of the northern gods. What also goes without saying is that she will ask me what she does ask me, her voice jagged, the sharp blades of her teeth cutting off the ends of her words, 'What's a nice Jewish boy doing in a place like this?'

Inger. Wouldn't it be! She is on an errand, this Inger. Herself, she doesn't know me from Abraham. But her boyfriend does. He knows me from the photographs on the dustjackets of my novels. And he has sent her over. Partly to invite me in; partly to show me what he's got. Because he too is English. And because he too is here, in the land of the northern gods, on account of the destruction of the Second Temple. That's him there, Inger shows me, right there in the throbbing smoking heart of it all, the one in the bib and braces, in the green embroidered Bavarian waistcoat, swaying with the mass, singing *Ein Prosit!*, smashing his foaming beer glass into whoever will smash his. Teuton to Teuton. Far deeper into the pornographic fantasy than I or anyone I know has ever had the nerve to venture. For all I can discern to the contrary he is in *Lederhosen*, and wears a jiggling charm chain of pagan phalluses around his middle. When he sees that I have been Ingered and have located him he waves to me, smiles, and then holds – no, covers – his nose. A Jewish joke shared by Jewish men the world over. A joke you make everywhere except Israel. 'What are you doing here with that thing showing? Hide it, man, hide it!' The freemasonry of the Jew. And seeing him cupping his nose, I cup mine.

Is this why we don't make good dancers, tumblers, jugglers, trapeze artists? Because we always have to keep one hand free to cover our nose? Is this why we can never relax into Dionysiac delirium?

No question, though, Inger: your boy is making a better job of it than I am.

Five months later I am at something more like a carnival proper. Venice. Still restrained by some critics' standards, not Rio, not Trinidad, and not anciently uninterrupted (as though anything is, as though anything ever has been), but a carnival for all that. I have been here since yesterday afternoon, scarfed against the cold, uncostumed, unmasked, doing the perimeter trick again, but determined to be abandoned once the opportunity for abandon comes my way. Last night I watched the transvestites having fun in the window of Florian's. Spectacular gowns and hairy cleavages. Outside, looking in, the tourists clicked their cameras. Not what carnival should be, everyone engaged, no distinction between players and spectators. But the camera has probably put paid to such ideas of integration for ever; the camera has sanctified spectatorship. And they are clicking everywhere in San Marco today. This seems to be what the masqueraders first and foremost parade through the great square for: to be admired, stopped and snapped. They disport themselves, *dispose* themselves, for the cameras. They fall into little tableaux, posed eighteenth-century costume pieces, exactly the requisite height and width for the average Japanese viewfinder. Apart from the transvestism, you can forget reversals and the World Turned Upside Down. The only inversion is the negative image seized by the camera. And that will ultimately be looked at the Right Way Round.

I roam the square, disappointed. People posing is not what I have come to the Venice Carnival to experience. One man, dressed as a monk, performs an antic Hippoclidean dance, lifting his cassock and waving a two-foot-long red knitted woollen prick. The sausage we used to make by pulling wool through bobbins in primary school. The older Catholic ladies in their Italian furs roar with laughter. Some of them deliberately put themselves in the way of it, dance with it, cover their faces, then allow it to take them from behind. At last – the obscenity, the irreverence, the liberty of carnival. But that's the only liberty I find. For the rest, it's all powdered wigs and buckled shoes. I go on wandering, waiting, primed for something. Then, just as I am thinking it is time to give it away for the morning, go and have lunch or a lie down, a couple of clowns – a woman dressed as

Harlequin and a young man got up as Charlie Chaplin – leap at me out of the crowd. A hand reaches for my nose. And a voice, a woman's voice, would-be comical, would-be carnivalesque, says, 'Let's see if this is real.'

My own hand moves like lightning. Catches the clown by the wrist before she can grab me. 'Don't you dare!' I hear myself saying. I am astonished by the asperity I hear in my voice. The clown falls back, as though she has been struck. As I release her wrist I see white indentations made by my fingers, the marks of my fingerprints; sufficient evidence, if she took her wrist to a police station, to have me arrested. That was how hard I held her in the fraction of a second she was in my grip.

She looks quickly at her companion in his silly moustache and chalky face paint, her mouth quivers, then they both disappear back into the crowd.

Dismayed by what I have done, utterly shaken by my primness and my violence, I fall into an outside seat at Florian's and order coffee. Make that two coffees. And a grappa. Make that two grappas.

Was I acting Jewishly? Remembering in the blood some ancient carnival offence committed in a square in Lithuania 400 years ago? No. I don't think so. I was just instinctively protecting my person – it could have been any part of my person – against violation. Insisting on my right to distance. The fence between individual and individual which no stranger has any right to climb. You want to play? You want to touch me? Ask, first. Put it in writing.

Writing, writing . . . How vitalizing carnival looks on the printed page. How irresistible in all its communal contortions. How touchingly its delicate central nerve impulse sends time flowing backwards, restores our perception of the wideness of the sacred day.

. . . On the page.

. . . As long as you never have to leave the house.

CHAPTER NINE

The Revenge of the Spider

But what happens when you *don't* leave the house . . .

The effects of the Black Death had not yet subsided, and the graves of millions

of its victims were scarcely closed, when a strange delusion arose in Germany, which took possession of the minds of men, and, in spite of the divinity of our nature, hurried away body and soul into the magic circle of hellish superstition. It was a convulsion which in the most extraordinary manner infuriated the human frame, and excited the astonishment of contemporaries for more than two centuries, since which time it has never reappeared . . .

(Pause, if you wish to interject that the twentieth century has seen the reappearance of *every* hellish convulsion and superstition, to consider that the author of this work on the dancing mania of the Middle Ages is a Professor J. F. C. Hecker, writing over a hundred years ago in the cloudless innocence of a department of historical pathology in a German university.)

It was called the dance of St John or St Vitus, on account of the Bacchantic leaps by which it was characterized, and which gave to those affected, whilst performing their wild dance, and screaming and foaming with fury, all the appearance of persons possessed.

The mention of Bacchantic leaps should be enough to remind us that

Europe has a long history of convulsive dancing. The Corybantes, followers of Cybele, the Great Mother, dancing ecstatically in her train, literally 'out of their minds', as she wandered torch-lit over the verdant mountains. Euripides' Bacchae, worshippers of Dionysus, maenads running like fauns with fire on their heads, their throats upturned, their hair flying, dancing 'where the darkness is deepest, where no man is'.

That these dances were necessary for their participants – both as expressions of religious feeling and from the point of view of mental hygiene (if you don't consider that to be splitting hairs) – the polytheistic ancients did not doubt. Plato argued for the treatment of some morbid conditions of the soul by music and rocking movements, and Euripides sent mad those who would not party, then had them torn limb from limb. But monotheism was bound to be more jealous and fearful of the dance. Dancing entails the worship of other, stranger gods. It draws attention to the genitals as well, encouraging the dancers first to thoughts, then to acts of libidinousness. (In seventeenth-century England, rises in bastardy rates were traced directly to the maypole. As a consequence of his assault on maygames, plays, pastorals and all the other glorious freedoms of merry England – a concept, like every fantasy of a golden age, forever in the process of being questioned and remade – the Puritan William Prynne, whose *Histrio-Mastix* was a fighting answer to the monarchical-popular *Book of Sports*, suffered the indignity of having his ears cropped in public. A nicely gauged punishment – not a million miles from the madding of Malvolio – to close the musical senses of one who feared what music could effect.) Horror of the dance, whether it's Moses rounding on the celebrants of the golden calf or American high-school principals forbidding the playing of Bill Haley records, is invariably driven by the belief that dancing is an encouragement, in the words of the Elizabethan naysayer, Phillip Stubbes, to 'filthy groping and unclean handling', and is thus 'an introduction to whoredom, a preparative to wantonnesse, a provocative to uncleanness, and an introit to all kinds of lewdness'. The truth of which, even leaving Baubo and Hippoclides, to say nothing of the maypole, out of it, will be admitted by anyone who has ever shaken a leg in mixed company.

However good a job Christianity made initially of damping down Dionysiac frenzy, substituting Satan for the old pagan gods of joy and wine, it couldn't damp it down for good. Throughout the Middle Ages outbreaks of maddened dancing and leaping were reported all over Europe. In 1278 the Moselle Bridge at Utrecht collapsed under the weight of 200 uncontrolled half-naked dancers, spilling them into the water and drowning every one. In 1374 'assemblages of women were seen at Aix-la-Chapelle . . . dancing, regardless of bystanders, for hours together, in wild delirium, until at length they fell to the ground and groaned as if in the agonies of death'. Cologne and Strasburg soon succumbed to the same plague, hundreds of foaming, garlanded women giving themselves up in the name of St John or St Vitus to 'a ruinous disorder' in which all their most secret desires, and all their most morbid sensitivities, were activated. The sexual consequences of unmarried women 'raving about in consecrated and unconsecrated places' need not detain us. Ruin, in that sense, is ruin the world over. Far more intriguing, from the point of view of the pathology of it all, was the form their morbidities took. To some the sight of a weeping person became abominable. Others could not abide red clothes. Others again took so violently against the fashion of wearing pointed shoes that they issued an ordinance, 'that no one should make any but square-toed shoes'. As for what relieved them of their 'spasmodic ravings': where the music and the dancing were not themselves sufficient, they offered up their afflicted parts to 'thumping and trampling', obtaining relief from 'kicks and blows which they found numbers of persons ready' – no doubt only too ready – 'to administer'.

That such pathological fastidiousness, alternating with abandonment of all self-regard, might also be accompanied by involuntary laughter, will not be problematic to anyone who has come thus far in this book. Paracelsus, studying the phenomenon of the St Vitus dancers in the sixteenth century, and noting their propensity to laughter, put it down to an internal pruriency to which some individuals are susceptible, their blood being the more easily set in commotion by an alteration of the vital spirits. Foremost among his cures for this malady was a course of fasting and solitary confinement, taking up an uncomfortable position to sit in, and making a wax image of oneself, heaping upon it all the blasphemies and sins one could think of, and then burning it. That the dancers were already taking care of their own health, that the exertion and the music and the laughter were themselves as much the cure as the disease, was a self-evident truth that played no part in his alchemy.

Of all these outbreaks of Christianized Maenadism – let the doctors call it whatever else they will – the most extraordinary occurred in Italy, specifically in the Apulian city of Taranto and its environs, an area rich in ancient associations and obviously possessed of a long memory. When the Roman fleet entered the port of Tarentum in 282 BC, none of the

citizens could be bothered to resist, so engrossed were they in the comedy they had gathered to laugh at in the city's theatre. Apulia was the region given over to the phylax play, you will remember, that species of comedy that was too low for classicists to bear to associate with the refined Aristophanean comedies of Athens. It was here that those red-figure vases, so painful to the sensibilities of Pickard-Cambridge – *go look at them elsewhere, if you must* – were manufactured in all their 'full hideousness and disgustingness'. But along with their taste for vulgar comedy, for vase-painting, for luxury, for a reluctance to forgo the arts of peace for war, the Tarentines and their immediate neighbours were also known to be worshippers of Dionysus, god of the ecstatic dance. Here, too, maidens had run like fauns, their throats upturned. So you could say that this dry and stony instep of Italy was already well-prepared ground for the dancing mania which reached it from northern Europe in the fourteenth century and hung on for several hundred years.

Taranto was well-prepared ground in other ways too. It had spiders. In particular the tarantula, the local hairy spider whose supposedly poisonous bite gave an extra justification to the frenzy, and added a musical twist to the tale – from Taranto the tarantula, and from the tarantula the tarantella. A strange rumour, common throughout Europe in the Middle Ages, held that whoever was bitten by a venomous spider 'ejected by the bowels and kidneys, and even by vomiting, substances resembling a spider's web'. For some people, among whom I count myself, just to see a spider, let alone be bitten by one and proceed to vomit spiders' webs, is to fall into a morbidity, a despair of all divine intention, a disbelief in anything but malignancy, for which not even maniacal dancing is a cure. But as hysterics of a more moderate order, the Tarantati, as the afflicted were called, believed that music and dancing helped to distribute the poison of the tarantula over the whole body and then expel it through the skin. Though 'if there remained the slightest vestige of it in the vessels, this became a permanent germ of the disorder, so that the dancing fits again be excited ad infinitum by music'.

Here, then, was a call to a sort of perpetual musical motion. You were bitten, you were poisoned (you weren't, in fact, but you thought you were, which is as good), you danced, you dropped, you danced again, and if you did not dance enough your system insisted that you dance some more. For it was only this dance, the tarantella, which could alleviate the paroxysms of alternating melancholy and lewdness into which, as the spider's victims, you had fallen. 'At the first sound of the musical instrument,' a learned eye-witness reported,

although the sick lie, as it were, in an apoplectick fit, they begin by degrees to move their hands and feet, till at last they get up and fall to dancing with wonderful vigour, at first for three or four hours; then they are put to bed, refreshed from their sweating for a short time, and repeat the exercise with the same vehemence, perceiving no weariness or weakness from it, but professing to grow nimbler and stronger the more they dance . . .

At this sport they usually spend 12 hours a day, and it continues three or four days, by which time they are generally freed from all their symptoms, which do nevertheless attack 'em again about the same time next year . . .

As musick is the common cure, so they who are bitten are pleas'd, some with one sort of it, some with another; one is rais'd with a pipe, another with a timbrel; one with a harp, another with a fiddle . . .

While the *Tarantati*, or affected, are dancing, they lose in a manner the full use of all their senses; like so many drunkards, do many ridiculous and foolish tricks; talk and act obscenely and rudely, take great pleasure in playing with vine leaves, with naked swords, red cloths, and the like . . .

Where the St Vitus dancers of northern Europe had expressed a horror of all things red, the Tarantati suffered 'a rage for colour', embracing objects in their favourite colours, 'like lovers ... weeping over them, kissing them, caressing them'. They found relief from their ravings by having the soles of their feet beaten. They loved to swing, or to hang upside down like the spider that had bitten them. They yearned for a sight of the sea. They became so sensitive to the music of the dance that they could not endure a false note; even the most musically uneducated among them acquiring a refined sense of hearing, as though their affliction had somehow 'initiated them into the profoundest secrets' of harmony.

Profound secrets of another sort were at work here too. For the tarantula, whether it bit or it didn't, is a venomless spider. Not on account of anything it injected did the Tarantati weep over red ribbons, hang upside down, and dance obscenely. Toxicologically speaking, the tarantula was entirely innocent of every indecorousness committed in its name.

Hecker, the German professor of pathology to whose work any student of dancing madness is indebted, insists that we get a sighting on the phenomenon from an arachnid-free perspective.

Let us here pause to consider the kind of life which the women in Italy led. Lonely, and deprived by cruel custom of social intercourse, the fairest of all enjoyments, they dragged on a miserable existence. Cheerfulness and an inclination to sensual pleasures passed into compulsory idleness, and, in many, into black despondency. Their imaginations became disordered – a pallid countenance and oppressed respiration bore testimony to their profound sufferings. How could they do otherwise, sunk as they were in such extreme misery, than seize the occasion to burst forth from their prisons and alleviate their miseries by taking part in the delights of music?

So instead of thinking of Tarantism and other associated outbreaks of uncontrolled Bacchante dancing as manifestations of morbidity, sicknesses of the soul or body, we would do better to see them as the human organism looking after its own soundness, knowing what's best for itself, attending to its welfare through pleasure. A significant part of that pleasure being the gratification to be found in society itself, the contriving of a communal cure for a communal malady. For no matter how privately this or that individual spider-bitten dancer succumbed to her affliction, the tendency was always to public display and consolation. Let her be apoplexed in the seclusion of her own bedroom, she still needed musicians and singers to raise her from her torpor. Little by little, one contemporary observer remarked, 'by means of intoxicating music, a kind of demoniacal festival for the rude multitude was established'. Demoniacal, presumably, in the sense with which we are familiar: the demons being first welcomed in order that they can then be dispelled. This festival became known as the Women's Little Carnival, for it was the women who arranged it, saving their money all year in order to reward the musicians who toured the country, looking to deploy their skills in playing the tarantella. A carnival, this, quite free of cynical manipulation; no one not of the 'rude multitude' granting them just sufficient taste of liberty to reconcile them again to servitude. A carnival entirely of the people's own making.

Nothing ever goes away completely. Neither the Bacchantes nor the Tarantati. Earlier this century a London singing teacher, Albert Visetti, reported seeing an unbridled dance break out in a cemetery in Dalmatia, the dancers eating broken glass and burning coal, the dance conducted from a tombstone by an 'abbot' who, for his finale, performed a somer-sault 'which aroused in the onlookers an incredible enthusiasm'. Embold-ened by this comparatively recent sighting, I decided to nose into the possibility of something remaining – anything would do; the smallest memorial or notice – in the environs of Taranto itself. But no. Nobody was aware of a thing. No little dance, no modest procession, no merely touristical allusion, nothing . . . Unless one counted a raggedy tradition, in truth more honoured in the breach than the observance, which saw a couple of old ladies paying an annual visit, if they happened to be well enough, to the Church of St Peter and St Paul, the patron saints of the bitten, in Galatina, some fifty or sixty miles from Taranto. And when did this happen? Oh, late June some time. But truly, truly, the chance of its happening at all was slim. And not worth the risk of a special visit.

Why do some discouragements have exactly the opposite effect to that intended? What does one hear in the voice of the discourager that tells you nothing is in fact something? A little too much feeling in the 'truly, truly'? A far too altruistic concern that a perfect stranger shouldn't waste his money on a plane ticket? Whatever the reason for suspicion, late June some time saw me in Galatina with a film-crew. The town was closed to traffic when we arrived in the late afternoon. The streets full of police on motorbikes and clerics in full regalia looking at their reflections in shop windows. A ferris wheel was turning. Music was playing. Restaurants had spilled their tables into the roads. This was more than a fun-fair or a street-party; this was a festival. By early evening, before there was time to take a lens cap off a camera, a procession of thousands was snaking its way through the crowds, bearing the Catholic icons you associate with one of the major holy days, to the Church of St Peter and St Paul.

I scrutinized the processionists, especially the women, for expressions of Tarantati excess. A little too much rhythm in the gait. Looks of libidinousness. A tendency to apoplexy. Vine leaves. Punctures of the flesh commensurate with the mandibles of the tarantula. But nothing that was not consistent with a conventional holy procession did I see. I followed them into the church. An organ was playing a hymn. No pipes or timbrels. No fiddles or tambourines. No one looking even remotely tempted to dance. So what did any of this have to do with Tarantism?

Outside the church, though, you could buy ribbons, yellow, green, red. I remembered the Tarantati's 'rage for colours'. And the stalls selling religious artefacts were festooned with twisted chilli phalluses, plastic versions of my Pompeii guide's humpbacked *malocchio* key-ring. Paganism, on the very steps of the *chiesa*; available for purchase, alongside plaster figurines of Our Lady, the same sacred member in whose name, and in this very corner of the classical world, the mad Bacchantes had leapt and foamed with fire in their hair.

But still the church filled, and still the hymns played, and still nothing specifically spidery disrupted the sacraments.

We asked questions. When we didn't encounter ignorance of our meaning we encountered resentment of it. Shrugs. Evasions. Discouragement of the sort that had encouraged us to come here in the first place. Until at last, thanks largely to a policeman on a motorcycle with an interest in languages and anthropology, we discovered that indeed we weren't seeing everything, that there was an alternative underlying meaning to this festival, an afterword, a second-kick in it, so to speak. Embarrassment lay behind the false information and the no information we'd been given. Fear of newshounds and interlopers. Local shame. Family disgrace. And if we turned up, at five the next morning, and stood not here in the square outside the grand church of St Peter and St Paul, but there in that little street outside the *chapel* of St Peter and St Paul, now deconsecrated, we would see why.

We were there, in the pearly blackness, at four-thirty. So were several dozen other people. Local journalists. Local TV men. Some academics. One or two authors. A handful of the merely curious, travellers, passersby of the night before, who'd accidentally picked up the odd rumour of this or that. By six we'd been joined by several dozen more of the same. Did we know what we were waiting for? Some of us thought we did. We

Den-

Jacques Callot

Scaramucia. *Fricasso.*

were waiting for Tarantati. Not folklorists recreating the hysterical dance, not a picturesque tarantella band turning it into a kitsch country knees-up for visitors – which was the very most, after all, that I'd originally hoped for – but the real thing, afflicted dancers, lewd maenads, spider-bitten Corybantes, still in thrall to the music more than half a millennium, counting from the first post-Christian outbreak, after it all began, but in truth going back a few millennia prior to that. Every year, on their saints' day, they came to this little chapel to make spiritual reparation, or give thanks, or pray for a cure, or do something – nobody was quite sure what. Every year the people of Galatina denied that it happened. And every year, despite these denials, the morbidly curious gathered in the early morning and waited.

Did we know what to look for? Only this – that the Bacchantes would not be young maidens, that they would not come leaping and foaming towards the chapel with their throats upturned, but would be old ladies, probably infirm, probably in the care of their relatives. And their relatives, going on past experience, would be aggressive, would not want to be observed and stared at, let alone filmed. For this was what their shame was. The ignominy they were bound to expose on St Peter and St Paul's day. Their terrible family secret. Granny was a Corybante.

Cap. Mala Gamba. ☉ Cap. Bellauita

Jacques Callot

We waited till seven. Seven-thirty. Seven-forty-five. A few Galatinans came and went to and from the chapel. Occasionally a hooped widow hobbled in, her weeds black as a tarantula. We all converged on her. But she only stood before the altar, made the cross, bent her head, prayed and left. Every female over fifty not carrying a camera became suspect. Why the young were exempt, given that we were witnessing – that's to say, hoping to witness – a phenomenon of such antiquity that the most ancient woman was a chicken by comparison, I don't know. An insane logic was at work: this had been going on for centuries, therefore it affected only the old.

Just before eight a small car drove into the street at speed and braked hurriedly outside the chapel. A man driving, a woman beside him, another man in the back seat, and beside him a black shape. Respectable city people; not quite bourgeois, but not peasants. Small tradespeople, perhaps. Upholsterers, or bakers. We moved towards the car. The driver started forward again, made for the news cameraman, swerved, swung into us, scattered us, reversed, swung into us again, cursing us through his open window. We backed off and then regrouped, incorrigible in our inquisitiveness. He came out of the car red with rage, shaking his fists, turning his shame on us. Again we fell back. He lowered his head, walked around the car a couple of times, then opened the rear door and took one end of the black shape. Only when it was half out of the car could we tell it was human. An old woman. Black scarf, black stockings. Prone. Conscious, but not moving. The second man took the other end, and together they carried her into the chapel. The fourth member of the family, the woman in the front passenger seat, walked behind them carrying pillows, turned, yelled at us, then slammed the chapel doors on us. We heard the bolts slide in. Then silence.

In a body we made for the doors. Wherever there was an aperture or a crack, somebody put his eye or his ear. A couple of kids flattened themselves on the ground, trying to get a look under the door. But there was nothing to see and nothing to hear. Except, every now and then, a curse from one of the unafflicted members of the family, realizing what we were about, and a thundering on the door from inside, to shoo us away. Once, the driver came out to move his car, his eyes lowered. Otherwise the pattern was unbroken: we crept back towards the chapel door, craned our necks like hungry birds, screwed up our faces, and listened, until the hammering repulsed us again. And then, quite suddenly, we heard a crooning sound, not quite singing and not quite sobbing, but something in between. The voice light, like a girl's, but not carefree and not really melodic either; an insistent ageless wail, without pain in it, but aimless, like the music of a mind wandering. One of the kids laughed, but the rest of us fell still and turned cold.

When the two men unexpectedly came out of the chapel we retreated, more respectful now, but more than ever desperate to get a look inside, to catch sight of the old Bacchante on the flagstones, crooning on her pillows, but they were too quick for us; no sooner were the doors opened than they'd shut again. We thought it was all over, that the abashed and angry relatives were fetching the car in order to bundle the last of the Tarantati back into it. But they had only gone to the car to collect something from it; they fished around in the boot and came back carrying a couple of plastic bags each. I manoeuvred myself as close to the chapel doors as decency permitted, so that I could see what they were bringing in. I suspected refreshments. Tea, biscuits, sherry. The kind of things ordinary old ladies like. But the bags contained nothing of the kind. They contained musical instruments. Let me be more specific: they contained tambourines.

And if we'd turned cold before, now, as the doors slammed again and the drumming began, our blood froze. A tambourine can make a fearful sound at the best of times; the violent rapping of the knuckles imparting a vibration to the parchment which no mere drum can match for harshness, the cymbals seeming to jeer at the rasping tympany. A boastful, bull-baiting, nerve-jangling sound, full of southern European derision. But the noise now, amplified in the tiny chapel and intensified by all that we could only imagine, was enough to make the heart stop. And just below it we could hear the crooning begin once more. The lost, wandering thread of melody. Then the drumming of the parchment, as though the walls themselves were being beaten, and the mockery of the cymbals, like the sound of nerves snapping. I remembered what I had read, that the Tarantati hung upside down like the spiders whose victims they considered themselves to be, that they writhed lewdly, that they liked to have the soles of their feet beaten, that the swellings of their abdomens could sometimes only be brought down by kicks and blows. What the hell was happening in there?

Whatever it was, it wouldn't stop. On and on it went. The incessant drumming, the ceaseless sardonic jingling. It was as though the entire chapel had become a throbbing tambourine. Too much, surely, for the constitution of a twenty-year-old maenad at the height of her possession, never mind a comatose invalid of eighty who had been carried in horizontally, one man at one end, one at the other. But when at last, a good hour or more later, the music finally did stop and the car was brought around and the doors of the chapel were flung open, we saw a sight that was sufficient to make converts to Dionysus of us all. The old Bacchante exiting under her own propulsion, wide awake, refreshed, indifferent to our stares, and fully erect.

CHAPTER TEN

Now Get You to My Lady's Chamber . . .

Tragically I was an only twin
An unused line of Peter Cook's

I

It is Hamlet, the black prince, who throws comedy its most material challenge. In that greatest of all meditations on death – Hamlet observing a grave being prepared, though ignorant as yet that it is a grave for Ophe-

lia – every player, save one, is a clown. Almost as though it is an orchestrated history of clowning (and therefore of civilization) itself, the scene progresses from the gross inurement of the cloddish gravedigger, through the wild gambols of Yorick (perhaps the most renowned jester in literature, famous to us precisely because we know him only in death), to the quicksilver morbidities of Hamlet himself: distracted, antic, punning, persistent, energized by what destroys energy, relentlessly outwitting death's humourless finalities. Only the soberly decent Horatio, the refuser of comedy's inquisitiveness ("'Twere to consider too curiously, to consider so'), is left out in the cold. Of all these soundings of mortality the most unquestioning, the most concerned to preserve the dignity of things, is the least liberating.

Where are we most vividly alive? In our laughter.

So what is death's greatest prize? The sound of our laughter.

Therefore in order to defy death . . .? We must show that we can still laugh.

Now get you to my lady's chamber, and tell her, let her paint an inch thick, to this favour she must come. Make her laugh at that.

The first and last challenge to comedy. If you are so clever and can do so much, make us laugh at death. Because if you can't, if you are unable to persuade us to go on laughing in the face of our universal fate, you have only ever been an evasion, a way of filling time, not conquering it.

Death and the Fool are frequently companioned. At times they are even mistaken one for the other. In the *danse macabre* of the morbid Middle Ages and Renaissance, fools laugh at death and buffet him, death dons a cap and bells, and together they mock the miserly and the prudent, those who think they can cheat their fate through accumulation and sobriety. We smell death on some comedians, whether it's their own consciousness of a battle they don't expect to win, as with Hancock, or a black refusal of it, let it singe and fry him as it will, as with Max Wall. Grimaldi's father, who brought an infamously cruel and melancholy Pierrot to England, could not stay away from tombs and graveyards. The nineteenth-century English 'philosophical' circus clown, James Boswell, much admired in France, would run around the ring in a stained white cloth resembling a winding-sheet streaked with blood, declaiming blood-curdling extracts from Shakespeare's goriest tragedies; he died at the age of thirty-nine while balancing upside down on the last upright spar of a self-disassembling ladder. Sepulchral? Does it help to call it that? Was it sepulchral of the poet Donne to have himself painted in his shroud betimes? *'Twere to consider too curiously, to consider so?* Not a bit of it. By taking to the grave before the grave can take to you, you may achieve a fierce, even a frenetic, release from it.

'Counterfeit?' muses Falstaff, rising up after wisely playing dead on the battlefield at Shrewsbury, 'I lie; I am no counterfeit. To die is to be a counterfeit, for he is but the counterfeit of a man who hath not the life of a man; but to counterfeit dying when a man thereby liveth, is to be no counterfeit, but the true and perfect image of life indeed.'

The which, in the eyes of his astonished companions who had seen him horizontal, amounts to little short of a resurrection.

JOHN:

> But soft! whom have we here
> Did you not tell me this fat man was dead?

PRINCE:

> I did; I saw him dead,
> Breathless and bleeding on the ground. Art thou alive,
> Or is it fantasy that plays upon our eyesight?
> I prithee speak. We will not trust our eyes
> Without our ears. Thou art not what thou seem'st.

FALSTAFF:

> No, that's certain, I am not a double-man . . .

A joking reference, no doubt, since he is shouldering another's corpse, to the carnival 'double-man', the costume that gives the upside-down impression of a Dead Man Carrying a Living Man – life and death on a temporary, festive job-exchange scheme.

Just as fools are forever seen keeping company with death, so are they forever resurrecting. Frazer documents any number of local 'jack-puddings . . . with motley countenances' willing to be their community's substitute sacrifice in return for a few brief days of fun and the promise of rebirth. Every Twelfth Night in Haxey on Humberside, a fool is still smoked over the festival fire. In the dance-play of the Plow Boys of Revesby, the fool fights first with the hobby-horse, then with the dragon-ish 'wild worm', and after being killed by the farmers is brought back to life by them. Sick with unrequited love, Harlequin tries to end it all by tickling himself to death, only to be restored to an energetic desire to go on living by the bodily pleasures of laughter. In another version, after being, as he supposes, poisoned by a rival, he finds himself entombed alongside a woman who declares she has 'been brought to this estate by a faithless lover on whom I doted too much'. Once again, Harlequin is too hot to settle for death. 'Come over here,' he propositions the woman. 'Although I am dead I feel I still have a taste for the ladies.' No flattened clown ever fails to come back up. If he goes on lying there, immobile among the debris and the custard, something other than comedy has intervened. And the best clowns know how to circumvent disaster before it befalls them, resurrect themselves, so to speak, in advance of their death. In *The Silent Clowns*, Walter Kerr marvels over Buster Keaton's casual adaptability, that 'superb serenity' which enables him, trapped inside a turning paddle wheel, to take a ruminative and apparently unper-

ilous evening stroll, or, threatened by a murderous stage manager and a
flooded orchestra pit, to climb aboard a bass and, using a violin as paddle,
canoe himself to safety. 'It is not a cheerful serenity; that would be too
much. It is simply the other side of resignation, the unruffled calm that
comes of having accepted whatever is.' Which itself presupposes, since
Keaton does not calmly accept defeat or annihilation, that whatever is is
death's opposite.

If the insouciance of Hippoclides is once again in play here, so too is
the optimism associated with excrement. Defecation is the mother of
hope and Keaton is always in the shit. Where the body dies, there the body
is reconstituted and reborn.

The Fifth Story of Boccaccio's *Decameron* prodigally exploits this invariable three-way relationship – the very bedrock of comedy – the fool,
the shit, prosperity.

Andreuccio has come to Naples from Perugia to buy horses. Spying
him conducting his business more openly than is the local custom, that is
to say making too free a demonstration of the contents of his purse, a
young and beautiful Neapolitan woman hatches a plot to relieve him of
his cash. She invites him to her house, persuades him she is his sister,
feeds him, plies him with drink, engages him in protracted and loving
conversation, and prevails upon him to spend the night under her roof.
The night being stifling, Andreuccio undresses, removing his hose and
breeches and money purse, which he places beneath the lady's very own
bolster. Needing to relieve himself, he asks instructions of the page, who
points to a door in the corner of the room. Whereupon, passing 'jauntily
through', Andreuccio falls into the sewer running between the houses,
and although mercifully suffering no injury, gets himself 'daubed from
head to foot' – just like the goose that shat gold coins – 'in the filthy mess
with which the place was literally swimming'.

Needless to say, Andreuccio is not granted readmission when, still
smelling foully, he raps upon his self-styled sister's door, reminding her of
their loving conversation of the night before and complaining of his
treatment. 'My good fellow,' she says, laughing at him from her window,
'you must have had a dream.'

'Look on the bright side,' a couple of passing rogues tell him; 'if you
hadn't fallen into the shit you certainly would have been murdered in your
bed. At least this way, although you've lost your money, you've kept your
life.'

His new friends lower him into a well so that he may wash the ordure off himself, but flee when some officers of the watch, in need of water from the well themselves, approach. The officers haul at the rope. The bucket seems heavy, but then they are expecting it to be full of water. Meanwhile . . .

when Andreuccio saw that he had nearly reached the top of the well, he let go the rope and threw himself on to the rim, clinging to it with both hands. On seeing this apparition, the officers were filled with sudden panic, and without a word they dropped the rope and began to run as fast as their legs would carry them.

Not satisfied with just one resurrection, Boccaccio reunites his accident-prone Perugian with the two rogues who had lowered him into the well and who now persuade him to climb into the tomb of the Archbishop of Naples – buried that very day – in order to steal a priceless ruby from his finger. Realizing that they will leave him in the vault once he has passed the ring out to them, Andreuccio pretends he is unable to find it. Fine by the rogues; they drop the lid of the vault on him just the same.

Dead again, Andreuccio collapses on the Archbishop's corpse. 'If anyone could have seen them at that moment, he would have had a job to tell which of the two, the Archbishop or Andreuccio, was the cadaver.' Not shit waiting for him this time, but shit's equivalents – the noxious odours of a corpse and the maggots that will grow from it. Make him laugh at that!

Fortunately – for there is no evil but good comes thereof – the rapacity of men is without limit. Another group, led by a marauding priest, also have their hearts set on the Archbishop's ruby. They creep into the cathedral and open the tomb. Scornful of his companions' terrors – 'What are you afraid of? Dead men don't eat the living' – the priest swings his legs into the vault. Where Andreuccio grabs him. The priest 'lets out an ear-splitting yell and hurls himself bodily out of the tomb'. Convinced that 'ten thousand devils' are after them, the rest of the gang run howling from the cathedral. Leaving the tomb open. And leaving Andreuccio to make his escape from it in his own good time.

And thus, 'contented beyond his wildest hopes', Andreuccio is able to put his experiences in Naples behind him and return to his native Perugia, the richer by a good story and an Archbishop's ruby.

The shit, the well, the tomb. Thrice dead and thrice revived. And all this, as the story-teller, Fiametta, reminds her auditors, 'in the space of a single night'. Small wonder 'the whole company, ladies and young men alike, rocked with laughter over Fiametta's account of Andreuccio's misfortunes'. They'd been given three resurrections for the price of one.

Radiant after the death of Norm and the plummet of a couple of stunt-spectators, reaching too far over the balcony to grab a gladdy, Dame Edna closes one of her shows by soaring up 'resplendent' on a cherry-picker fifty feet above the audience. 'A parody of the Assumption,' Barry Humphries calls it. He might, without seriously compromising theological veracity, risk a wickeder sally still. He might observe that the Assumption is itself already a sort of parody of phallic regeneration, a travesty of the ascent of the Dionysiac comedian. But then maybe that would only be to spell out what for a long time has been latent in Dame Edna's act – her superior divinity.

II

In the course of a characteristically breezy stop in Banaras, the Indian city of the dead, towards the end of his characteristically inconsequential amble down the Ganges, Eric Newby is made an offer he can't refuse: 'If you wish I am taking you to see this Aghori. He is living at City Post Office . . . It is a very strange sect. These men are eating their excrements . . .'

The first Aghori he is taken to see – though there is some dispute as to whether he is really an Aghori at all – is lying completely naked on his stomach across the entrance to the Banaras post office. On spotting the Newbys he rolls over, so that they might the better inspect his sexual organs – 'of an impressive size'. The second Aghori, who has rather more to say for himself, drinks rum out of a human skull and explains the purpose of subsisting on the excrement and actual bodies of persons and animals, a subsistence which can be refined to eighteen days on his own water should there be nothing stronger available – 'to teach indifference'.

Among further examples of holy adroitness to which this Aghori lays claim, or at least claims for others of his sect, is the skill to suck up liquids with the penis, to enjoy intercourse without emission, and to make a barren woman fertile with a 'special kiss between legs'.

So who are these Aghori whose existence was meant to illuminate Newby's sojourn in Banaras but whose messy mysticism made so small an impression on his spiritual convictions? 'The epithet *aughar* by which the Aghori is widely known and which implies uncouth carefreeness,' explains

Jonathan Parry in *Death in Banaras*, 'is one of the names of the god [Shiva] . . .'

Like Shiva, who ingested the poison which emerged from the Churning of the Oceans and thereby allowed creation to proceed, the Aghori is a swallower of poison who liberates the blocked-up fertility of women. Like his prototype he is addicted to narcotics, is master of evil spirits, is touched with madness and his most salient characteristic is his moodiness. He is *arbanghi*: one who follows his whims with truculent intransigence. He adorns his body with the ornaments of Shiva, plays Shiva's part as spoiler of the sacrifice when denied admission to it. In the rite of *chakra-puja*, the Aghori becomes the Lord of Forgetfulness wrapped in a deathless embrace with his consort, while his necrophagy on the cremation ground

– hence the attraction of Banaras to him; much to eat here –

may be seen as an act of communion in which he ingests Shiva (represented by the corpse) and thus re-creates his consubstantiality with him . . . Above all, like Shiva – the Great Ascetic and Destroyer of the Universe whose emblem is the erect phallus and whose sexual transports shake the cosmos – he transcends the duality by uniting opposites within his own person, and thereby acquires Shiva's role as *Mahamritunja*, the 'Conqueror of Death' . . .

Sound familiar? Follower of a phallic god; eater of shit and swallower of piss; taker of sexual licence; whimsical spoiler; Lord of Forgetfulness; connoisseur of indifference; conqueror of death . . .? Do we not now recognize in the Aghori all we know of clowns?

Parry describes scenes of Aghori manhandling and abuse, nakedness, obesity, the flinging of the contents of chamber-pots into the midst of grateful crowds, the throwing of urine as a blessing, which exactly recall the festive clowning of the Hopi and the Zuni and only fail to resemble a western circus because western circuses have lost their way.

But what exactly, Parry asks, is the connection between the discipline of the Aghori – for it is a discipline to cultivate carelessness and intransigence to this degree – and the conquest of death? 'By scavenging from the dead . . . the Aghori escapes the clutches of the living,' and so achieves the ascetic ideal of autonomy. Inversions and opposites again. 'The ascetic becomes the consort of the prostitute, the menstruating prostitute becomes the goddess . . . the cremation ground a place of worship, a skull the food-bowl, excrement and putrid flesh become food, and pollution becomes indistinguishable from purity.' And the Aghori himself 'passes out of the world of creation and destruction and into an existence which is beyond time.'

He has broken the linear logic which completes itself in death. That he calls it asceticism rather than clowning is neither here nor there. What's in a name?

III

But mere bodily ascension, finding prospects for a new life in the destruction of an old one, rising ruby-rich from the shit or replenished from the cremation grounds – these are relatively easy tricks for comedy to perform. A more difficult feat is the overcoming of what is deathly in us while we are still alive. And this it does, often against our wishes, by dogging us with our shadows, by forcing us into the company of our other selves – our secret sharers – by insisting we have another voice to speak with than the one we customarily use. Jung understands the near-universality of the trickster figure, haunting the mythology of all ages, this way: 'as a faithful copy of an absolutely undifferentiated human consciousness' – us as we once were, and to an extent that embarrasses us, still are.

The bread-and-butter ventriloquist's dummy manifestly works at this level, its grotesque and knowingly unperturbed features a travesty of childlikeness (our selves unsocialized), its waywardness an expression of the unadmitted violence of its tight-lipped owner, its impertinence rooted in the secure knowledge that it speaks only on another's visceral say-so. The gothic horror conceit of a dummy taking over the life of the person who works it and perpetrating crimes in his name, is a cumbersome and otiose refinement: a schizophrenic *frisson* is already intrinsic to the very notion of a talking doll. Emu's attack on Michael Parkinson released hysteria partly because of the horror associated with the relentless beak of a giant demonic bird; but we never for a moment forgot that the energy for cruelty was Rod Hull's, that we were watching a demonstration of live violence in a public place which we could not have tolerated but for the convention of the ventriloquist and his doll, and that the doll was acting as much on behalf of our unacknowledged aggression – which of us didn't secretly want to savage Michael Parkinson in those days? – as Rod Hull's.

From sitting one's psychological innards on one's knee and giving them leave to speak, to allowing that one's body, too, may lead an independent and sometimes frightening existence, is only a short step backwards. Once again, the gothic horror fancy – hands of a murderer grafted on to arms of a pianist, say – imports anxiety where there is already anxiety enough. Our limbs and organs are unruly; our physical wants do not obey the dictates of our conscience; the phallus rises when it chooses and doesn't when it doesn't. The hands of the Winnebago trickster, Wakdjunkaga, fight each other over food. He burns his anus with a brand, to teach it a lesson. Identification with 'lower and more primitive states of consciousness,' Jung reminds us, 'is invariably accompanied by a heightened sense of life'. We have to go down in order to come up. A strange exaltation is released whenever a clown suddenly finds or treads on or is molested by a part of himself that he doesn't at first recognize. It is as though we are witness to some multiplication of himself: a physiological ignorance that is also a freedom from mere physiological limitation. The Russian clown Slava Polunin makes love to himself through the sleeve of an overcoat, balancing existential pathos with sexual risk – how far will that self-caressing hand go, what further liberties will it dare take? Driven still further into lonely despair (fellow-feeling with which might have been what drove me to pursue him to St Petersburg), he makes preparations to hang himself, only to find a second despairing clown making preparations to hang himself at the other end of the same rope. Does that make for community, discovering that we are all lonely together? Ogo-Yuguru, trickster of the Dogon, is forever searching for his twin, his complimentary other half. In both the above brief pantomimic sketches Slava Polunin finds a sort of consolation, an accrual of energy, precisely in a complimentary version of his isolated self. He doubles what he is, in other words; makes himself plenteous by the negative power of two.

Far more than any opportunity for fun with mistaken identity, it is just this spectacle of increase – ridiculous in the precision and conscientiousness with which it duplicates – that explains the frequency of twins in comedy. Seniority, precedence, authority – all go hang, however temporarily, as Dromio of Ephesus and Dromio of Syracuse, the twin-servants of *The Comedy of Errors*, exeunt hand in hand, 'not one before the other', and thereby block the doorway. One twin is always one too few, and two is always one too many. That other half of our divided self becomes pre-posterous to reason when at last we find it, and makes an optical absurdity of both of us.

Why should this be?

'Two faces that are alike,' says Pascal, 'although neither of them excites laughter by itself, make us laugh when together on account of their likeness.' But *why* do we laugh? Bergson thinks we laugh, as it were cor-rectively, as a matter of ophthalmic vigilance, on behalf of our creative intuition that 'a really living life should never repeat itself'.

An idea of our individual dignity, that something sacred attaches to our particularity, lies behind this argument. Some of us can bear to be fol-lowed by a street clown who mimics what we look like, the way we walk and how we hold or hang our head, some of us cannot. I am of that party that abominates such mimicry, no matter whether I'm the victim or someone else is. But if I care so dearly about my individuality, am I right to withhold laughter when it is threatened? Might not laughter be mobil-ized, exactly as Bergson would have it, precisely in individuality's defence? God made the first man noble in his uniqueness. So necessary was this uniqueness to his original design, that only special pleading got him someone even vaguely like himself to play with. Would God and his angels have laughed had Eden been peopled with a horde of identical Adams? Assuredly they would have done if our reactions to the Monty Python sketch of the mental ward of would-be Richard IIIs, or the wealthy playground of identikit Alan Whickers carrying microphones and breathing after millionaires, are anything to go by. The argument that it is not the one that is absurd, but the many, might be a little hard to press in that latter case, but it remains true that the many are always more absurd still. We become ridiculous to others, as indeed we become ridiculous and a shame to ourselves, the moment we are *exactly* reproduced. Good for our powers of ridicule. For if we mock physical duplication we must also mock its intellectual and spiritual equivalents – agreement, collusion, sects, cults, factions, parties, all the tyrannies of likemindedness. By this reasoning, Bergson need not have feared the conformist tendency of laughter, for laughter which defends uniqueness against repetition is on the side of conservatism only when conservatism is on the side of individuality.

But even this may be to put too rigid a clamp of ridicule around the comic business of imitation and repetition. A really living life may never wish to repeat itself *exactly*, but uniqueness is an anguish from which, like

Jacques Callot

Scapino. *Cap. Zerbino*

Ogo-Yuguru, we dream of liberation. When we laugh at replication, at mimicry and doubles, at clowns and parrots that get us to a T, is it not possible that we are simultaneously protecting what is single from duplication *and* preserving it, by repetition, from extinction? We don't want a really living life to lose itself in copies, but we don't want it to disappear entirely either. *Einmal ist keinmal* – 'What happens but once,' Milan Kundera laments, 'might as well not have happened at all.' Doubling gives life a second chance. *Zweimal.*

Nor is pure repetition or replication exactly what we're getting anyway. The parrot offers an animal gloss on our human selves; the street clown a public and dishevelled transliteration of our introverted dignity. Though in appearance bafflingly the same, the twins of farce are in fact often fundamentally different, of opposite sex or opposite character, harbouring distinct expectations, arousing contrary passions. And even that machine-precision musical routine, still so popular in English pantomime, in which humans become a sort of engine or conveyor-belt, performing split-second functions quite alien to Bergson's 'elastic' and 'unrepeatable ... inner suppleness of life' – even that apparent subjugation of every human irregularity to the smoothness of a mechanical necessity is not

Jacques Callot

Cap. Babeo.   *Cucuba.*

mechanical in Bergson's life-defeating sense. Quite the opposite. The comedy, the yield of pleasure, depends on the marvel of each distinct element (or person) exerting itself and surviving by a whisker (i.e. by a triumph of timing) in potentially lethal combination with others performing contrary tasks; in other words, differentness – not sameness – asserting itself and miraculously dovetailing to make the pattern, and *that* then splendidly amplified and repeated in a way that suggests it could go on, getting bigger and more complicated, and just avoiding catastrophe, for ever. Our laughter hangs upon the breaking of linear expectations of the way things happen, so that an improbable million-to-one chance comes to seem inevitable. The same mechanical certainty, in defiance of all the odds, catches up with Oedipus. Only there we don't laugh. Because in Oedipus' case the hand at the machine is not human. As always, it takes comedy to return us to ourselves.

Put that another way: it is comedy – specifically the comedy of repetition and doubling, duplication and stand-ins – that frees up chance. Not just by giving the unbearably light human life the weight of a second opportunity – its *zweimal* – but by working on time, slowing it, reversing it, refusing gravity, making a reality out of illusion, making what has vanished materialize again, restoring a body that has been sawn in half, or otherwise raising one that has been felled – all the death-defying and resurrectionary stunts of the variety palace and the music hall and the circus ring.

These comic mirror-images, of course, are nothing other than the topsy-turvy of carnival kept strictly to the horizontal. The ass riding on the back of its master, fish flying in the sky while deer gallop in the deep, the man nursing the baby while the woman smokes the pipe – what are these great liberating images of a loosened world but distorted replicas, broken reflections in a parodical mirror, humankind seeing itself in perpetual ironic flux, as-it-would-be confronting as-it-is, stagnancy eyeing metamorphosis?

Transitional, anthropologists like to call the condition induced by these slithering reflections. A state of becoming. A stage in the violation of accustomed boundaries facilitated by such other familiar festive paraphernalia as masks, animal disguises, behavioural and linguistic transgressions, imaging oneself upside-down or inside-out, cross-dressed, cross-specied, cross-sexed. Of all images of reversal, of all the ways of figuring ourselves extended, mirrored way beyond ourselves, the most universal – and therefore, we must suppose, the most effective – is transvestism. It is difficult to find a culture that does not employ it, a festival that doesn't need it, a mode of comedy that won't exploit it. Deuteronomy warned against it – 'the woman shall not wear that which pertaineth unto a man, neither shall a man put on a woman's garment blah blah' – with too great a vehemence for there to have been nothing to warn against. Those depilated piggie-wiggies, exposed to the prying eyes and fingers of Aristophanes' audience, were played by men. Nero was said to have opened his legs and given birth on stage. Roman men put on women's finery at the Kalends processions to mark the New Year, as they still need scant prompting to do at the modern carnival in Venice. Celebrating the Saturnalia away from home, Roman soldiers wore plaited wigs and exchanged ribaldries in high falsetto. Christianity failed to keep the sexes distinct, abominable as was such confusion to the Lord. Witness the terpsiphobe Fetherston again, inveighing against those who

doe use to attyre men in womens apparrell, whom you doe most commenly call maymarrions, whereby you infringe that straight commaundment whiche is given in Deut. 22. 5 That men must not put on womens apparrell for feare of enormities. Nay, I myselfe have seene in a maygame a troupe, the greater part wherof hath been men, and yet have they been attyred like unto women, that theyr faces being hidde (as they were in deede) a man coulde not discerne them from women. What a horrible abuse was this: what horrible sinnes might have hereupon ensued.

The rest – whether it's Shakespeare's women-acting-as-men exploiting the conventions of men-acting-as-women, or the courtesans of carnival, 'apparelled like men, in carnation or light-coloured doublets and breeches' (according to the seventeenth-century English traveller, Fyles Moryson) 'and so playing with the racket at Tennis with young men', or the Hopi personators of old women, licking their chops and rubbing their bellies after a generous draught of urine, or the gross night-club drag act, or the more modest but no less knowing pantomime dame – is now utterly familiar to us. Wherever laughter is appealed to to commemorate a change in the season or mark a transition from ordinary to ritual time, or simply to effect a change in the community's mood, some person of one sex is to be found assuming the dress and appearance of the other. That the whole business of dressing-up works a miraculous transformation in the personality of the dresser is a commonplace. I know of teachers of arts and crafts who have had to give up making masks with their pupils, so drastically do the masks affect the children's behaviour once they put them on. And the effects of dressing-across are still more dramatic. If you want the best of Lily Savage, it's Lily Savage in full rig you talk to, not the quiet man in the open-necked shirt she otherwise is. To be herself, even on radio, Dame Edna Everage has to be dressed and equipaged as Dame Edna Everage. The principal carnival buffoon at the St Peter Festival in the southern Colombian Andes was, for many years, a wildly sacrilegious transvestite with any number of outrageous *alter egos*, nuns, harlots, film-stars, each one more shocking to the devout mountain people than the last; in daily life he was a poor, modest, lonely, preternaturally shy wood-worker named Tobito, under orders for the rest of the year to wear no disguises and create no public spectacles.

But transvestism would not be so successful a festive intervention were it not able to effect a more general transformation as well. Go to Fou Fou's Palace in Manchester any Friday or Saturday night and the trans-gressions you see are all the work of people in (or frequently out of) their normal clothes, keeping to their normal sexual categories. Their ab-normalities of behaviour, though – carnivalesque might be a better de-scription, for it's always a hen night or a stag night at Fou Fou's – are absolutely the consequence of Fou Fou herself being quite brutally a man in a sequinned evening gown. Loosen the categories anywhere in the ritual performance, loosen it for only one of the officiants, and a general liberty follows. I am not saying that it becomes Sodom or Gomorrah in Fou Fou's the minute Fou Fou starts referring to her cock, or that Mancunians require a transvestite comedian to show them the way to their vulgarity, but Fou Fou's slippage unmistakably frees the audience from some of the more usual social inhibitions. Would the girls let a man *not* dressed as a woman make quite so free with their bodies? Even allowing for the conventions of a stag night, would the boys lower their pants for a man dressed as a man, would they allow an unequivocal *him* to trace the contours of their buttocks with his painted fingernails or knock their 'dickie-wickies' with his microphone? Would they be able to *take* any of it, come to that, from a woman dressed as a woman?

By dispensing with all the assumptions and associations of strict sexual definition, the presiding and not altogether unpriestly transvestite – for priests, too, officiate and make their magic in women's dress – frees his/her congregation from the restrictions and shames which those same strict sexual definitions normally impose. It's no coincidence that show-time at Fou Fou's begins with a male stripper teasingly unfurling his youth, like an imago from a chrysalis, out of the figure of a skeleton.

The accustomed forms shatter and fall apart. Freed from the deathly patterns of certainty and conformity, life shakes its lewd limbs.

IV

We have not, of course, been putting our mind here to the womanly in man or vice versa. Sexual orientation is not the issue. With ritual transvestism we have entered the grotesque world again, the world where nothing is calm or stable or as it should be, nothing completed or completable, Bakhtin's world of 'pregnant death', confounding categories, outraging nature's rigid instinct for position and propriety, jangling her nerves. And as with the ritual transvestite, so with those other untouchable trespassers into forbidden anatomical territory, the performing dwarfs, midgets, hunchbacks; in their case, too, no social services agenda or vocabulary is appropriate, the intention in all instances being neither to advocate nor to mock an appearance or a lifestyle. By taking liberties, so to speak, with the shape and organs of the body – its material topography – such cross-categorizing clowns throw into chaos prevailing notions of the body's limits, our timid expectations of its normality and order.

We have already alluded briefly to the ancients' penchant for amusing their dinner guests with monsters of simplicity, but monsters of other sorts also have a long history in the entertainment business. Some say that the pharaohs were the first to fetishize deformity, the young Neferkare writing in the Sixth Dynasty of the eager anticipation with which he awaited the gift of 'a dwarf of divine dances from the Land of the Spirits' who will 'dance the divine dances to cheer the heart of the King of Upper and Lower Egypt'. But this is surely an accommodation which no one culture can be said to have begun. You throw away a deformed baby or you prize it; either way, as a significant deviation from what is normal it reawakens you to the arbitrary and accidental nature of the normalcy-making powers, and for good or evil provides you with a fleeting access to them. Some people detect the handiwork of God when they behold a child; I myself am able to see traces of it only in the travestied lineaments of a homunculus.

They got about, these manikins, anyway, whoever first thought about employing them for mirth. According to Athenaeus, Sybarites kept them like lap-dogs. Dwarfs ran about naked in the salons of aristocratic Roman women. A sexual perversion? I'd be very surprised if not. Clement of Alexandria noted that 'delicately reared ladies' liked to have a deformed moron or two to pet while at table. Cleopatra – herself no stranger to carnivalesque contradiction, 'for vilest things become themselves in her' – had her dwarf and her eunuch, as did, of course, Volpone, whose tastes were so refined that they required a fool to be thrown in to boot. According to all accounts it was hard to have a meal at Montezuma's court without 'some little humpbacked dwarf' dancing attendance on you. Peter the Great took pleasure in periodically throwing one of his favourite dwarfs, 'the King of Siberia', over his head. Lucrezia Borgia gave a banquet at which a couple of her midgets were served up with the fruit, and Charles I found the eighteen-inch Jeffrey Hudson waiting for him when he cut into his cold baked pie. More recently there were outbreaks of competitive dwarf-throwing in France and Australia, and although these contests were subsequently banned on the grounds that they outraged public taste and violated the dignity and human rights of dwarfs, some of the dwarfs in question are still said to be trying to sue the French and Australian governments for taking away their livelihoods.

We live in dainty-stomached times. Koestler's argument, that we have travelled too far along the tracks of spiritual and intellectual progress to find amusement in malformation – 'to civilized man, a dwarf is comic only if he struts about pretending to be tall' (i.e. the only comedy accept-able to us is comedy of manners) – has won the day. 'Please use the term "person with restricted growth",' pleads the Royal Association for Dis-ability and Rehabilitation, 'as opposed to "dwarf" or "midget".' Those who hold themselves to be 'restricted' must of course decide the ap-propriateness of such vocabulary for themselves; but does the new abir-ritant terminology offer either party – the 'restricted' or the 'unrestricted' – any genuine liberation? And is Koestler right to suppose that our un-willingness to be amused (supposing that we truly *are* unwilling to be amused) by what gave pleasure to Cicero and Francis Bacon and Dickens (Koestler's own list) is evidence of our greater civilization?

'We do not want to see,' the critic Santayana observed in his famous essay on Dickens; 'we gloss the fact over; we console ourselves before we are grieved, and reassert our composure before we have laughed. We are afraid, ashamed, anxious to be spared. What displeases us in Dickens is that he does not spare us; he mimics things to the full; he dilates and exhausts and repeats; he wallows.' The thing he wallows in most – hence his inclusion in Koestler's list – being the comedy of the disordered and the deformed. But – Santayana again – 'the most grotesque creatures of Dickens are not exaggerations or mockeries of something other than themselves; they arise because nature generates them, like toadstools . . .' A fecundity all round. Nature cannot stop her sportive multiplying, nor the grotesque comedian his rolling in the riches.

'Cultivated English feeling winces at this brutality,' Santayana goes on, 'although the common people love it in clowns and in puppet shows; and I think they are right.'

We have only to think of Mr Punch to recall the seemingly invariable association of brutality and invigoration. If Mr Punch is imperturbable, it is not *in despite* of his hump and his falsetto squeak. Similarly with Dick-ens' dwarf, Quilp. 'How are you now, my dear old darling?' he enquires of his mother-in-law, having shown her, only a moment before, his reflection in the mirror – 'a horribly grotesque and distorted face, with the tongue lolling out'. After which, leading her with 'extraordinary politeness' to the breakfast-table, he proceeds to eat his eggs with their shells on, his prawns with their heads and tails on, drink boiling tea without winking, while at the same time chewing tobacco and watercress and biting his spoon and fork until they bend. That his little family should be in doubt as to whether he is really a human creature at all, is of course his intention. But it is not any diminution of the will to live that his grotesque dwarfishness presages; quite the contrary, an inexpugnable energy shakes his frame until he is finally drowned in the slime of life, his hair stirred by the damp breeze into a kind of mockery of death – 'such a mockery as the dead man himself would have revelled in when alive'.

Revelry the last word about him.

There is a scene in Fellini's *Casanova* in which Casanova intemperately consoles himself – a professional lover always has something to console himself for – in the arms of a lubricious, red-haired, long-and-loose-tongued, humpbacked woman. Whether she is otherwise 'restricted' or 'impaired' we are never privileged to discover. But our minds riot with curiosity. Fellini was no admirer of Casanova's compulsive eroticism, and therefore we cannot suppose him to have approved, especially, the epicureanism with which he eroticizes the humpbacked woman's departures from the conventional. Nevertheless, the scene as Fellini shot it is tumultuously alive, funny, full of movement and laughter, not drowsily or mechanically sensual as are the many other couplings in the film, but fervid and adventurous, hot with all the bountiful excitements of taboo-breaking and transgression. Whatever his thoughts about Casanova specifically, Fellini never took pains to conceal his own cinematic predilection for the outlandishly erotic. Think of the gigantic Saraghina doing her grotesque thinness-impaired rhumba on the sand. Saraghina's great bulk helps mythologize sex for the young Fellini *alter ego*, Guido, and his school pals, who watch her rhapsodically on the beach, urging her on to even grosser movements. In her the promise of sex grows simultaneously wondrous and absurd, mixing desire and laughter, threatening the proprieties of his Catholic education as no conventional sex object ever could. The degree to which she is not physically contained, of no ordinary proportions, is the degree to which she liberates the young Guido's imagination. Similarly, the humpbacked woman's misproportions and 'impairments' release the normally rigid and heartless Casanova ('unborn, still in the placenta') into a virtual carnival of sex, nothing where it should be, everything out of place, an ecstatic consummation of irregularity, deformity and laughter.

Life triumphant, in other words. But not in the social services sense, not disability winning out over adversity. More along the lines of that 'greater latitude in living' which Kundera speaks about, that beneficent relief which the laughter of the devils, as opposed to the bogus laughter of the angels, or the social workers, makes available to us. What those uncivilized fondlers of dwarfs and bakers of midget-pie understood – though they were never called upon to justify their merriment in such terms – was that the spectacle of deformity and abnormality confirmed the looseness, the variety, and the unpredictability of life. Hence the queer and almost universal instinct that it is lucky to touch the misshapen, that they enjoy and confer immunity from the evil eye. Are possessed of a protean creative power capable of defeating that imperviousness, that rigidity of category which is malevolence's domain.

To be truthful, 'persons of restricted growth' is a phrase full of the conviction of defeat. We are speaking, as always, imaginatively and not of lifestyles, but rather than understanding one's identity as an aspirant to growth who didn't quite make it, would it not be preferable to be shot out of the mouth of a cannon or to come in with the fruit?

V

Race-hatred, as Sartre explained it, is the ambition to be stone. To feel and know only one thing. To combine the impermeability of mineral with the certainty – craved by ideologues of all parties and all faiths – of death. Our subject has all along been contrariety. In the physical grotesque there is a never-to-be-resolved argument between the human and the something-else. When he puts on the mask of an animal or a devil (or of a stranger, come to that) the reveller oversteps his own limits. Clowns and jesters everywhere are parti-coloured, striped, part black part white, neither half a true mirror-image of the other. It is of the essence of comedy to kaleidoscope extremes, to jam together opposites so that they are simultaneously true; in this it defeats the laws of an inexorable linear logic of cause and effect, beginning and end, action and consequence. This is why those who would promulgate the certainties of the dead fear comedy, imprison clowns, outlaw jokes.

In so far as man has an interest, other than in just staying alive, in so far as he invests in a moral or ideological system, comedy is always against it. The sign of a great comic writer is not that he necessarily makes us laugh, not that he peoples his world with grotesques, not that he engorges the phallus or flings the excrement about – though we are pleased when he does all or any of these things – but that contrariety is able to have its way with him.

Late in Dickens' *Little Dorrit*, as the shadows of prison and disappointment gather around everyone and everything, a jaunty figure makes an inopportune appearance. No single cause can be given for Arthur Clennam's incarceration in the Marshalsea or for the spiritual malaise which has progressively reduced him. *Little Dorrit* is the great novel of Victorian England because it brings the dead weight of a heartless self-punishing social system, a wilful economic and intellectual gullibility, and an exhausted faith – nothing less than a morbidity infecting the entire national character – to bear on every individual life, no matter how resolutely or independently lived. But of all visitors, the one Clennam is least likely to want to receive is Ferdinand Barnacle of the Circumlocution Office, that branch of government dedicated to ensuring that nothing ever happens, and to that degree a body instrumental in Clennam's collapse. If Clennam's lifelong struggle has been with cynicism and defeatism, then no one is more naturally his enemy than 'the easy and agreeable' Barnacle. 'We must have humbug, we all like humbug, we couldn't get on without humbug. A little humbug, and a groove, and everything goes on admirably, if you leave it alone.'

At this grave stage of the novel, with moral fervour declined into moral fatigue, you would think that Ferdinand Barnacle's breezy practicalities would be peremptorily dispatched. But in fact his brief passage through the Marshalsea illuminates it like a comet. Imprisonment had begun to tell on Clennam. 'Anybody might see that the shadow of the wall was dark upon him.' Barnacle, on the other hand, comes and goes all cheerfulness . . .

'Good day! I hope that when I have the pleasure of seeing you next, this passing cloud will have given place to sunshine. Don't come a step beyond this door. I know the way out perfectly. Good day!'

With these words, the best and brightest of the Barnacles went downstairs, hummed his way through the Lodge, mounted his horse in the front courtyard, and rode off to keep an appointment with his noble-kinsman . . .

It is not that Dickens gives Barnacle his dues in spite of himself. Strictly speaking the novelist should have no 'self' to spite. But it is as though the flow of the novel's sympathies is re-routed at this moment; an indomitableness of character and personality insists itself, quite contrary to the novel's prevailing mood, but in answer to some other inner necessity. Call it the necessity of comedy. The requirement, which is an insistence of warm life itself, for rough vitality, for callousness, for that greed for prosperity and high spirits which sets no store, at last, by morality or the decencies or fear of death and retribution.

It's this principle that we recognize when we lend ourselves, for the short duration of his performance, to Mr Punch. He isn't us. We cannot live like him. He is contrary to us, and therefore our deformed reflection.

But if we are to be anything other than the regulated sequence of timidity and compromise which gets us through our sublunary lives without our doing too much harm or causing too much sorrow, only to wash us up in blind terror, finally, at the mouths of our deaths, then we cannot do without that deformed reflection.

Tragedy flatters us into believing we are grand, when put to the test; something more than flesh that falls away. Comedy answers to our suspicions that we are not grand at all, *only* flesh that falls away – but how much the more remarkable *then* our exuberant persistence!

George Cruikshank

THE END

Bibliography

Adams, Patch (1993) *Gesundheit!*, Healing Arts Press, Rochester, Vermont

Alpert, Hollis (1986) *Fellini: A Life*, Atheneum, New York

Andersen, Jorgen (1977) *The Witch on the Wall*, Allen and Unwin, London

Aristophanes (1978) *The Knights, Peace, Wealth*, transl. Alan H. Sommerstein, Penguin, London

—— (1993) *Archanians, Lysistrata*, transl. Kenneth McLeish, Methuen Drama, London

Babcock, Barbara (1984) 'Arrange me into disorder: fragments and reflections on ritual clowning', in *Rite, Drama, Festival, Spectacle*, ed. John J. MacAloon, University of Pennsylvania Press, Pennsylvania

Bains, Roly (1993) *A Call to Christian Clowing*, Marshall Pickering, London

Bakhtin, Mikhail (1984) *Rabelais and His World*, Indiana University Press, Bloomington, Indiana

Bandelier, Adolph F. (1971) *The Delight Makers*, Harcourt Brace and Company, New York

Banks, M., and Swift, A. (1987) *The Joke's on Us*, Pandora, London

Barnes, Peter (1985) *Red Noses*, Faber and Faber, London

Baudelaire, Charles (1956) *The Essence of Laughter and Other Essays, Journals, and Letters*, ed. Peter Quennell, Meridian Books, New York

—— (1989) *Le Spleen de Paris: Petits Poèmes en prose*, transl. Edward K. Kaplan, as *The Parisian Prowler*, University of Georgia Press, Athens, Georgia

Bergson, Henri (1911) *Laughter*, Macmillan, London

Bettelheim, Bruno (1978) *The Uses of Enchantment*, Penguin Books, London

Billington, Sandra (1984) *A Social History of the Fool*, The Harvester Press, Sussex

Blickle, Peter (1988) '"Zu mercklichem Nachtheil gemeines Nutzens"', in Schultz

Boccaccio, Giovanni (1972) *The Decameron*, transl. G. H. McWilliam, Penguin Classics, Penguin Books, London

Bollas, Christopher (1995) *Cracking Up*, Routledge, London

Bourke, J. G. (1891) *Scatalogic Rites of All Nations*, W. H. Lowdermilk and Co., Washington

Brenman, Margaret (1954) 'On teasing and being teased: and the problem of moral masochism', in *Psychoanalytic Psychiatry and Psychology*, vol. 1 (ed. R. P. Knight), International Universities Press, New York

Brookner, Anita (1967) *Watteau*, Paul Hamlyn, London

Bunzel, Ruth (1932) *Zuni Origin Myths*, Forty-seventh Annual Report of the Bureau of American Ethnology, Washington DC.

Burke, Peter (1988) *Popular Culture in Early Modern Europe*, Wildwood House, Aldershot, Hampshire

Byrom, Michael (1972) *Punch and Judy: Its Origin and Evolution*, Shiva Publications, Aberdeen

Cheesman, Tom (1993) 'Performing omnivores in Germany *circa* 1700', in George and Gossip

Collier, John Payne (1828) *Punch and Judy*, S. Prowett, London

Cook, William (1994) *Ha Bloody Ha: Comedians Talking*, Fourth Estate, London

Corbett, P. B. (1986) *The Scurra*, Scottish Academic Press, Edinburgh

Cornford, Francis Macdonald (1961) *The Origin of Attic Comedy*, Anchor Books, New York

Cousins, Norman (1979) *Anatomy of an Illness*, Norton, New York

Davis, Natalie Zemon (1984) 'Charivari, honor, and community in seventeenth-century Lyon and Geneva', in *Rite, Festival, Spectacle*, ed. John J. MacAloon, University of Pennsylvania Press, Pennsylvania

Dodds, E. R. (1973) *The Greeks and the Irrational*, University of California Press, Los Angeles, California

Douglas, Mary (1966) *Purity and Danger*, Routledge, London

Douglas, Mary (1975) *Implicit Meanings*, Routledge, London

Duchartre, Pierre Louis (1966) *The Italian Comedy*, Dover Publications, New York

Durant, John, and Jonathan Miller (eds.) (1988) *Laughing Matters*, Longman Scientific and Technical, London

Elliott, R. C. (1960) *The Power of Satire: Magic, Ritual, Art*, Princeton University Press, Princeton, New Jersey

Euripides (1969) *The Bacchae*, in Greene, David, and Lattimore, Richmond (eds.) *Greek Tragedies*, vol. 3, University of Chicago Press, Chicago

Fetherston, Christopher (1973) *A Dialogue Agaynst Light, Lewde and Lascivious Dauncing* (facsimile of 1582 edition), Guizer Press, Leicester

Freud, Sigmund (1978) *Jokes and Their Relation to the Unconscious*, Pelican Freud Library, Penguin Books, London

Fuchs, E. (1912) *Geschichte der Erotischen Kunst*, Albert Langen, Munich

George, David J., and Gossip, Christopher (eds.) (1993) *Studies in the Commedia dell'Arte*, University of Wales Press, Cardiff

Goethe, Johann Wolfgang (1962) *Italian Journey*, Collins, London

Gilbert, Douglas (1940) *American Vaudeville*, Whittlesey House, New York

Griffiths, Trevor (1976) *Comedians*, Faber and Faber, London

Halperin, David M., Winkler, John J., and Zeitlin, Froma I. (eds.) (1990) *Before Sexuality*, Princeton University Press, Princeton, New Jersey

Harrison, Tony (1990) *The Trackers of Oxyrhynchus*, Faber and Faber, London

Hazlitt, William (1907) *Lectures on the English Comic Writers*, OUP, World's Classics, Oxford

Henderson, J. (1991) *The Maculate Muse*, OUP, Oxford

Hickman, Katie (1993) *A Trip to the Light Fantastic: Travels with a Mexican Circus*, HarperCollins, London

Hird, John (1991) *The Comic Inquisition: Conversations with Great Comedians*, Virgin, London

Holden, Robert (1993) *Laughter the Best Medicine*, Thorsons, London

Hutton, Ronald (1994) *The Rise and Fall of Merry England*, OUP, Oxford

Jacobson, Howard, and Sanders, Wilbur (1978) *Shakespeare's Magnanimity*, Chatto and Windus, London

Johns, C. (1982) *Sex or Symbol: Erotic Images of Greece and Rome*, British Museum Publications, London

Jonson, Ben (1989) *The Selected Plays of Ben Jonson*, CUP, Cambridge

Jung, C. G. (1992) *Four Archetypes*, Ark Paperbacks, London

Kapferer, Bruce (1991) *A Celebration of Demons*, Berg and Smithsonian Institute Press, Washington DC

Kerr, Walter (1980) *The Silent Clowns*, Da Capo Press, New York

Knight, Richard Payne (1992) *A Discourse on the Worship of Priapus*, Dorset Press, New York

Koestler, Arthur (1989) *The Act of Creation*, Arkana, London

Kundera, Milan (1980) *The Book of Laughter and Forgetting*, Penguin Books, London

Lahr, John (1984) *Automatic Vaudeville*, William Heinemann, London
—— (1991) *Dame Edna Everage and the Rise of Western Civilisation*, Bloomsbury, London
—— (1992) *Notes on a Cowardly Lion*, Bloomsbury, London
—— (1996) *Light Fantastic*, The Dial Press, New York
Lawrence, D. H. (1927) *Mornings in Mexico*, Martin Secker, London
Le Roy Ladurie, Emmanuel (1979) *Carnival*, Scolar Press, London
Lea, K. M. (1934) *Italian Popular Comedy*, Clarendon Press, Oxford
Leach, Robert (1985) *The Punch and Judy Show: History, Tradition and Meaning*, Batsford Academic and Educational, London
Legman, Gershon (1968) *Rationale of the Dirty Joke: An Analysis of Sexual Humor*, Grove Press, New York
—— (1975) *No Laughing Matter: Rationale of the Dirty Joke* (Second Series), Breaking Point, New York
Leone, Matthew J. (1992) 'The Shape of Openness: Bakhtin, Lawrence, Laughter', unpublished thesis, submitted to Colgate University, Hamilton, New York
Levin, Harry (1987) *Playboys and Killjoys*, OUP, Oxford
Lincoln, Kenneth (1993) *Indi'n Humor*, OUP, Oxford
Lissarrague, François (1990) 'The sexual life of satyrs', in Halperin *et al.*
Lorenz, Carol Ann, and Vecsey, Christopher (1991) 'The Emergence and Maintenance of the Hopi People', in Vecsey, C., *Imagine Ourselves Richly*, HarperSanFrancisco, New York
Mallory, M., and Rose, M. (1993) *The Comedians' Quote Book*, Sterling Publishing Co., New York
Mann, Thomas (1954) *Felix Krull*, Secker and Warburg, London
—— (1961) 'A Man and His Dog', in *Stories of a Lifetime*, Mercury Books, London
Mantzius, K. (1901) *A History of Theatrical Art*, transl. Louise von Cossel, Duckworth, London
Marcus, Leah S. (1986) *The Politics of Mirth*, University of Chicago Press, Chicago
Monkhouse, Bob (1993) *Crying With Laughter*, Century, London
Mulkay, Michael (1988) *On Humour*, Polity Press, Cambridge
Napier, A. David (1986) *Masks, Transformation, and Paradox*, University of California Press, Los Angeles, California
Neihardt, John G. (1988) *Black Elk Speaks*, Bison Books, University of Nebraska Press, Lincoln, Nebraska
Newby, Eric (1983) *Slowly Down the Ganges*, Picador, London

Nicoll, Allardyce (1986) *The World of Harlequin*, CUP, Cambridge

O'Farrell, Pedraic (1993) *Before the Devil Knows You're Dead: Irish Blessings, Toasts and Curses*, Mercier Press, Dublin

Olender, Maurice (1990) 'Aspects of Baubo: Ancient texts and contexts', in Halperin *et al.*

Oreglia, G. (1968) *The Commedia dell'Arte*, transl. Lovett F. Edwards, Methuen, London

Parry, Jonathan P. (1994) *Death in Banaras*, CUP, Cambridge

Parsons, E. C., and Beals, K. L. (1934) 'The sacred clowns of the pueblo and Mayo-Yaqui Indians', in *American Anthropologist*, 36:4

Pelton, Robert D. (1980) *The Trickster in West Africa: A Study of Mythic Irony and Sacred Delight*, University of California Press, Los Angeles, California

Pershing, Linda (1991) 'There's a joker in the menstrual hut', in Sochen

Petzoldt, Leander (1988) 'Narrenfeste, Fastnacht, Fasching, Karneval in der Bürberkultur der frühen Neuzeit', in Schultz

Phillips Barker, E. (ed.) (1932) *Seneca's Letters to Lucilius*, vol. 1, Clarendon Press, Oxford

Rabelais, François (1983) *Gargantua and Pantagruel*, transl. J. M. Cohen, Penguin Classics, Penguin Books, London

Radcliffe-Brown, A. R. (1940) 'On Joking Relationships', in *Africa*, xiii, 195–210

—— (1940) 'A Further Note on Joking Relationships', ibid., xix, 133–40

Radin, Paul (1972) *The Trickster: A Study in American Indian Mythology*, Schocken Books, New York

Reik, Theodor (1941) *Masochism in Modern Man*, transl. Margaret H. Beigel and Gertrud M. Kurth, Farrar, Straus and Company, New York

Richards, K., and Richards, L. (1990) *The Commedia dell'Arte: A Documentary History*, Blackwell, Oxford

Richlin, Amy (ed.) (1992) *Pornography and Representation in Greece and Rome*, OUP, Oxford

Rigby, Peter (1968) 'Joking relationships, kin categories and clanship among the Gogo', in *Africa*, xxxviii, 133–55

Sahl, Mort (1976) *Heartland*, Harcourt Brace Jovanovich, New York

Santayana, George (1968) *Selected Critical Writings of George Santayana*, ed. Norman Henfrey, CUP, Cambridge

Schröder, Hans-Christoph (1988) 'Der Pope's Day in Boston und die Verfassungsfeier in Philadelphia', in Schultz

Schultz, Uwe (ed.) (1988) *Das Fest*, C. H. Beck, Munich

Segal, Eric (1987) *Roman Laughter*, OUP, Oxford

Sochen, June (ed.) (1991) *Women's Comic Visions*, Wayne State University Press, Detroit

Stephen, Alexander M. (1936) *Hopi Journal*, Columbia University Press, New York

Stevenson, Matilda Coxe (1904) *The Zuni Indians: Their Mythology, Esoteric Fraternities and Ceremonies*, Twenty-third Annual Report of the Bureau of American Ethnology, Washington DC.

Storey, Robert (1978) *Pierrot: A Critical History of a Mask*, Princeton University Press, Princeton, New Jersey

—— (1985) *Pierrots on the Stage of Desire*, Princeton University Press, Princeton, New Jersey

Stubbes, Philip (1972) *The Anatomie of Abuses*, facsimile of 1583 edition, Da Capo Press, New York

Sypher, Wylie (ed.) (1991) *Comedy*, Johns Hopkins University Press, Baltimore

Taplin, Oliver (1994) *Comic Angels*, Clarendon Paperbacks, Oxford

Tedlock, Barbara (1992) *The Beautiful and the Dangerous: Dialogues with the Zuni Indians*, Penguin, New York

Thomson, George (1972) *Aeschylus and Athens*, Haskell House Publishers, New York

Tich, Mary, and Findlater, Richard (1979) *Little Tich, Giant of the Music Hall*, Elm Tree Books, London

Tietze-Conrat, E. (1957) *Dwarfs and Jesters in Art*, The Phaidon Press, London

Trubshaw, Bob (1991) *Good Gargoyle Guide*, Heart of Albion Press, Loughborough, Leicestershire

Tyler, Hamilton A. (1964) *Pueblo Gods and Myths*, University of Oklahoma Press, Norman, Oklahoma

Tynan, Kenneth (1980) *Show People*, Weidenfeld and Nicolson, London

Unterbrink, M. (1987) *Funny Women: American Comediennes 1860–1987*, McFarland & Co., Jefferson NC

Welsford, Enid (1927) *The Court Masque*, CUP, Cambridge

—— (1935) *The Fool: His Social and Literary History*, Faber and Faber, London

Williams, Elsie A. (1991) 'Moms Mabley and the Afro-American comic performance', in Sochen

Wilson, Elkin Calhoun (1973) *Shakespeare, Santayana and the Comic*, George Allen and Unwin, London

Wolfenstein, Martha (1978) *Children's Humor*, Indiana University Press, Bloomington, Indiana

Zijderveld, A. C. (1982) *Reality in a Looking Glass: Rationality Through an Analysis of Traditional Folly*, Routledge, London

Index

abuse
  of audience, 114–18
  rituals, 132–4
Academy of Fools, 86
Adams, Patch, 151
Addison, Joseph, 174–5
Adiani, Placido, 79
aggression, 95–6, 105–38
Aghori, 227–9
Aix-la-Chappelle (Achen), Germany, 212
Allen, Woody, 29
Alpert, Hollis, 63
Altdorfer, Albrecht, 178
American Indians
  anthropomorphism and, 4
  Apache laughter, 14
  Chuku, 75
  Heyokas, 194, 198
  Hopi, 33–4, 48–51, 72–4
  Kokopelli figures, 51
  Navajo
    baby's first-laugh rite, 10–14
    ridiculed by Hopi, 33–4
  Newekwe, 75
  phallic rituals, 48–51
  Sioux, 194–5, 198
  urine-throwing, 72–3
  Winnebago, 23–4, 62, 143, 230
  Zuni, 48, 50–51, 72–4
animals
  anthropomorphism, 4
  comedic use of, 4–6
  laughter in, 3–7
  man's resemblance to, 2–4. 8–9
anticlimax and bathos, 63–5
Antimachos, 116
Apulia, Italy, 212–15
Archilochus, 114, 118, 121

Aristophanes, 44, 56–7. 63, 64, 115–16, 121, 156,
  168, 174
Aristotle, 11, 13, 41–2
Armin, Robert, 111
Arnobius, 56
arses, 68–72
aspirations and actuality, 1–2
Athenaeus, 114, 237
Austen, Jane, 147

babies' laughter, 10–16
Bacchae, 154, 211, 216, 221
Bacchus, 46–7
Bacon, Francis, 238
Bains, Roly, 184–5
Bakhtin, Mikhail, 56, 156, 189, 198, 236
Ball, Lucille, 65
Banaras, India, 227–9
Bandelier, Adolf, 50
Barnes, Peter, 192–3, 200
Barrault, Jean-Louis, 90–91, 178
Basehart, Richard, 184
Basil the Blessed, Saint, 164
'The Bastard from the Bush' (Australian poem),
  120–21
Baubo, 56, 57, 59, 61, 66–7. 72, 116, 118, 151,
  200, 211
Baudelaire, Charles P., 6–7, 137, 172, 178–83
Beardsley, Aubrey, 43, 76
beauty, 66
Beham Barthel, 159
Bergson, Henri, 6, 63, 201, 206, 231, 233
Bettelheim, Bruno, 19
Black Death, 210
Black Elk (Sioux holy man), 194–5
Blackpool, 134–7
Blake, William, 14
Blyden, Larry, 111

Boccaccio, Giovanni, 225–7
Bollas, Christopher, 14–16, 51
Borgia, Lucrezia, 237
Bosch, Hieronymus, 107, 156
Boswell, James (clown), 223
Brand, Jo, 76
Brenman, Margaret, 145–6
British Folk Studies Forum, 106
Brookner, Anita, 178
Brooks, Mel, 1–2
Brown, Arnold, 14, 30–31, 37
Brown, Roy 'Chubby', 36, 72, 135–7
Bruce, Lenny, 112–13
Bum Holes (Gilbert and George picture), 71
Bunzel, Ruth, 50
Burton, Sir Richard, 77
Byron, George Gordon, 6th Baron, 147

Caliban, 120, 128
Callot, Jacques, 107–8
Calvin, (Navajo baby), 10–13
'Candid Camera', 27, 30
Carlin, George, 130
Carnal Knowledge (film), 62–3
carnival
    Conservatism of, 201–6
    European, 198–200
    Lord of Misrule, 198
    parades distinguished, 187–8
    pathos of change and transience, 198–200
    public amusement, 192–3
    role-reversal and anti-rules, 193–8, 205–6
    Roman, 200
    taboos abandoned, 195
    transvestitism, 208–9, 234–6
    universality of, 198
    in Venice, 208–9
    Women's Little Carnival, 216
Chaplin, Charles, 8, 47, 64, 147
charivari, 201–3
Charles I, 237
Charton, Charles, 79–80
Chaucer, Geoffrey, 84
Chicot (Henry IV's fool), 169
children
    masks affecting behaviour, 235
    recapturing childhood, 94
Christensen, Michael, 25
Cicero, 238
The Circus (Chaplin film), 8
Circus Harlequin, 64–5
Circus Space, 185
City Dionysia, 115
Cleese, John, 14, 65, 144
Clement, 56

Clement VI, Pope, 200
Clinton, Kate, 66
Clownade, 90, 96
clowns, *see* comedy and comedians
Collins, Cecil, 184, 191
Cologne, Germany, 212
Colombian carnival, 235
comedy and comedians
    abuse of audience, 114–18
    aggression towards audience, 95–6, 105–38
    'alternative', 173–4
    audiences' familiarity with dramatic
        conventions, 36
    black comedy, 31
    cheating death, 109, 151, 172, 222–42
    clowns
        aggression of, 95–6. 105–38
        animal-like humour of, 8–9
        Clown Care Unit, 25
        fear of, 85–6, 94–5, 105
        Heyokas, 194, 198
        Hopi, 33–4
        in hospitals, 24–5
        and innocence, 88
        Lanarkshire clowns, 105
        melancholy of, 223–4
        poignancy of, 184–5
        as policemen, 74, 153
        Slava Polunin, 85–101
        as teachers, 51
        tragic, 149–50
    Cora Indians, 152
    correct attitudes to, 174
    court fools, 111, 127
    cruelty and, 34, 185, 236–9
    degradation and, 64–5
    dramatic make-believe of, 35–6
    dying on stage, 110–11
    expectations of comedy, 97
    expressions of hate, effect of, 36
    grotesque, the, 7–8, 33–4, 42, 55–61, 106–7,
        156, 236–41
    gurning, 59–61
    inflexibility, 63
    lavatorial humour, 75–7
    modern burgeoning of, 185
    no drawing of lines with comedy, 37
    racial and ethnic comedy, 32–7, 141, 240–41
    repetition and doubling, 193–8, 205–6, 228–
        35
    and revenge, 30
    rivalry between comedians, 30–31, 110–13
    self-deprecatory humour, 66–7
    on side of plenitude, 80–81
    trickster figures, 229

comedy and comedians – *contd*
  see also phalluses; women comedians
commedia dall'arte, 77–9, 108, 110, 120, 180
community opprobrium, 201–4
conferences on humour
  Freud Society, 14–15
  Health and Comedy Seminars, 30–31, 37
  Humor Convention, Saratoga Springs, 107, 194
  'Positive Power of Humor and Creativity', 25–7
Congo comedy, 9
congress of Fools, 98–9
Conrad, Joseph, 9, 157
contrariness, 193–5
Cook, Peter, 127–8, 222
Cook, William, 110
Corbett, P. B., 123–5
Cornford, Francis, 117–18
Cornwell, David, 106
Corybantes, 211, 218
Cousins, Norman, 26–7, 30, 31
The Craft of Comedy (Banks and Swift), 107
cruelty, 34, 185, 236–9
Crystal, Billy, 139
cursing, 117–33
Cybele, 211

DMT 31 (British Folk Studies Forum
    publication), 106
Dalmatia, 216
dancing madness, 210–16
Dante Alighieri, 158
Davidson, Jim, 113, 174
de la Halle, Adam., 158
death and comedy, 222–4, 229, 242
Deburau, Jean-Gaspard (French Pierrot), 79, 91,
    172, 178–82, 191
Debussy, Claude, 178
Decameron (Boccaccio), 225–7
defecation the mother of hope, 81
deformity
  amusement from, 237–9
  of clowns, 240–41
  cultivated feeling versus love of the grotesque,
    236–40
  dwarfs, 15–16, 70, 237–8, 240
  fetishizing, 237–8
  guide to disability terms, 125, 238, 248
  handicap humour, 34
  and sex, 239
  taking liberties with topography of the body,
    236–40
  value of freaks, 167–8, 177
  see also political correctness

degradation, 64
Demeter, 55–7, 66, 151
derision, 4–5, 37, 114, 146
devil
  as clown, 162
  equipment of, 156
  exorcism, 204–5
  expulsion, 53–8, 151–6
  horns, 160–62
  in religious drama, 156–7
Dickens, Charles
  Great Expectations, 71
  Hard Times, 192
  Little Dorrit, 241
  The Old Curiosity Shop, 174, 238
Diderot, Denis, 166
Diller, Phyllis, 66, 142
Diocletian, Emperor, 163–4
Dionysia, 186
Dionysus, 44–5, 51, 115–16, 117, 120, 154, 211
dirt-affirmation, 72–84
disdain, 71
Dodd, Ken, 47, 156
Donne, John, 144, 147, 223
Douglas, Mary, 5–6, 74
'Dozens', 129–32, 134
Duchartre, Pierre Louis, 104, 124, 158–60, 161
Dürer, Albrecht, 178
dwarfs, 15, 70, 237–8, 240

Eclair, Jenny, 147
Egremont, Cumbria, 59
Egyptian festivals, 116, 237
Einstein, Albert, 37
Eisen, Charles, 54
Elisha, 119–20
Elton, Ben, 174
Embassy Club, Manchester, 31–2
Les Enfants du Paradis, 79, 91, 178, 181
Epistemon, 69, 70
Ervine, St John, 59
ethnic jokes, *see* racial and ethnic jokes
euripides, 46
Evans, Lee, 62, 110, 141
Everage, Dame Edna, *see* Humphries, Barry
Everett, Kenny, 68
exaggeration and hyperbole, 36, 79–80, 156, 172,
    238
Extempo War, 132–4

faeces, 1–2, 81–4
fairy stories, 16–19, 24
Fantoni, Barry, 86
farting, 79–80
Feast of Fools, 166, 184, 195–8

Fellini, Federico, 62–3, 66, 184, 239
  Casanova, 62–3, 66, 239
  8, 239
  La Strada, 184Fescennine Verses, 126–7, 201
Fescennine Verse, 126–7, 201
Feste, 168–9, 170–71
Fetherston, Christopher, 153, 172, 234–5
Fielding, Henry, 122–3, 173, 174
fools
  court and family (*allowed* fools), 111, 127, 167, 168–71
  Court of Fools, Grosselfingen, 203
  and death, 223–4
  debilitated, 183–5
  elevation of, 204
  Feast of Fools, 166, 184, 195–8
  naturals, 167–9, 170–71
  saints as, 163
  in Shakespeare, 111, 144, 168–72
  visionary, 176–7
Formby, George, 63
Fou Fou, 235–6
Francis of Assisi, Saint, 164–6
Frazer, Sir James, 117, 151–2, 198, 224
freaks, *see* deformity
Frederick I (Barbarossa), 70
French, Dawn, 67
Freud, Sigmund, 64–5, 134, 140
Fry, Dr William, 28
Funambules, Paris, 181, 182

Galatina, Italy, 216–21
Gautier, Théophile, 79, 96, 157, 180–82
Gelasius, Saint, 163
Genesius Saint, 163–4
'Gesundheit!', West Virginia, 151
Gilbert and George, 71, 81
Gilles (pantomime figure), 178
Godeau, Antoine, 169–70
Goethe, Johann Wolfgang von, 200, 203
The Golden Goose (fairy story), 18
Goldoni, Carlo, 180
de Goncourt, Edmond and Jules, 178
Goodman, Dr Joel, 25–6, 51
Graves, Robert, 117
Greece and the Greeks
  Fescennine Verses, 126–7
  festivals, 193
  gods' junketings, 23
  grotesque figures of antiquity, 7
  invective, 125–6
  masks in Comedy, 107–8
  phallus-centred comedy, 41–4, 114–18
  phylax vases, 42, 213
  satyr plays, 46–8, 55–6, 156, 158–60

Green, Mort, 21–2
Gregory, Philippa, 64
Griffiths, Trevor, 35
Grimaldi, Joseph, 47, 223
Grimm, Jacob and Wilhelm, 18, 24
Gros, Jean, 133
Grosselfingen, Germany, 203
Guinness, Alec, 107
gurning, 59–61

Hageseth, Dr Christian, 25
Hammerstein, Willie, 21
Hancock, Tony, 144, 147, 223
handicapped people, *see* deformity
Hardy, Thomas, 19, 202
Harlequin, 5, 47, 78, 108, 152, 224
  appearance of, 158–60
  in religious drama, 157–8
Harrison, Tony, 46
Haxey, Humberside, 224
Hazlitt, William, 2, 6
Hecker, J. F. C., 210, 215
Herakles, 47
Herodotus, 39–41, 116
Hickman, Katie, 152
High Anxiety (film), 1
Hippoclides, 39–41, 46, 57, 67, 177, 211, 225
Hitler, Adolf, 36, 64
Hobbes, Thomas, 29–30
Hobbs, Sandy, 106
Hogarth, William, 202
Holden, Robert, 28, 29
holidays, *see* carnival
Hollis, Sir William, 111
Holy Innocents' Day, 195
Hopi Indians, *see* American Indians
Horace, 123–5
Hordern, Michael, 49
horns, 160–62
Hos, India, 117
Hudd, Roy, 75
Hudson, Jeffrey, 237
Hughes, Geoffrey, 75
Hull, Rod, 229–30
humiliation, 21
humour, *see* comedy and comedians
Humphries, Barry
  as Dame Edna Everage, 48, 72, 137–8, 147, 227, 235
  on Jews, 147
  as Sir Les Patterson, 48, 113–14
Hutton, Ronald, 153
Huysmans, Joris Karl, 183

Iambe, 55–6

India, 97, 117, 227–9
indifference, 39–41, 67, 176, 227–8
invective
    cursing, 117–22
    as dialectic, 127
    enjoyment of insults, 127
    Fescennine Verses, 126–7
    Horatian, 123–6
    insult contests, 127–37
    in marriage, 122–5
    see also obscenity
    inversions and opposites, 193–8, 205–6, 228–
        35
Isaiah, 160
Israel, Lee, 107

Jack and His Bargains (fairy story), 18–19
James, Henry, 91
Jellicoe, Ann, 20
Jerome, Saint, 160–62
Jews
    carnival role, 205–6
    masochism of, 147
    in Mexican ceremonial, 152–3
    noses, 207–9
    sadism of Jewish jokes, 140–41
John, Saint, dance of, 210–12
Johnson, Samuel, 167
jokes
    abusive, 134–7
    failure to get, 140
    Freud on, 134, 140
    Jewish, 140–41
    joking relationships, 131–3
    listening to, 139
    on misfortunes of others, 136–8
    mother-in-law, 174
    racial and ethnic, 32–7, 140–41, 240–41
    as structured dialogue, 36
    unfunny, 139–40
    see also comedy and comedians
Jonson, Ben, 111, 147, 237
Joyce, James, 129, 147
Jung, Carl, 185, 229

Kapferer, Bruce, 204
Kaplan, Brian, 30–31
Keaton, Buster, 224–5
Kemp, Lindsay, 90–91
Kerr, Walter, 224
Kikuyu tribe, 69, 70
Killer Klowns from Outer Space (film), 103–6, 176
Klenze, Leo Von, 187–8
Knight, Richard Payne, 52–3
Koestler, Arthur, 2–3, 238

Kokopelli, 51
Konyot Clown Company, 64–5
Korah, 71
Kundera, Milan, 150–51, 232, 240

Ladurie, Emmanuel Le Roy, 198
Lahr, Bert, 59, 75, 111
Lahr, John, 69, 75, 147
Lamb, Charles, 175–6, 200
Lanarkshire clowns, 105
laughter
    in animals, 3–7
    Baudelaire on, 6
    as communication, 6
    contrariness releasing, 194
    correcting erring individuals, 201–3
    as cure for ailments, 24–34, 194–5
    death's greatest prize, 223
    at deviance from normal, 63
    devil's, 150–51
    different types of, 12
    as expression of existential disappointment, 2,
        5–8, 10
    as gasp of horror, 107
    giving birth to gods, 24
    giving masochistic gratification, 145
    jollified, 107
    laughting at and with, 30–31
    Laughter Clinic, Birmingham, 28–9
    Laughter Therapy, 25
    as malady itself, 183
    at misfortunes of others, 113–18, 137–8
    naked intimacy of, 13
    Navajo baby's first-laugh-rite, 10–14
    at one's own superiority, 29–30
    as refined disillusion, 3
    sexual potency of, 19–23
    as sign of at-homeness in the world, 14
    stupid, 15
    tragic, 149–50
    unsmiling princesses, 16–21
'lavatorial' humour, 75–7
Lawrence, D. H., 4, 8, 70
Lawson, Henry, 121
Lea, K. M., 158
Legrand, Paul, 180–82
Lenia (feast of mad women), 115
Leo X, Pope, 169
Levin, Harry, 174
Lewis, George R., 57–8
Lewis, Jerry, 110
Lithuania, 205–6, 209
Little Tich, 106–8
Loki (Norse evil spirit), 20, 129
Lord of Misrule, 198

Lumley, Joanna, 66
Lycambes, 114, 118, 121, 126

McPhail, Donna, 110
Maenads, *see* Bacchae
Mailer, Norman, 69
Major Doyle's Revenge, 69–70
'Make Me Laugh' (TV game show), 21–3
Mali, West Africa, 203–4
Mallarmé, Stéphane, 178
Mann, Thomas, 3, 8–9, 103, 146, 148
Manning, Bernard, 31–2, 34, 36, 115
Mantzius, K., 156
Marceau, Marcel, 90–91
Mariano, Fra, 169
marriage, 122–6
Martial, 167
Martin, Steve, 142
Marx Brothers, 27, 30
masks, 107–8, 235
Melmoth the Wanderer (Maturin), 183
Melville, Herman, 176
Mesnil, Eustace de, 196
Michelangelo, 160
Middleton, Thomas, 171
Miller, Jonathan, 171
mime, 86, 90–91
misanthropy, 30–31
mistaken identity, 230–31
monkeys, 8
Monkhouse, Bob, 21–2, 112
Montezuma, 237
mooning, 59, 68–71
Moore, Dudley, 127–8
Morton, Bruce, 110
Moryson, Fyles, 235
Mr Saturday Night (film), 139
Munich, Germany, 186–92, 207–8

Naked Shit Pictures, 71
Naples, Italy, 52–3
naturals, 167–9, 170–71, *see also* fools
Navajo Indians, *see* American Indians
Neferkare, 237
Nero, Emperor, 234
Newby, Eric, 227–8
Newman, Cardinal John, 164
Newton, Alfred, 5
Nicholson, Jack, 62–3
Norse mythology, 20–21, 129

Oates, Jack, 111, 142–3, 146
obscenity
    mecessity for, 31–2
    pleasurableness of, 117–33

see also invective; phalluses
Oedipus, 233
Ogo-Yuguru, 230, 232
Oktoberfest, Munich, 186–92, 207–8
opera, 114, 149
ordure into treasure, 77

Pagliacci, I (Leoncavallo), 149
Pantagruel, 68–9, 79
Pantalon, 108, 120
pantomime
    aggression in, 113
    English, 172
    French, 79, 96, 178–84
    origins of, 5
    poeticization of characters, 178
    romantic, 96
    Russian, 91, 98
    Wroclaw Pantomime Theatre, 90
    see also Harlequin; Pierrot
Panurge, 69, 70, 80
Parkinson, Michael, 229–30
parrots, 5, 8, 37
Parry, Jonathan, 228
Pascal, Blaise, 231
Patterson, Sir Les, *see* Humphries, Barry
Paul, Saint, 165
Peacock, Thomas Love, 147
Perrucci, Andrea, 120
Pershing, Linda, 66
Peter the Great, 237
phalluses
    Aghori, 227–9
    apotropaic, 41
    in Attic comedy, 41–4
    Bavarian adornments, 189
    bladders, tickling sticks and gladdies, 47–8
    carvings at Pompeii, 52–3
    and comedian interchangeable, 62–3
    fear of failure, 63–4
    flashing, 39
    gives comic its dynamic pattern, 62
    and grand democracy of things, 41
    Kokopelli figures, 51
    as model of indifference, 41–7
    padded, 42–4
    phallic revival, 62
    phallic rituals, 48–51
    phallic singing, 41–2, 50–51, 114–15, 121, 160
    Phallophoroi, 114–15, 117–18, 121, 126
    in Pueblo Indian culture, 48–50
    'quantitive contrast' and, 64–5
    visible attributes of, 61–5
    see also satyrs
Philip Neri, Saint, 164

Philip of Burgundy, Duke, 170
Phochophoboch (the shining one), 24
phylax vases, 42, 213
Pickard-Cambridge, Arthur W., 42, 213
Picong (abuse ritual), 132
Pierrot
    in English pantomime, 172
    in French pantomime, 79, 91, 178–82
    interpreters of, 178–82
    in Italian pantomime, 5, 180–81
    pathos of, 182–3
Piers Plowman, 167
Pinsky, L. E., 65
Plautus, 193
Play of Adam, 155–6, 162
Plow Boys of Raseby, 224
Plutarch, 55, 167
political correctness
    amusement at the human condition, 15
    more threatening than ethnic jokes, 35
    off-limit jokes, 174–6
    vocabulary of, 125, 238, 240
    see also deformity
Polunin, Slava, 85–101, 230
Pomos of California, 151, 157, 160
Pompeii, Italy, 52–3, 133
Pope, Alexander, 147
Priapus, 52–3, see also phalluses
Priestley, J. B., 106–7
princesses, unsmiling, 16–19, 20–21
Procopius of Ustyug, Saint, 164
Prynne, William, 211
public amusement, see carnival
Pulcinella, 79, 108–10, 113, 166–7, 200–203
Punch and Judy, 47, 109, 122–3, 172–3, 174, 238
Puritanism, 211

RADAR (Royal Association for Disability and
        Rehabilitation), 15, 238
Rabelais, François, 53–5, 65, 68–9, 71, 81, 127,
        154
racial and ethnic comedy, 32–7, 141, 240–41
Radcliffe-Brown, A. R., 131
Rapping Rebbe, 141–2
Recueil Fossard, 108
Red Indian tribes, see American Indians
Red Nose (Barnes), 192–3, 200
La Regle du Jeu (Renoir film), 20
Reik, Theodor, 145–7
religion and comedy
    ceremonial, 50–51
    cheerful Christianity, 174–5
    Christian martyrs providing entertainment,
        163–4
    Christianizing satyrs, 177–8

clergy ordinances against jesting, 166
dancing madness, 210–16
devil turned into clown, 156–7, 166–7
devil's role in, 156–7, 166–7
Feast of Fools, 166, 195–8
foolery for Christ's sake, 164–6
foolish saints, 164–6
Holy Innocents' Day, 195
la chasse Arlequin, 157–8
Passion Plays, 154
priest-clowns, 184–5
Punch at Actors' Church, 173
sacrilegious roistering, see carnival; Saturnalia
Rémy, Tristan, 182
ribaldry, 41–2
ridicule, 15, 66–7, 114
Rigoletto (Verdi), 114
rituals
    abuse, 132–4
    opposites necessary to understanding of, 190
    phallic, 48–51
    and sense of humour, 33
Rivers, Joan, 66, 107
Roman entertainments
    Christian martyrs, 163–4
    freaks, 167–8, 237
    Kalends, 234–5
    Saturnalia, 193–4, 198
Rops, Félicien, 41
Roth, Philip, 82–3, 119

Sadler, Rosalin, 85–6, 93, 95, 96, 100
sado-masochism, 142–8
Sahl, Mort, 111–13
St Petersburg, Russia, 85–101
Santayana, George, 238
sarcasm, 146
Sartre, Jean-Paul, 240
satire, 117–18, 129, 146–7
Saturnalia, 193–4, 198
saturs
    Christianizing of, 177–8
    satyr-babies, 178
    satyr plays, 47–7, 55–6, 156, 158–60
    Strabo on, 162
Savage, Lily, 235
scatology, 72–84
Schlön, Erhard, 6–7, 157
self-deprecatory humour, 66
Semos of Delos, 114–15
Seneca, 193
sense of humour
    absence of, 15–17
    English and American compared, 26–7
    ritualism and, 33

unfunny jokes, 139–40
see also comedy and comedians
sex and humour
   deformity, 239
   frigid princesses, 16–19
   male ritualistic responses, 33
   potency of laughter, 18–23
   religious ceremonial, 000
   sacred circus sex, 50
   secrets revealed, 53–5
   'sexism', 174
   transvestitism, 208–9, 234–6
   see also phalluses; women and humour
Seyler, Athene, 107
Shakespeare, William
   fools in plays, 111, 144, 149, 168–72
   tragedies, 94
   Antony and Cleopatra, 193
   Comedy of Errors, 230–31
   Hamlet, 91, 222
   Henry IV, Pt 2, 122, 223–4
   King Lear, 171–2
   Twelfth Night, 168–9, 170, 211
   Sonnet 109, 144, 149
Shaw, George Bernard, 129
Sheela-na-gig, 58–9, 72
Ship of Fools, 99
Sibyl, 68–70, 82, 115, 116, 118, 129, 166
Silenus, 55
'Silliness' meaning 'blessedness', 29
Simon, Saint, 164
singing, phallic, 41–2, 50–51, 114–15, 121,
   160
sinhalese exorcism, 204
Sitwell, Sacheverell, 107, 108
skimmingtons, 202–3, 205
Skinner, Frank, 110
Sober, Sue, 21
Socrates, 168
Somers, Will, 169
Sophocles, 46
Stephen Alexander M., 33–4, 49–50, 73
Stevenson, Matilda Coxe, 49, 72–3
Storey, Robert, 79
Strabo, 162
Strasburg, France, 212
Stubbes, Philip, 153, 211
'superiority humour', 29–30
Sutherland, Donald, 63
Swearing
   beneficence of, 137
   as expression of affection, 127
   joys of, 37, 118–22, 127–38
   lighting the way to infinity, 128

Swift, Jonathan, 70, 147
Sylvester, David, 71

taboos, 195
Taper-Tom Who Made the Princess Laugh (fairy
   story), 17–18
Taplin, Oliver, 42
Tarantism, 210–21
Taranto, Italy, 212–16
tarantula spider, 213–15
teasing, 145
Tedlock, Barbara, 74
Theophilus (East Roman Emperor), 195
Thomas, Mark, 110
Thomson, John, 37
Tiepolo, Domenico, 108–9, 113, 166
Tomaszewski, Henryk, 90
tragedy, 62–3, 94, 96, 149–50, 195, 241–2
transvestitism, 208–9, 234–6
Trinidad, 132–3
Trubshaw, Bob, 59
twins, 230–31
Tynan, Kenneth, 1

United States of America
   'Dozens', 129–32, 134
   expectations of comedy, 97
   Pomos of California, 151, 157, 160
   see also American Indians
Unterbrink, M., 66
Up Pompeii (film), 48
Updike, John, 82
urine-throwing and -drinking, 72–84, 228
Utrecht, Netherlands, 211–12

Venice, 166, 208–9, 234
ventriloquists' dolls, 229–30
Vidal, Gore, 63
Visetti, Albert, 216
Vitus, S., dance of, 210–14

Wakdjunkage (Winnebago trickster), 23–4, 62,
   143, 230
Walker, Nancy, 66
Wall, Max, 223
Wallace, Nellie, 107
Watteau, Antoine, 178
Webster, John, 171
Weilditz, Hans, 81
Whicker, Alan, 231
wilde, Oscar, 129
Wisdom, Norman, 62, 112, 144
witches, 82–3
women and humour

women and humour – *contd*
  blushing and laughter, 19–20
  comedians
    beauty not funny, 66
    drag artists, 65
    loss of dignity, 66–7
  Crazy Women venture, 98
  genitals
    aged vulvas, 55–6
    as horseshoe gargoyles, 58–60, 162
    lack of visible play, 61
    religious symbolism, 58
    shooing away malignity, 53–8

  gurning, 60–61
  making women laugh, 21–3
  outsmarting the phallus, 66–7
  putting genitals where mouth is,
    57
  sexual frigidity, 16–17
  unsmiling princesses, 16–19
  Women's Little Carnival, 216
  see also sex and humour
Wright, Thomas, 58, 162
Wroclaw Pantomime Theatre, 90

Youngman, Henry, 21